RESURRECTION AND THE NEW TESTAMENT

STUDIES IN BIBLICAL THEOLOGY

A series of monographs designed to provide clergy and laymen with the best
work in biblical scholarship both in this country and abroad

Advisory Editors:

C. F. D. MOULE, *Lady Margaret's Professor of Divinity
in the University of Cambridge*

PETER ACKROYD, *Samuel Davidson Professor of Old Testament Studies,
University of London*

JAMES BARR, *Professor of Semitic Languages and Literatures,
University of Manchester*

C. F. EVANS, *Professor of New Testament Studies,
King's College, London*

FLOYD V. FILSON, *Formerly Professor of New Testament Literature
and History, McCormick Theological Seminary, Chicago*

G. ERNEST WRIGHT, *Professor of Old Testament History and
Theology at Harvard University*

STUDIES IN BIBLICAL THEOLOGY

Second Series · 12

RESURRECTION AND THE NEW TESTAMENT

C. F. EVANS

ALEC R. ALLENSON INC.
635 EAST OGDEN AVENUE
NAPERVILLE, ILL.

SBN 8401 3062 7
FIRST PUBLISHED 1970
© SCM PRESS LTD 1970
PRINTED IN GREAT BRITAIN

CONTENTS

PREFACE

These pages had their origin in three lectures delivered in 1964 in Liverpool Cathedral at the invitation of the Liverpool Diocesan Board of Divinity, and in a modified form to the Faculties of Theology of Cardiff and Swansea. As the Board at the same time requested publication I must apologize for their very belated appearance now. But it did not seem proper on such a profound and complex subject to publish the somewhat bald and sweeping statements which are all that are possible within the scope of a lecture without adding more detailed notes in support. In the end the notes, turned out to be more numerous and much longer than intended, partly owing to the considerable literature on the Resurrection which has appeared in the last five years, and eventually they came to exceed the original text. I am more indebted than I can say to Mr J. S. Bowden for the time, care and skill which he has expanded in rearranging the manuscript and in making it far less unreadable than it would otherwise have been.

King's College, London
December 1969

ABBREVIATIONS

EvTh	*Evangelische Theologie*
ExpT	*Expository Times*
HTR	*Harvard Theological Review*
IDB	*The Interpreter's Dictionary of the Bible*
JBL	*Journal of Biblical Literature*
JEH	*Journal of Ecclesiastical History*
JTS	*Journal of Theological Studies*
LXX	Septuagint
NS	New Series
NovT	*Novum Testamentum*
NTS	*New Testament Studies*
SJT	*Scottish Journal of Theology*
TDNT	Kittel (translated Bromiley), *Theological Dictionary of the New Testament*
TZ	*Theologische Zeitschrift*
VT	*Vetus Testamentum*
ZNTW	*Zeitschrift für die neutestamentliche Wissenschaft*

I

THE IDEA OF RESURRECTION

To a greater extent than it is anything else, Christianity – at least the Christianity of the New Testament – is a religion of resurrection; and it is this to a greater extent than is any other religion. Or, rather, it is a religion of cross and resurrection, with the emphasis falling on the whole on resurrection, especially if along with resurrection is taken the cognate and more embracing concept of exaltation.

'For them (the first disciples) the Gospel without the Resurrection was not merely a Gospel without its final chapter; it was not a Gospel at all . . . Christian theism is Resurrection-theism. Similarly Christian ethics are Resurrection ethics.'[1] 'Just as certainly as – even in a completely historical sense – there could be no gospel, not one account, no letter in the New Testament, no faith, no Church, no worship, no prayer in Christendom to this day without the message of the resurrection of Christ, even so difficult and indeed impossible is it to gain a satisfactory idea of how the Easter events took place.'[2] 'If there is one link (in the chain of saving events) which really bears the weight, or – to alter the picture – if there is a link on which the whole chain is hung, it is, so far as the New Testament is concerned, the Resurrection.'[3] 'References to the Resurrection are ubiquitous in the New Testament with the exception of a few writings (II Thessalonians, Titus, Philemon, III John, II Peter, Jude and James). On the whole it is clear that the Easter event is the central point of the New Testament message. Resurrection by God and appearance to his disciples form the basis of the New Testament witness to Christ; it is from this

[1] A. M. Ramsey, *The Resurrection of Christ* (1945), pp. 7f.
[2] G. Bornkamm, *Jesus of Nazareth* (1960), p. 181.
[3] H. Grass, *Ostergeschehen und Osterberichte* (1962²), p. 268.

standpoint that the New Testament is written.'[4] 'The *kerygma*, in so far as it is and sets out to be God's message, stands or falls with the Easter message at its centre, . . . the Resurrection is the presupposition of the emergence of the Church, . . . the basis of the specifically Christian belief in God, . . . of the Christian concern with man's life in the world.'[5] 'What happened at Easter overwhelmed the Church to such an extent that it dominated all its thought and became the very centre of all its preaching.'[6]

Particularly eloquent on this subject are the writings of Bishop Westcott, who saw the resurrection as 'the central point of history, primarily of religious history and then of civil history of which it is the soul',[7] while his oft-quoted statement that the resurrection was for the first Christians 'not an article of their creed, but the life of it'[8] points to one of the main difficulties, which is that of describing an event which is not one of a series but governs the whole series. In the Creed itself the statement of the resurrection stands as one alongside other statements without special emphasis or interpretation.

That despite the position of Easter in the Christian year from primitive times (one of the earliest disputes, the Quartodeciman controversy, was concerned with its celebration) the resurrection could lose its centrality even in the liturgical tradition which did most to maintain it, is illustrated by the absence of any reference to the resurrection in the eucharistic liturgy of the English Book of Common Prayer. W. Künneth sketches briefly the loss of this centrality in the theology of Schleiermacher and his followers,[9] and this is also the background of the detailed study of R. R. Niebuhr, who observes that 'the intense analysis of the New Testament produced by the great age of historical investigation has emphasized, among other things, this fact that belief in Jesus as the risen Lord informs every part of the early church's thought. But the rise of historical criticism has also made it increasingly difficult for theologians

[4] G. Koch, *Die Auferstehung Jesu Christi* (1959), p. 25.
[5] K. H. Rengstorf, *Die Auferstehung Jesu* (1960[4]), pp. 37f.
[6] E. Schweizer, *Lordship and Discipleship* (1960), p. 37. See also H. Anderson, *Jesus and Christian Origins* (1964), pp. 185f.
[7] B. F. Westcott, *The Gospel of the Resurrection* (1866), p. 5.
[8] Westcott, *op. cit.*, p. 111.
[9] W. Künneth, *The Theology of the Resurrection* (1965), pp. 16ff.

and biblical scholars to accept the New Testament order of thought. They have felt obliged to remove the resurrection of Jesus from its central position, and place it on the periphery of Christian teaching and proclamation, because the primitive resurrection faith conflicts disastrously with modern canons of criticism.'[10] E. Fascher, however, writing in 1927,[11] and promising an extended study which would show the understanding of the resurrection to be linked with the outlook and critical method of each succeeding generation, was able to assert that the question of the resurrection was of central concern, and to point to critical scholars who saw it as 'the basis of Christian faith' (Wellhausen) or 'the centre of the new understanding in theology' (Bousset). Nevertheless, the reassertion of the centrality of the resurrection was in fact made somewhat apart from critical studies by the dialectical theologians, as, for example, in E. Brunner's *The Mediator*.[12] Most recently W. Pannenberg and his school have placed the resurrection in the centre in a very special way with their interpretation of Christianity as a theology of the whole of human history, and of the resurrection as an historical event from which such a theology can proceed.[13]

The various types of Christian faith and life which are represented in the New Testament, with only rare exceptions, make their contribution to this emphasis on resurrection, each in its own fashion. The author of Acts, writing perhaps at the end of the first century and looking back over the growth of the church, chooses to put into the mouths of apostles at crucial points a message which is predominantly a gospel of the messiahship of Jesus through resurrection, and which at one point can be summarized as 'preaching Jesus and the resurrection' (17.18). Paul, for all the emphasis he is led by his controversies to put on the cross, attests the centrality of the resurrection both in statements which arise from and express his own theology, and in formulae which he has adopted as already traditional by his time. He connects it with the

[10] R. R. Niebuhr, *Resurrection and Historical Reason* (1957), pp. 1f.
[11] E. Fascher, 'Die Auferstehung Jesu und ihr Verhältnis zur urchristlichen Verkündigung', *ZNTW* 26 (1927), p. 1.
[12] E. Brunner, *The Mediator* (1934), ch. xxiii, 'The King Manifested'.
[13] See pp. 177ff. below. See also Neville Clark, *Interpreting the Resurrection* (1967), a brief but penetrating study of the stages of development of the idea of resurrection in the early church.

deepest things, and at one point can affirm categorically that denial of the resurrection amounts to a denial not of one element in the Christian faith, nor of one truth among others, but of the Christian faith itself (I Cor. 15.12ff.).

The case with the author of the Johannine writings and the author of Hebrews is somewhat different, since both operate in the main with the wider conception of exaltation, and this governs their presentations. The Johannine Christ is the Son, the Son of man, who makes the double journey of descent from heaven in incarnation and ascent to the Father through the cross (cf. John 7.33); the Christ of Hebrews is the Son of man who by virtue of obedient suffering mounts as pioneer to the heavenly places and is installed there as priest. Both authors, however, are sufficiently traditional to express this exaltation also in terms of resurrection, the former by concluding with narratives of resurrection appearances which are not strictly necessary to his thought, the latter by concluding his homily with a benediction from the God who has 'brought again from the dead' (not a normal expression for resurrection) the great shepherd of the sheep. The deutero-Pauline letters, Ephesians (and Colossians?), exhibit the same combination. The dominant theme is the heavenly places to which Christ, and Christians with him, are exalted, but the means thereto can be described in such an extraordinary concatenation of terms as 'the exceeding greatness of his power . . . according to the working of the strength of his might which he wrought in Christ, when he raised him from the dead' (Eph. 1.19f.).

Of the synoptic gospels it would not be sufficient to say simply that they conclude with resurrection narratives, for it is only in the light of faith in the risen Lord that they were written at all, and that the units of which they are composed were handed down in the tradition, so that in them it was the authoritative and living Lord who now spoke through the lips of Jesus of Nazareth. At the other end of the scale, Revelation, as a whole and in its parts, is a communication direct from this living Lord, the Son of man and the Lamb who was dead and is alive, and he is able to make this communication by virtue of his resurrection. The Pastoral Epistles (as already I Cor. 15) show that the resurrection, which some are declaring to be already past (II Tim. 2.18), has become a matter of acute debate, and such Christian writings of the second century as have survived, including now the newly-discovered Letter to

Rheginos, suggest that in that century resurrection had moved into the centre of controversy both within the church itself and between Christians and unbelievers.

These facts would seem to require that the subject be given constant attention in Christian thinking, since a false or inadequate understanding of what resurrection means must involve a false or inadequate understanding not of one element, but of Christianity itself. This attention it can hardly be said to have received. What is surprising is not the extent to which resurrection has been discussed in Christian history, but the extent to which it has lain unexamined.

A. M. Ramsey remarks that 'there has yet to be written a great book telling of what the Resurrection has meant in the thought, doctrine and worship of Christians down the ages'.[14] But while there might be much to be said on the subject in relation to worship, especially that of the Eastern church, it is doubtful whether there would be a great deal to record, so far as thought and doctrine are concerned, after the third century.[15] In his two articles on the above-mentioned Gnostic Letter to Rheginos on the Resurrection, W. C. van Unnik argues that the available evidence points to the resurrection having been the storm-centre in the second century to an extent to which it had not been previously and has not been since.[16]

In the comparatively small amount of surviving literature from the second and early part of the third centuries, the subject certainly has frequent mention. To this period belong Tertullian's full-scale treatise *De Resurrectione Carnis* (63 chs.), that of Athenagoras *On the Resurrection of the Dead* (25 chs. – if this is the discourse on the resurrection promised at the end of his *Legatio*, and not, as R. M. Grant argues,[17] an anti-Origenist work of the third or fourth century), and just possibly the 10 chapters on the resurrection preserved by John of Damascus, though his attribution of them to Justin is certainly ruled out by their style, language and arrangement. Irenaeus devotes the first 15 chapters

[14] A. M. Ramsey, *op. cit.*, pp. 115f.
[15] See J. McLeman, *Resurrection Then and Now* (1965), ch. 19; J. N. D. Kelly, *Early Christian Doctrines* (1956), ch. xvii.
[16] W. C. van Unnik, 'The Newly Discovered Gnostic "Epistle to Rheginos" on the Resurrection', *JEH* 15 (1964), pp. 141ff., 153ff.
[17] 'Athenagoras or Pseudo-Athenagoras', *HTR* 47 (1954), pp. 121ff.

of *Adversus Haereses* V to the subject, and there are briefer passages in Justin (*Apol.* 1.8, 18f., 52f.; 11.9; *Dial.* 69, 80f.), Tatian (*Orat.* 6), Tertullian (*Apol.* 48) and Theophilus (*Ad Autol.* 1.7f., 13; 11.14). According to the list of works on his statue, Hippolytus wrote *Concerning God and the Resurrection of the Flesh.*

These works differ in character, varying from the diffuse and scriptural *Apologies* and *Dialogue* of Justin to the philosophical treatment of Athenagoras,[18] which is based on an appeal to the natural reason and is almost devoid of scriptural reference; and from the biblical and dogmatic theology of Irenaeus to the ordered rhetorical argument of Tertullian. Each has individual insights, as when Athenagoras (ch. 14), departing from what appears to have been the common tradition, argues that the cause of resurrection is not the necessity of judgment but the nature of man as divine creation; or when Irenaeus (V. 8ff.) emphasizes the Spirit as already imparting life and so preparing for a future incorruption; or when Theophilus (1.7) sees resurrection as meaning that men are to see God; or when Tertullian (57) sees the pledge of resurrection in the exaltation of manhood to God in the exaltation of Christ. But the chief impression left by these works is that they all cover very much the same ground and meet the same objections with certain stock arguments and theological commonplaces. They would appear to be reproducing a common developing apologetic tradition on the subject, and in some cases to be dependent on one another. Thus Justin's reference (*Apol.* 1.8) to Plato's belief that the wicked are judged by Rhadamanthus and Minos reappears in Tatian (6); the argument that Christ's miracles were pledges of a final wholeness of resurrection is found in Irenaeus (V. 12), Tertullian (57f.) and Ps.-Justin (4); and Tertullian's lengthy discussion (48–56) of the Pauline text 'flesh and blood shall not inherit the kingdom of God' is dependent on that of Irenaeus (V. 9), who calls it a favourite text of heretics (V. 13).

This common tradition appears to have grown from two sources. In the first place, the resurrection was felt to be the specifically new Christian thing in the climate of thought of the Greco-Roman world. 'The resurrection of the dead is

[18] 'Probably the best early Christian treatise on the subject', B. F. Altaner, *Patrology* (1960), p. 130.

Christian men's confidence. By believing it we are what we claim to be.'[19] 'For indeed it was a strange and new thing for God to promise that he would not keep incorruption in corruption, but would make corruption incorruption.'[20] This was so not only for the predominantly lay theologians who wrote about it, but for the ordinary Christian whose faith is probably more reflected in a work like *The Acts of Paul and Thekla*, and especially for the martyrs, who were regarded by some as passing straight to paradise.[21] In the second place, it was a doctrine peculiarly subject to attack. As van Unnik observes, 'the manner in which this subject is brought up in various circles shows that it has become highly controversial. It would not be unfair to say that at no time in the long history of Christianity has the resurrection of the dead been so much debated as during that period. In the third century the front had shifted.'[22]

In part, the controversy was occasioned by the necessity of facing the outsider's ridicule of the doctrine as crude, and of reducing its apparently irrational and fantastic nature. Since the apologists took over from popular philosophy some form of the immortality of the soul, which is unaffected by death, and sought to combine it with the already traditional 'resurrection of the flesh', they had to show that man is a permanently compound creature of soul and flesh, and that resurrection was to the flesh, which is affected by death, what immortality was to the soul, and that both must come to judgment.[23] The fact that all these writers, and especially Tertullian, go to such great lengths to extol 'the flesh' and its dignity as divine creation shows that they were arguing on the background of a deep and widespread repudiation of the physical as having anything to do with God or the spiritual realm. In this type of argument, however, the word 'flesh' tended to be used in a different way from that of the Bible to denote one part of a man, whereas in the Bible it means the whole man, body and soul, in his natural or sinful condition. Thus Tertullian (18) can argue that the language of

[19] Tertullian, *De Resurrectione Carnis* 1.
[20] Pseudo-Justin 10.
[21] Justin, *Apology* 1.8; Tertullian, *De Anima* 55.
[22] van Unnik, *op. cit.*, p. 156.
[23] Tertullian, *De Resurrectione Carnis* 15–18; Ps-Justin 7–10; Irenaeus, *Adv. Haer.* V. 7; Athenagoras, 12f., 15, 18.

resurrection applies only to the flesh, since only that can 'rise up' which has previously 'fallen down', and the soul does not fall down as the body does.

There are, however, clear indications that the controversy not only arose from the concern of apologists with what outsiders were saying, but was also present within the church, and arose from what some counted as unbelief there. Thus Justin (*Dial.* 80) warns Trypho that he may meet some who called themselves Christians who assert that there is no resurrection, and that souls pass straight to heaven. Tertullian, at the beginning and the end of *De Resurrectione Carnis* (2, 63), refers to 'many unlearned, and a number doubtful of their own faith, and not a few plain men who need to be equipped, guided and protected', and to the 'heat of questionings' from which the illumination of the Paraclete will deliver them. He also speaks (19) of those who used orthodox language, but tricked the faithful, since they meant by resurrection the present state of the baptized and the knowledge of special truth. Irenaeus (V. 31) speaks of the faithful who, through deriving their views from heretical sources, are ignorant of the resurrection of the just. The objections against which Ps.-Justin frames his arguments come from those who 'maintain the wrong opinion', and include not only the unbelievers who are hindered by the devil from believing, but the faithful who are in danger of being seduced by him from the faith, and those who profess in word that they are believers but prove themselves more unbelieving than the unbelievers (1.2, 5). Athenagoras defends his method of first dealing with objections before going on to expound the truth on the grounds that he had found some utterly disbelieving in the matter, others doubting, 'and even among those who have accepted the first principles some who are as much at a loss what to believe as those who doubt', though they do not know why (1). So also Celsus could appeal to the fact that some Christians did not hold the doctrine as evidence of its repulsiveness.[24] Sometimes there seems to have been a denial of both resurrection and judgment: 'Whoever perverts the sayings of the Lord to suit his own lusts, and says that there is neither resurrection nor judgment, such a one is the first-born of Satan' (Pol., Phil. 7), and: 'Let none of you say that this flesh will not be judged

[24] Origen, *Contra Celsum* V. 14.

and rise again' (II Clem. 9). They are frequently found defended together.

It is therefore a question whether behind this denial there lay a Gnostic conception of salvation, and whether this had not had a continuous existence in the church from the time when Paul asked the Corinthians, 'How can some of you say that there is no resurrection of the dead?'. That the destruction of death could be part of a Gnostic conception of salvation would appear from Clement of Alexandria's reference to Valentinus having written in a homily: 'You are originally immortal and children of eternal life, and you would have death distributed to you that you may spend and lavish it, and that death may die in you and by you; for when you dissolve the world and are not yourselves dissolved, you have dominion over creation and all corruption' (*Strom.* iv.13). Irenaeus refers to Basilides as teaching that the soul alone received salvation while the body persists in corruption (1.26). For such Gnostics, the denial of resurrection would not be a denial of salvation but the assertion of it, and it would not have been difficult to take in this sense certain Pauline and Johannine statements about the Christian being already risen with Christ and already possessing eternal life. Thus Irenaeus refers to Menander as teaching that resurrection for his disciples consisted in receiving baptism (1.17, cf. Tert. *De Anima* 50), and when Tertullian sprinkles his scriptural proof of resurrection with attacks on those who were prepared to allegorize anything in scripture, he shows that he was faced with those who interpreted statements of the New Testament about resurrection figuratively of the present new life in Christ. It is remarkable that while Ignatius insists as strongly as possible in anti-gnostic fashion on the physical nature of the incarnate and risen Lord, he does so because it guarantees that union of flesh and spirit and that anticipation of immortality which Christians already experienced, and he barely refers to a future resurrection of believers,[25] and not at all to the judgment, despite his preoccupation with death and with the issue of his life and theirs. How complex the situation may have been can be seen from the Letter to Rheginos. Here Pauline thought, including its stress on faith, its mixture of realized and unrealized eschatology, the resurrection of the believer with Christ and the

[25] Only in the Introduction to Trallians.

putting on of Christ, is repeated and extended, but is combined with language reflecting a Gnostic milieu, and there is no reference to God or to a *parousia*; on the one hand resurrection is a deliverance from a world of illusion, which reflects a background of an anthropological dualism, and yet there is to be a resurrection body.

In contrast to the New Testament period, the discussion was almost entirely about the resurrection of the flesh (body) of believers, and reference is made to the resurrection of Jesus only indirectly and as bearing on that.[26] A discussion in these terms was unlikely to lead to any profound development of the doctrine of resurrection, and 'resurrection of the flesh' probably exercised its greatest influence in the sphere of popular piety, where it was the basis for asceticism and for exhortation to purity of the flesh, i.e. sexual continence.[27] The discussion tended to revolve round two stock arguments, which are already found together in I Clem. 23–27. The first was an appeal to the natural order as exhibiting pointers to the possibility and truth of resurrection, such as the rising of the sun, the growth of human beings from a drop of seed, the phoenix, sleep, and the changes which take place in mortal life. This was to some extent a substitute for the appeal to scripture; passages such as *De Res. Carn.* 26ff. show how hard put these writers were to prove resurrection from the Old Testament. The second argument was a somewhat wearisome reiteration of the text 'With God all things are possible', to show that he who created out of nothing could raise the dead, could gather the flesh however dispersed or eaten by other beings, and could reassemble it for resurrection.[28] Origen later refused to go along with those whom he called 'the more simple' in 'taking refuge' in this text, and he steered a course between the literalism of a reconstituted body and the Gnostic exclusion of the body altogether. He held that the material of the body, like all matter, was a subject of constant mutation but was constituted by a λόγος or εἶδος, a seminal

[26] van Unnik notes as a feature of the Epistle to Rheginos that it makes a closer connection between the two. See M. L. Peel, *The Epistle to Rheginos* (1969), pp. 125f. on the resurrection of Jesus as bringing about the resurrection of the Elect.

[27] See, for example, *The Acts of Paul and Thekla*.

[28] See R. M. Grant, 'The Resurrection of the Body', *Journal of Religion* xxviii (1948), pp. 120ff., 188ff.

principle or form which gave it its continuing identity. In the resurrection, the body is completely transformed as to its qualities, while remaining the same in identity, a view which in its own mode could be held to be a continuation of Pauline thought.

Subsequent exposition in the third and fourth centuries, in so far as it has come down to us, took the form of either bitter opposition to Origen for spiritualizing the doctrine away to the point of Neo-Platonism (so Methodius, Adamantius, Eustathius, Epiphanius, Jerome), or a partial or whole-hearted use of Origen (so Cyril of Jerusalem, Hilary, Gregory of Nyssa). Revealing is the charming episode of Synesius, the aristocratic, ostrich-hunting squire of Cyrene, who, when pressed by his grateful countrymen to be their bishop, agreed to consecration on condition that he was allowed to retain his Neo-Platonist convictions and to interpret the resurrection of the flesh allegorically (*Ep.* 105). The doctrine plays peculiarly little part in the vast thought of Augustine, and neither the Middle Ages nor the Reformation could be said to have made any particularly distinctive contribution to its development.

This very centrality of the resurrection in the New Testament faith is itself in some respects puzzling, and needs to be accounted for. For a doctrine of resurrection does not appear to have been one of the tenets long established in Judaism by New Testament times, but rather a comparative newcomer to it. There is no straight road here from the Old Testament to the New. Throughout the period covered by the Old Testament itself, the Jews seem to have remained content with the traditional idea of Sheol as the abode of 'the shades' of all the departed, where life is hardly worth living. The Old Testament knows of a post-mortem existence, but not of a future hope in terms of a further life. Since a religion can hardly be said to be mature until it has really grappled with the problem of death, this is remarkable. There is in the Old Testament only one unambiguous reference to resurrection, and that in its latest book.[29] Although it early became part of the church's apologetic that the resurrection of Jesus, like the cross and much else, was 'according to the scriptures' (I Cor. 15.4), that is, in fulfilment of the Old Testament and thus of the ultimate purpose of God, it is

---

[29] Daniel 12.2. There is another possible reference, also late, in Isa. 26.19, but this is disputed.

evident from the New Testament itself that the church was hard put to it to substantiate this claim. Thus, in contrast to the passion narratives, which are laced with Old Testament quotations and echoes designed to show that the cross was 'according to the determinate counsel and foreknowledge of God' (Acts 2.23), the resurrection narratives are almost entirely free from such, and those Old Testament passages which came to be used in apostolic preaching to argue the resurrection of Jesus are plainly being forced into service, and are made to bear a sense other than the original.

That somehow the resurrection of Jesus is the fulfilment of scripture in general is already contained in the traditional formula quoted by Paul in I Cor. 15.4, where the phrase 'according to the scriptures', a peculiar expression apparently without parallel in the rabbis, who referred to a specific passage of scripture, may already reflect controversy over the subject with rabbis. However, no use is made of scripture in the argument of I Cor. 15 itself, except the echo of Hos. 13.14 in 15.55 and the reference to Gen. 2.7 in 15.45 (or to an apocryphal writing, if 'it is written' refers to the whole verse). A general appeal to scripture is found on the lips of Jesus in Luke 24.27, 44f., but again without any particular scripture being adduced. This is in marked contrast with the passion narratives, though they are, of course, much longer than the comparatively brief resurrection stories.

In the sermons of Peter and Paul in Acts 2 and 13, the particular scripture is Ps. 16, especially 16.10: 'Thou wilt not suffer thy holy one to see corruption'. The similarity of argumentation in the two sermons – David said this; but he cannot be referring to himself, since he is dead and buried; he must therefore have been referring to the Messiah (concerning him, or with him in view, 2.25) – suggests that we do not have here the words of Peter and Paul, but of the author of Acts or of a form of preaching familiar to him. That the exegesis itself is a product of a Hellenistic church is evident from the fact that the force of the argument depends at times on the use of the LXX text at points where it differs in wording and sense from the Hebrew. In the Hebrew version, the psalmist says that he lives 'in confidence', because God will preserve him from adversity and from an untimely death; only in the Greek version does he speak in 'hope' of deliverance out of the corruption of death into eternal life in the presence of God (Acts 2.28; 13.34f.). Thus Acts 2.25–26a could apply to Jesus' life and death, 2.26b–27 to the period in the tomb, and 2.28 to the resurrection.

In both Acts 2 and Acts 13 it is not the resurrection of Jesus simply as an individual which is argued, but the establishment through his resurrection of the promise of a permanent dominion of the house of David,[30] and this is a Lukan theme (Luke 1.26–33, 69). In Acts 2 the argument is carried forward by the use of Ps. 110.1: 'The Lord said unto my Lord, Sit thou on my right hand, till I make thine enemies the footstool of thy feet.' This appears to have been originally an assurance of divine protection to the king on his enthronement, but it may lie behind every statement in the New Testament of the exaltation of Jesus to the right hand of God.[31] This is synonymous with resurrection if Acts 2.33 is to be rendered 'exalted by the right hand of God', but carries the thought forward if the meaning is 'exalted at the right hand of God'. In Acts 13 the argument is supported by the use of Ps. 2.7: 'Thou art my son, this day have I begotten thee' (also connected with the enthronement of Jesus in Heb. 1.5; 5.5), which is regarded as fulfilled, when taken in conjunction with II Sam. 7.14, in the enthronement by resurrection of Jesus as king in the permanent kingdom promised to David. To this is added Isa. 55.3: 'I will give you the holy and sure things of David' (the connection with Ps. 16.10 is partly verbal – 'I will *give* the *holy* things . . .'/'Thou wilt not *give* thy *holy* one . . .'), which is interpreted of a permanent house for David through the incorruptible life of the resurrection. Ps. 118.22: 'The stone which the builders rejected is become the head of the corner', may lie behind Eph. 2.20, and is quoted of the resurrection and exaltation in Acts 4.11; I Peter 2.4ff.; Mark 12.10f. par., where it is evidently a later addition to the parable.[32] This is a somewhat meagre selection of Old Testament texts, and indicates how unpromising a basis for a doctrine of resurrection the Old Testament was. There is no trace of these

[30] Acts 2.30; 13.33ff. See E. Lövestam, *Son and Saviour* (1961); B. Lindars, *New Testament Apologetic* (1961), ch. ii.

[31] Heb. 1.3, 13; 8.1; 10.12; 12.2; Eph. 1.20; Col. 3.1; I Peter 3.22; Rom. 8.34; Acts 7.55; Mark 12.36; 14.62; I Cor. 15.25.

[32] For Hosea 6.2, see pp. 48f.

passages in the resurrection narratives (except possibly Ps. 2.8 in Matt. 28.18ff.), which appear to have been moulded by different interests.

Resurrection is certainly not something which could have been arrived at by reflection on the Old Testament. It is only when to the Old Testament is added the Apocrypha, and to the Apocrypha are added certain books, chiefly apocalyptic, which were not included in it, and which have only come to light again in the last hundred years, that the situation is changed. From this more immediate hinterland of the New Testament a doctrine of resurrection becomes perceptible and intelligible; within the Apocrypha, for example, in II Esdras, II Maccabees and the Wisdom of Solomon; outside the Apocrypha in I and II Enoch, II Baruch, Jubilees, the Assumption of Moses, the Apocalypse of Moses, the Psalms of Solomon, IV Maccabees, and – if they are to be reckoned pre-Christian – the Testaments of the Twelve Patriarchs. These books at least put a question-mark against any idea of a normative Judaism in the first centuries BC and AD, to be deduced from the Old Testament and rabbinic exegesis of it. They point rather to a considerable ferment of thought and speculation. R. H. Pfeiffer describes the Judaism of this period as 'so alive, so progressive, so agitated by controversies, that under its spacious roof the most contrasting views were held – until a greater uniformity was reached after AD 200'.[33]

These writings, however, are not easy to handle, nor is their evidence easy to assess. They vary considerably in character, content and status; some are composite works, some difficult to date with precision. Generally speaking they stretch from the point reached by the latest book of the Old Testament, Daniel (*c.* 165 BC), to the end of the first century AD; that is, they cover a period of more or less acute crisis, beginning with unprecedented military and political success in the Maccabaean war, declining into an independence under the Hasmoneans which was full of bitter disappointments for the nobler spirits, and then declining further into subjection to a foreign power, and finally into hopeless revolt and extermination as a political entity. In some measure this was a

[33] R. H. Pfeiffer, *History of New Testament Times with an Introduction to the Apocrypha* (1949), p. 53. See also A. T. Nikolainen, *Der Auferstehungsglaube in der Bibel und in ihrer Umwelt* (2 vols. 1944, 1946); R. Martin-Achard, *De la mort à la resurrection d'après l'Ancien Testament* (1956).

literature of revolt, when a Judaism which was now more conscious of itself than previously was both at loggerheads with alien powers and also open to their influence. In Jewish eyes what was at stake could never be conceived in purely political, military or cultural terms. It concerned God, his ultimate purpose and his people, and the tensions involved in being the people of God in the world were now heightened. In this context, the older belief in Sheol begins to be replaced by something more adequate to the case, and 'resurrection' appears as one way of describing the action of God in relation to that which embodies or frustrates his purpose. This, however, takes more than one form.

In what may have been its earliest form it can be seen in II Maccabees, arising more immediately out of the passion of conflict and from reflection upon that conflict. The struggle of which I Maccabees (written probably about the beginning of the first century BC) is a straightforward, sober, historical account, is in II Maccabees (written perhaps some fifty years later) cast into the heroic mould. Here a doctrine of resurrection can be seen being born as a twin with a doctrine of martyrdom. Israel's oppression is a punishment of divine justice upon her sin, but to be chastened is a sign of being beloved by God so much is no more than the old prophetic view. What is new is that the hero martyrs, who are part of sinful Israel but not completely so, since their witness to the laws of God in their torments is such as to expiate the sins of their brethren, hurl their defiance at the tyrant out of full confidence in a resurrection to eternal life. Since this eternal life is to be a reunion with their brethren in order to participate in the kingdom on earth, resurrection takes the crudest form of restitution of the actual tormented body (II Macc. 7.14–38; 14.46). This combination of the ideas of martyrdom, expiation and a hope for the future may have had more influence on New Testament thought than has generally been recognized,[34] but the particular doctrine of resurrection which went along with it was hardly profound, or likely to be creative. Its limitations, and their origin in the particular crisis

[34] See C. K. Barrett, 'The Background of Mark 10.45', in A. J. B. Higgins (ed.), *New Testament Essays in Memory of T. W. Manson* (1959), pp. 1ff.; J. Downing, 'Jesus and Martyrdom', *JTS*, NS xiv (1963), pp. 279ff.; E. Lohse, *Märtyrer und Gottesknecht: Untersuchungen zur urchristlichen Verkündigung von Sühntod Jesu Christi* (1955), *passim*. For the concept of martyrdom in Judaism, both in itself and in its relation to the New Testament, see W. H. C. Frend, *Martyrdom and Persecution in the Early Church* (1965), chs. ii and iii.

to which the doctrine was tied, can be seen in the curious form it takes in Dan. 12.2 (which is also written on the background of the Maccabaean struggle), of a resurrection of Israelites only, and of these, apparently, only the best and the worst, viz. those who had performed superlatively well by resisting the tyrant to the death, who are to be resurrected to life, and those who had apostatized from Judaism, who are to be resurrected to 'abhorrence'. That is, resurrection is both limited in its scope, and is not in itself positive and saving.

A second form of the doctrine is less immediate and passionate, and more metaphysical. It also starts from the old prophetic teaching of the divine righteousness and judgment, which it now asserts in cosmic and dualistic terms, which probably betray that somewhere in the background lies the influence of Iranian Zoroastrianism. Its primary concern is not with resurrection at all, but with a universal judgment whereby God will bring to an end the present age (now conceived of as irretrievably evil) and the evil angels responsible for it, and will assert his righteousness over all. Resurrection is here part of a *schema*; it is the necessary prelude for assembling all men before God in a suitable form for judgment. And that means in a body, since in Jewish thinking a man is not fully himself, and therefore capable of being judged, without a body to establish his identity as the man he was. Thus, in II Baruch 50–51, the resurrection body is not itself a body of glory, but the previous physical body restored from earth for the purpose of a man's identification by his fellows, and of proof that resurrection has taken place. Only after the judgment is it then transformed into a body of glory for the purposes of eternal life. While this doctrine, in the various and sometimes contradictory forms in which it is found,[35] had a strong ethical content through its connection with

---

[35] For these variations see D. S. Russell, *The Method and Message of Jewish Apocalyptic* (1964), ch. xiv, and P. Hoffmann, *Die Toten in Christus* (1966), chs. iv–vi. The main ones are:

(a) resurrection of the righteous (Israelites) only (so Psalms of Solomon, I Enoch 83–90);

(b) resurrection of the righteous and unrighteous in Israel for judgment (so Dan. 12.2; I Enoch 6–36; II Baruch);

(c) resurrection of all men for judgment (so Sibylline Oracles, II Esdras, Testament of XII Patriarchs).

There are differences about place (resurrection to earth, to a renewed earth, to Paradise), time (to a messianic period belonging to this age, to eternal life in perpetuity), and form (a reconstituted body, a transformed body, without

a universal moral judgment, it is in itself singularly sterile, and can hardly avoid R. H. Charles' charge of being a 'mechanical conception'. He writes: 'Severed from the spiritual root from which it grew, it was transformed into a sort of eschatological property, a device by means of which the members of the nation were presented before God to receive their final reward.'[36] It is only loosely connected to the nature of that reward.

A third form is more directly concerned with the problem of death as such, and betrays a greater or less influence from the Greek side in being not a doctrine of resurrection, but of immortality. This is so in Jubilees, where it is said of the righteous that their 'bones rest in the earth and their spirits will have much joy' (23.31); in the Assumption of Moses, where Israel is to be exalted by God straight to heaven and her foes to Gehenna (10.9f.); in some parts of I Enoch, where the righteous dead pass in their spirits into heavenly life from Sheol, while the wicked are left behind there; and especially in the Wisdom of Solomon and IV Maccabees. It is never the pure consistent philosophical conception of immortality, which means 'undieableness' as an inalienable property of the soul, and which logically requires a doctrine of the eternal pre-existence of the soul as its accompaniment, but always some sort of hybrid between this and the Hebraic conception of God as the giver of life, here and beyond, and as active and intervening in human affairs. Thus, in the Wisdom of Solomon man is on the one hand created for immortality, and is so because he is created by God as an image of his own incorruptible being. His pre-existent soul enters a corruptible body on earth, and in the case of the righteous, who is maintained in the root of immortality by incorruptible wisdom, only seems to die, death being the creation

---

body). These variations, some of them sometimes found within a single work, reflect a considerable fluidity of thought, which was probably brought about by the impact upon Israel of new modes of belief, especially the Iranian, to which resurrection and the final judgment were by this time indigenous. Cf. J. H. Moulton, *Early Zoroastrianism* (1913); R. C. Zaehner, *The Teaching of the Magi* (1956); N. Söderblom, *La vie future d'après le Mazdéisme* (1901). It is a matter of some importance for the history of religions that the doctrine of resurrection, which was to move into the centre in Christianity, was a comparative newcomer in Israelite belief, and did not belong to the main stream of 'biblical' religion.

[36] R. H. Charles, 'Eschatology', in: T. K. Cheyne and J. S. Black (eds.), *Encyclopedia Biblica*, vol. II (1901), p. 1355, col. 1.

not of God but of the devil; in the case of the wicked it continues for
ever in the spiritual death which ungodliness has already meant on
earth. Yet, on the other hand, there will be a day of visitation when
God comes to judgment. Similarly IV Maccabees teaches the
immortality of spirits both righteous and unrighteous, but in the
case of the righteous this immortality is not thought of as an
inalienable possession, but, in continuation of the heroic mood of
II Maccabees, though on a loftier plane, as a prize conferred by
God for victory in the conflict.³⁷ When Josephus (B.J. 2.162ff.)
says of the Pharisees that they 'attribute everything to Fate and to
God' and that they hold that 'every soul is imperishable, but the
soul of the good passes into another body, while the souls of the
wicked suffer eternal punishment', and of the Sadducees that they
'do away with Fate altogether, and remove God beyond not merely
the commission, but the very sight of evil', it is probable that with
the expression 'imperishable soul which passes into another body'
he is doing his best to translate a Jewish doctrine of resurrection
into terms with which the Roman world for which he is writing
was familiar, as he is certainly doing when he uses the rootedly
Greek but totally un-Jewish concept of Fate. This form of the
doctrine of a future life was naturally more characteristic of
Alexandrian Judaism, which was open to Greek influence, and has
its most explicit development in Judaism in Philo. Nevertheless, in
rabbinic writings at least as early as the second century AD, and
possibly earlier, alongside speculations about the resurrection,
sometimes of the greatest crudity, are to be found both statements

³⁷ R. H. Pfeiffer, *op. cit.*, p. 336, comments on the Wisdom of Solomon:
'Since our author attempted to combine mutually exclusive Hebrew and Greek
ideas about life after death, his thought was inevitably indefinite, if not
actually inconsistent. His interpreters have consequently reached opposite
conclusions in their attempts to understand his teaching.' And on the Maccabaean books (p. 220): 'While II Maccabees repeatedly speaks of the resurrection of the body as the hope of martyrs, and only once (7.36) of "eternal life"
(which may be a loose way of speaking of resurrection), IV Maccabees, like
the Wisdom of Solomon, teaches the doctrine of the immortality of the spirit
(14.5; 16.13) – "pure and immortal souls", 18.23 – both of the pious (14.6)
and of the wicked (13.15); the pious are honoured by God and have an abode
in heaven (17.5) after achieving "the prize of victory in incorruption in everlasting life" (17.12), or better, with a slight change in the Greek, "the prize of
victory *was* incorruption". They shall stand beside the throne of God and
live in blissful eternity (17.18) "unto God", having obtained a divine inheritance (18.3). On the contrary, eternal torments are the lot of the wicked (9.9;
10.11; 15.21; 12.12).' For immortality, cf. possibly II Enoch 50.2; 65.6.

of the immortality of the soul, as of the specifically spiritual and God-given element in man, and also statements of its pre-existence in a kind of heavenly storehouse before the creation of the world. It does not appear to have exercised much influence on the New Testament, though the hybrid can be seen in Paul's statement that with the resurrection body a man will put on immortality.

The evidence provided by this literature is not easy to estimate with any confidence that the resultant picture is in focus. The conceptions of the future life in it are not uniform, but various, and sometimes incoherent. That may itself argue that they were widespread and well established, and this would seem to be the conclusion drawn by most of the authorities. Thus Guignebert judges that 'belief in a resurrection was of primary importance in the religious beliefs of the Jews in Jesus' day, so much so that it may be said to have transformed the old Jahwism into a new religion', and that 'only the somewhat sceptical aristocrats of the Temple staff . . . denied it'.[38] Mowinckel's view is that in the time of Jesus, belief in a general resurrection was prevalent and was taken as 'the distinguishing mark between believers and unbelievers'[39]

[38] C. Guignebert, *The Jewish World in the Time of Jesus* (1939), pp. 117, 120.
[39] S. Mowinckel, *He That Cometh* (1956), p. 274; cf. G. F. Moore, *Judaism*, ii (1927), pp. 295ff., and others. Moore prefaces his study of the development of the ideas of the after-life in Judaism with the observation that 'the resurrection of the dead, or in their (sc. the Pharisees) own phrase the revivification of the dead, thus became a cardinal doctrine of Judaism', and concludes it with: 'On the premises of Scripture the only logical way in which the Jews could conceive the fulfilment of God's promises to the righteous was that they should live again on the earth in the golden age to come, and share in the salvation of Israel. The resurrection seems, indeed, so necessarily the consequence of the whole teaching of Scripture concerning the salvation of the righteous and their reward that it is not strange that the Pharisees found it explicit or by intimation in all parts of their Bible' (pp. 313f.). K. H. Rengstorf, *Die Auferstehung Jesu*, p. 87, has it that the hope of resurrection had by the turn of the first century BC long obtained in the circles of traditional Jewish piety the position of an uncontested doctrine, and refers to the evidence of Strack-Billerbeck, IV, p. 1216. On the other hand, it has frequently been complained (as e.g. by Morton Smith, 'The Dead Sea Sect in Relation to Ancient Judaism', *NTS* 7 (1960–61), pp. 355ff.) that Moore was misleading in his identification of normative Judaism with that of the Pharisees. J. Bonsirven, *Palestinian Judaism in the Time of Jesus Christ* (1964), p. 164, is more cautious, and argues that it 'was unavoidable that there would be great divergence of opinion in these matters', because they involved a radical departure from the old idea of Sheol and a growing conviction that man is composed of body and soul, the soul being able to enjoy a separate existence after leaving the body. He concludes that 'in the first Christian century, belief in resurrection was far from being commonly accepted among the Jews . . . By the end of the first century

Christianity on this basis could be regarded as a resurrectionist sect within Judaism, as one of the groups of Samaritans is said to have been,[40] or somewhat as various Jewish groups are said to be manifestations of a widespread baptizing movement before and during the first century AD. Certainly Christians did not invent the idea of resurrection; the way it was thought about and the terminology for expressing this thought will have been already current.

The vocabulary of resurrection in the New Testament may be a further indication that the concept was a comparatively late and foreign one in Israel. The concept, in what came to be its principal form, belonged with apocalyptic and was unintelligible apart from that context. But apocalyptic in Judaism was a syncretistic phenomenon, which was only in part a development from Israelite tradition. As H. Koester observes,[41] the language of the New Testament is to a considerable degree syncretistic language, and none more so than the language of resurrection.

The words chiefly involved are the two verbs ἐγείρειν and ἀνιστάναι, which are already found in inter-testamental writings where these are extant in Greek. The former, which is hardly, if ever, used in ordinary Greek in connection with death and resurrection, is the word used in Dan. 12.2 (ἐξεγείρειν; cf. Isa. 26.19); II Kings 4.31; Ecclus. 48.5; I Enoch 22.13 (μετεγείρειν). It is the more frequent of the two in the New Testament, and is used absolutely (in Matthew, Mark, Luke, John, Acts and Paul), with ἐκ τῶν νεκρῶν ('from among the dead': so Matthew, Mark,

---

it seems to have become a dogma for the Pharisees' (p. 227). This can be seen in the second of the Eighteen Benedictions: 'Thou art mighty, strong, that quickenest the dead. Blessed art thou, O Lord, who quickenest the dead.' Mowinckel, *op. cit.*, p. 273, after remarking that the doctrine was characteristic of later Judaism, goes on to say that 'the fact that the Sadducees rejected it shows how new it really was, and how alien to earlier Judaism'. W. R. Farmer, *Maccabees, Zealots and Josephus* (1956), p. 190, holds that the normative Judaism of the first century is to be defined in terms of a nationalist theology of the Jewish resistance movements, and that the belief in the resurrection of the body was a part of this, accounting for 'the astonishing phenomenon of mass martyrdom as well as mass military heroism on the part of the Jews in the Greco-Roman period'. But it could be argued the other way round, especially from a comparison of I and II Maccabees, that the doctrine arose later out of reflection upon the nationalist activity and enterprise.

[40] M. Black, *The Scrolls and Christian Origins* (1961), p. 63.
[41] H. Koester, 'Häretiker im Urchristentum als theologisches Problem', in: E. Dinkler (ed.), *Zeit und Geschichte* (Bultmann Festschrift, 1964), pp. 67ff.

Luke, John, Acts, Hebrews, I Peter), and with ἀπὸ νεκρῶν ('away from (the) dead': so Matthew only). The noun derived from it, ἔγερσις, which is occasionally found in classical and Hellenistic Greek for resurrection of the dead, occurs in the New Testament only at Matt. 27.53. The latter verb, ἀνιστάναι, which is common in classical and Hellenistic Greek in connection with death and life from the dead, is the word used in II Maccabees (7.9, 14; cf. Isa. 26.19). In the New Testament it is used (*a*) transitively, 'to raise', either absolutely (John, Acts) or with ἐκ νεκρῶν (Acts); and (*b*) intransitively, in the second aorist and all middle forms, 'to rise', both absolutely (Mark, Luke, John and Paul) and with ἐκ νεκρῶν (Mark, Luke, John, Acts, Ephesians). The noun ἀνάστασις, from which the verb is derived, is found occasionally in classical and Hellenistic Greek for resurrection, and in II Macc. 7.14; 12.43, but not in Josephus or Philo in this sense. In the New Testament it is used absolutely (Matthew, Mark, Luke, John, Acts, Pastorals, Hebrews, Revelation), with (τῶν) νεκρῶν ('of (the) dead': Matthew, Acts, Paul and Hebrews), with ἐκ νεκρῶν (Luke, Acts, I Peter), with 'of Christ (him)' (Acts, Paul, I Peter), with 'of the righteous' (Luke 14.14), with 'of the righteous and unrighteous' (Acts 24.15), with 'of life' and 'of judgment' (John 5.29f.). That the two verbs are synonymous can be seen from their interchange in I Cor. 15.

The subject of ἐγείρειν is always God, or else the verb is used in the passive, which then always has the sense 'raised by God'. This establishes the resurrection as the act of God towards Jesus, and hence the theocentric character of the whole gospel. God can be characterized as 'he who raised Jesus (our Lord)' (Rom. 4.24; 8.11; II Cor. 4.14; Gal. 1.1; Col. 2.12; I Peter 1.21). The subject of ἀνιστάναι is God (this usage is confined to Acts; in John 6.39–54 Jesus is the subject in raising others), and the intransitive, which is not frequent, intends the sense 'he was raised by God' (cf. I Thess. 4.14: 'If we believe that Jesus died and rose (ἀνέστη), so also God will bring with him those who sleep through Jesus'). This is not so clear, however, as with ἐγείρειν, and ἀναστήσεται ('he will arise' – by his own power) in the Son of man predictions in Mark 9.31; 10.34; cf. 8.31; 9.9f., pars, is probably secondary.

The only clear exceptions to this usage are in the Johannine writings with their advanced christology. In John 2.19, Jesus is said to be the raiser of his own body; in 10.17f., he has the right (power), in obedience to a command of the Father, both to lay down his life in death and to resume it; in 5.21ff., as Son of God and Son of man, he possesses as delegated qualities and powers from God the capacity to have life in himself, to raise and quicken the dead, and to execute the final judgment, and it is through hearing his voice that the dead will come to life and emerge to a resurrection of life or judgment; as also in 6.39f., 44, 54, in obedience to the Father's will, he is to confer the final resurrection as the consummation of that eternal life which he already gives to the believer who feeds on him. In 11.25, all this is taken to a final stage where resurrection itself is identified with Jesus, and subsumed in his person. In Revelation Jesus is not said to have been raised, but to be alive, and to have the keys of death and Hades (Rev. 1.18; 2.8). It is a further step along this line when Ignatius says: 'He truly suffered, even as he also truly raised himself' (Smyrn. 2.1), and a very considerable further step when the author of the Epistle to Rheginos says not only that 'we have believed that he arose from among the dead' (46.15), but that 'He transformed (himself) into an imperishable Aeon and raised himself up' (45.17ff.), for here Jesus is the sole agent, and there is no mention of any Father God behind him.

Whether the perfect passive of ἐγείρειν (ἐγήγερται) which is found in the formula in I Cor. 15.4 and subsequently in the argument of I Cor. 15 (cf. II Tim. 2.8), has, in distinction from the normal aorist passive ἠγέρθη, the special nuance that the resurrection of Jesus was to a permanent and effectual state, is not clear. Rengstorf's objection[42] that if so 'he died' would also have to be in the perfect, since the death is said to be for our sins, is hardly cogent; the permanent significance of the once-for-all death of Christ is differently expressed and drawn out in the New Testament than is the permanent significance of the resurrection.

The meaning of resurrection suggested by the two verbs, though possibly the same in both cases, is not immediately evident:

(i) Since 'to awaken' is a primary meaning of ἐγείρειν, and a possible meaning of ἀνιστάναι in Greek writing (though less frequently in the LXX), the thought may be of death as a sleep

[42] *Op. cit.*, p. 55n.

and of resurrection as an awakening of men by God out of sleep. However, the idea of awakening the dead is very rare in secular Greek. It is found in the single Old Testament resurrection text (Dan. 12.2), and in what is probably a quotation from an early Christian hymn in Eph. 5.14: 'Awake (ἔγειρε), sleeper, and rise (ἀνάστα, get up?) from the dead.' In the New Testament, the thought is more closely connected with ἀνιστάναι (I Thess. 4.13–16; 5.10?; John 11.11ff., 24), but is found in connection with ἐγείρειν in Matt. 27.52; Acts 13.36f.; I Cor. 15.20. The idea of death as sleep, based no doubt on a certain resemblance between them, is a commonplace from Homer onwards, chiefly in literary or philosophical texts.[43] 'To fall asleep' was a conventional euphemism for 'to die'. As such it is found, though comparatively seldom, in the Old Testament and always with some addition, e.g. 'in the dust'. In itself it simply expresses the fact of dying, and does not, without further specification, denote the state of the dead as being a state of sleep. Thus the Old Testament phrase 'he slept with his fathers' does not mean that he joined his fathers in a state of sleep, but that he died and was buried in the ancestral grave. Thus the idea of sleep is not brought into connection with the Old Testament conception of Sheol as a shady and lifeless existence. The dead are not said to sleep in Sheol, nor are they awoken from there. In later Hellenistic poetry and philosophy the metaphor was filled out, and the state of the dead is there sometimes described as a state of permanent sleep. In the Jewish tradition, this idea appears, not as a development of Old Testament thought, but as a borrowed expression in later, and chiefly apocalyptic, books. It is used with particular reference to the state of a certain class of people – the patriarchs, or the righteous dead – whose state is one of rest, from which they will be awoken at resurrection (Jubilees 23.1; 36.18; I Enoch 91.10; 92.3; 100.5; cf. I Enoch 49.3; IV Ezra 7.85–95; II Baruch 11.4; 30.2; Test. Reub. 3.1; Test. Jud. 25.1, etc.).

In the New Testament also, 'to fall asleep' is a conventional expression for 'to die' (Matt. 27.52; Acts 7.60; 13.36; I Cor. 7.39; 11.30; 15.6), and 'those who have fallen asleep' for 'the dead' (I Thess. 4.13, 15). The Christian dead are those who have fallen asleep 'in' or 'through' Christ (I Thess. 4.14; I Cor. 15.18;

---

[43] Cf. P. Hoffmann, *op. cit.*, pp. 186ff.

cf. II Baruch 30.2: All those who have fallen asleep through hope in him (sc. the Messiah) shall rise again), and the risen Christ is the first instalment of those who sleep (I Cor. 15.20). John 11.11ff. (cf. Mark 5.39?) plays on the double meaning. But the expression is so conventional that it can hardly be pressed to convey real information about the condition of the dead, and it plays no part in the development of New Testament thought about resurrection. It could hardly do so because even there it is a reduced metaphor, which points only indirectly to the reality, and it gives no hint of any transformation. If it had pointed directly to the resurrection, it would have suggested a corpse which gets up and walks, and this is not meant, at least by the resurrection of Jesus. When Paul contemplates his own death in Christ, he does not appear to envisage it as a sleeping existence, but rather as life with Christ, and as a further sharing in the present resurrection experience (Phil. 1.21–23; 3.10f.), and even in I Thess. 4.14–16, in the expressions 'asleep through Jesus' and 'the dead in Christ', it is probably 'in Christ' rather than 'asleep' that is stressed. The idea of awakening does not fit well with ἐκ νεκρῶν (to awake from (among) the dead), and would require something like ἐκ θανάτου (from death: as Ecclus. 48.5; cf. Rom. 13.11, ἐξ ὕπνου : from sleep).

(ii) Both ἐγείρειν and ἀνιστάναι have another meaning, 'to raise upright', 'to set erect', 'to erect', of a statue or building (cf. John 2.19f. of the temple which is the body). Here the picture suggested is of one who is prone, and of death as that which places men in this position of incapacity (cf. 'I fell at his feet as one dead', Rev. 1.17). Resurrection is, then, that which restores men to a position of being upright and active. There is an analogous use in the gospel miracle narratives: 'taking hold of his (her) hand he raised him (her) up' (ἤγειρεν: so Mark 9.27; Matt. 9.25; Mark 1.31; Mark 5.41, where it is followed by 'and she immediately got up and walked'). In Eph. 5.14, two ideas may be combined: Awake, sleeper, and get up from the dead. This conception of 'raising' is also hardly a natural extension and development of Old Testament thought, as may be seen from the ambiguity in Paul's sermon in Acts 13.33. After summarizing Israel's history as God's acts in exalting the people, giving them judges and 'raising' for them David as king, he goes on to say that God has fulfilled his promises in 'raising'

Jesus, and it is uncertain whether the reference here is to the resurrection of Jesus or to his being brought on the historical scene, like David.

On the other hand, in Zoroastrianism, which undoubtedly influenced Jewish eschatology in its doctrine of rewards and punishments, this conception is present. There death was thought of as one of the chief weapons of the devil, and the eschatological restoration of the world, the defeat of the powers of darkness and the establishment of the divine kingdom, involved the reversal of the destruction of creatures through death. The language used to describe what was to happen as regards the dead is almost entirely based on the verb 'to raise'. Thus, 'in fifty-seven years Sosiyans will raise all the dead'; 'they rise from that place where the life went out from their bodies';[44] 'let the dead arise and let bodily life be sustained in these now lifeless bodies'.[45]

This meaning of ἐγείρειν and ἀνιστάναι would fit well when the verbs govern a direct object and in the phrase ἀνάστασις (τῶν) νεκρῶν (the raising of the dead); it would not fit so well ἀνάστασις ἐκ τῶν νεκρῶν (raising up from among the dead).

(iii) There is a further possible background to sense (ii). In Rom. 10.6ff., Paul, in arguing that righteousness by faith is present and available to the believer in the confession that Jesus is Lord and that God has raised Jesus from the dead, interprets the words of Deut. 30.13 in the form 'Who will descend into the abyss?', as meaning 'to bring Christ up (ἀναγαγεῖν) from the dead'. Here the picture is one of drawing the dead out of the pit of Sheol. With this may be compared I Enoch 51.1: Sheol shall give back that which it has received, and IV Ezra 7.32: the earth shall restore those that sleep in her, and the dust those that rest therein. Something of this sense could attach at least to ἐγείρειν, as when sabbath healing is defended by appeal to the action of a man who takes hold of an animal and draws it (ἐγερεῖ) out of a pit (Matt. 12.11). It is possible that the combination of death with Hades, the abode of the dead (as in Rev. 1.18; 6.8), and the more apocalyptic conception of Hades

[44] Zand-Ākāsīh, *Iranian or Greater Bundahišn*, translated by B. T. Anklesaria (1956), p. 287; *Pahlavi Texts, Part I*, translated by E. W. West (Sacred Books of the East, ed. F. Max Müller, Vol. V, 1880), p. 386.

[45] An Avestan fragment; see L. H. Mills, *Avestan Eschatology compared with the Books of Daniel and Revelation* (1908), p. 41.

as a rival kingdom which is to be made to yield up its captives
(Rev. 20.13f.; cf. Matt. 16.18; Acts 2.31), may have contributed
to the quasi-personification of death as a power and to the consequent thought of resurrection as final victory (cf. Acts 2.24:
loosing the pangs of death = destroying its power). This
appears especially in Pauline theology, where death rules
through sin (Rom. 5.14ff.), and has no more rule over Christ
because his resurrection shows his death to have been a death
to sin once and for all (Rom. 6.8ff.), where sin and death are
powers which take men captive (Rom. 7.7ff.), but the spirit of
God who raised Jesus from the dead brings them freedom and
righteousness (Rom. 8.8ff.), and where death is the last enemy
due for destruction and resurrection is the final victory (I Cor.
15.26, 54f., quoting Isaiah and Hosea). Also may be compared
II Tim. 1.10, Christ bringing death to destruction and life and
immortality to light; Heb. 2.14, Christ by death destroying the
devil who has the power of death; Rev. 1.18, Christ as possessing the keys of the domain of death and Hades.

Except as possibly lying behind sense (iii), neither ἐγείρειν
nor ἀνιστάναι appear to have contributed much to a positive
understanding of resurrection. This is conveyed rather by such
expressions as 'to live', 'to make alive', and 'to glorify'. God
is the living God, and as such is God not of dead men but of
the living (Mark 12.27; Luke 20.38; I Thess. 1.9; I Peter 1.21–
25). The living Father has sent the Son, who lives through the
Father, and the believer in the Son lives even in death (John
6.57f.; 11.25). The resurrection of Christ is a living after death,
and the conquest of death, so that he has dominion over all men
(Rom. 14.9), and being the conquest of sin is a life lived permanently to God (Rom. 6.13). This life is, or will be, shared
by those who are 'in Christ' (Rom. 6.13; 14.8f.; II Cor. 13.4;
Phil. 1.21; Col. 3.1ff.), and who will be 'made alive' (ζωοποιεῖν
John 5.21; Rom. 4.17; 8.11; I Cor. 15.22, 36, 45; I Peter 3.18).
Since the word 'glory' is the biblical word which comes nearest
to expressing the being and nature of God himself, it is inevitably
connected with the thought of resurrection as entry into the
divine life. This is so, first of the resurrection or exaltation of
Jesus as his elevation to the divine presence and life, especially
in the Gospel of John (John 7.39; 12.16; 17.1–5), but also elsewhere (Acts 3.13; Heb. 2.9; 5.5; Luke 24.26; Rom. 6.4; I Tim.

3.16; I Peter 1.11, 21); and then of those who share his resurrection (John 17.22; Rom. 5.2; 8.17f.; I Cor. 15.43; II Cor. 3.18; 4.17; Phil. 3.21; II Thess. 2.14; II Tim. 2.10; Titus 2.13; Heb. 2.10; I Peter 4.13f.; 5.1). In this connection the word φανεροῦσθαι ('to be made manifest') also appears (Col. 3.4; I Peter 5.4; I John 3.2).[46]

When full account has been taken of the apocryphal and pseudepigraphical literature referred to above in its testimony to some doctrine of resurrection, there is still ground for hesitation. This literature is that which has happened to survive, and its very survival may be due to the interest in it of later Jews and Christians, who, from their own point of view, were concerned with what it had to say. It is not altogether clear how far the views it expresses were widely held, or were the views of restricted but more articulate groups, or of individuals. Its very incoherence could argue that resurrection was not a universally held belief and badge of orthodoxy, but a subject of considerable speculation and debate. The phenomenon of the Sadducees remains. As they were the losing party which did not survive the fall of Jerusalem, their literature, assuming that there was any, is among that which did not survive; it would not have been of interest to later generations. Hence we are almost totally in the dark about them and their position, which may have been less that of the odd man out in the general scene than it must now appear. It is true that both Josephus and Luke represent belief in resurrection as a hallmark of Judaism, the former by limiting his description of the two main parties, the Pharisees and Sadducees, to their tenets in this matter and in the matter of free-will, as also in the prominence which he gives to it in his description of the Essenes; and the latter by making the later career of Paul in Acts a test case of the Pharisaic doctrine of resurrection, which is described as the hope of the whole Jewish race (Acts 26.6ff.). It has, however, to be remembered that both these authors, writing towards the end of the first century AD, are addressing the Greco-Roman world, to which this particular doctrine was the most eminently exportable.

The latest addition to this kind of literature, the Qumran scrolls, also apparently gives reason for hesitation. Here the matter is, of

---

[46] For a discussion of the resurrection vocabulary, see E. Fascher, 'Anastasis–Resurrectio–Auferstehung', *ZNTW* 40 (1941), pp. 166ff.; U. Wilckens, *Die Missionsreden der Apostelgeschichte* (1963), pp. 137ff.

course, still under debate amongst the experts, but some of them
are able to state categorically that in the scrolls so far available and
deciphered no indication is to be found of a belief in resurrection,
and while this may still be put down to chance, it is striking in a
sect with such strongly marked apocalyptic inclinations, which
contemplated a dénouement in a war of the children of light against
the children of darkness, in which some of the former would
perish. Those who maintain that the scrolls do refer to resurrection are so far only able to do so either in respect of one or two
passages which are themselves either conjectural or open to more
than one interpretation (words such as 'rise' or 'eternal life' are
notoriously ambiguous in this connection), or by an *a priori* argument that in the light of the sect's known beliefs it must have
believed in resurrection.

The diversity of opinion here is considerable.[47] This is due to
uncertainty whether the surviving documents are representative
of all the sect, or contain all its major tenets, to the fragmentary
condition of some of the texts, and to a possible ambiguity in
some words and expressions (e.g. in the word 'arise'). M.
Mansoor takes the expression in Hodayot 6.34, 'those who lie
(dwell) in the dust' as a definite reference to the resurrection of
the body, which he can call 'a belief highly developed by the
sect'.[48] Others, however, translate differently and Millar Burrows comments: 'In the highly poetic language of the Psalms, it
is not clear whether this passage speaks of the dead or the
living'.[49] J. van der Ploeg considers that 'the obvious kinship
of the sect with the Essenes would lead us to expect a belief in
the immortality of the soul apart from the body',[50] and this he
believes is borne out by the texts, which have little to suggest
a renewed bodily existence, but much to suggest a life in a world
of light, angels and God. H. H. Rowley also thinks that the
scrolls reflect a belief in the immortality of the soul rather than
in the resurrection of the whole person, body and soul together,
and that the sect stood closer to some other non-biblical works
of the second century BC: 'The members of the sect knew the

---

[47] See the discussion in Millar Burrows, *The Dead Sea Scrolls* (1956),
pp. 270ff.

[48] M. Mansoor, 'Studies in the *Hodayot* – IV', *JBL* 76 (1957), p. 146.

[49] Millar Burrows, *More Light on the Dead Sea Scrolls* (1958), p. 345.

[50] J. van der Ploeg, 'L'Immortalité de l'homme d'après les textes de la Mer
Morte', *VT* 2 (1952), pp. 171ff.

book of Daniel, in which this hope (of resurrection) is expressed, for fragments of it have been found at Qumran. Yet nowhere in our surviving texts is any thought of the resurrection of the faithful expressed.'[51] E. F. Sutcliffe states that 'no passage in the scrolls reveals an expectation of the resurrection. The word "arise" does not of itself suggest it. Both in the Old Testament and New Testament the word is used of kings and prophets appearing, coming on the scene . . . The texts which have been misunderstood to speak of the resurrection actually treat of arising for action or arising from the dust of humiliation as in Isa. 26.19.'[52] He notes that its absence is particularly surprising in the War Rule, where, when some of the sons of light are said to fall in battle, one might have expected some encouragement from the thought of future resurrection. H. J. Cadbury suggests that this may illustrate 'how attention when concentrated on apocalyptic hope may leave out as relatively unimportant the question what happens to those who do die'.[53] T. H. Gaster makes no mention of the resurrection in his analytical index of the community's tenets.[54] The conclusions of G. Vermes are as follows: 'The doctrine of the resurrection does not seem to have been a major preoccupation of the Community. It may be reflected in a few passages such as the following: "Hoist a banner, O you who lie in the dust! O bodies gnawed with worms, raise an ensign" (Hymn 10). But it is not impossible that the phraseology is metaphorical. On the other hand, considering the beliefs and expectations of the sect as a whole, it is difficult to conceive that the members would have denied their dead brethren and the saints of the past a full share in the eternal joys of the Messianic Kingdom.'[55] Matthew Black, discussing the Manual of Discipline and taking account of the eschatology of the Damascus Document, concludes that 'the general type of eschatology would appear to be that of an expected Kingdom of God (or New Creation) of eternal duration on the present earth, with Jerusalem (and the Temple) as

[51] H. H. Rowley, *The Dead Sea Scrolls from Qumran* (1958), p. 18.
[52] E. F. Sutcliffe, *The Monks of Qumran* (1960), p. 88.
[53] H. J. Cadbury, 'Intimations of Immortality in the Thought of Jesus', in: M. C. Perry (ed.), *The Miracles and the Resurrection*, Theological Collections 3 (1964), p. 104.
[54] T. H. Gaster, *The Scriptures of the Dead Sea Sect* (1957), pp. 303ff.
[55] G. Vermes, *The Dead Sea Scrolls in English* (1965²), p. 51.

its centre', and in relation to the Hymn of Deliverance he disagrees with Dupont-Sommer that it implies the immortality of the soul, and denies that there is any evidence that the Qumran Essenes believed in the immortality of the soul as distinct from the body. He sums up: 'It is virtually certain that the sect had some form of belief in the Resurrection, though, so far, no unambiguously clear evidence for such has been produced. Indeed, on the contrary, a number of passages appear to imply the old Biblical doctrine of Sheol, which seems to rule out, not only every form of belief in the Resurrection, but also, no less, any kind of hope of immortality.'[56] The conclusions of G. R. Driver are: 'The opinions of the Covenanters on a future life are not altogether clear. Possibly three passages more or less imply a bodily resurrection . . . At the same time many passages prove beyond doubt that the righteous, i.e. the elect or members of the Community, looked for "everlasting peace and perpetual salvation", expecting to live for ever . . . The conclusion, then, seems to be that the Covenanters had some vague notions of a physical resurrection, and certainly believed in a future angelic existence in eternal bliss in communion with God, if only as a corollary to the eternal damnation of their enemies, but perhaps not in any resurrection of the body.'[57] P. Hoffmann fails to find any evidence for a doctrine of a future state, and accounts for it by the community's imminent expectation of the end, but he refers to Père de Vaux's study of the graves at Qumran as indicating that Qumran was to be the scene of this end, and that the dead were to be raised for it.[58]

There is a curious statement in the Gospel of Mark which continues to embarrass the commentators. After the Transfiguration, Jesus is represented as enjoining the three disciples who had witnessed it not to disclose what they had seen until the Son of man had risen from the dead, and Mark adds that they kept the saying in mind and discussed what rising from the dead should

[56] M. Black, *The Scrolls and Christian Origins*, pp. 135ff., and cf. his strictures on the bad philology of translating 'arise' by 'resurrection' in M. Black (ed.), *The Scrolls and Christianity*, Theological Collections 11 (1969), p. 115 n. 21. In the same volume John Pryke, 'Eschatology in the Dead Sea Scrolls', pp. 45ff.

[57] G. R. Driver, *The Judaean Scrolls* (1965), pp. 74f.

[58] P. Hoffmann, *op. cit.*, pp. 131ff.

mean (Mark 9.9f.). If, as the commentators remark, resurrection was a familiar idea by this time, and almost a mark of orthodoxy, the disciples can hardly have treated it as a mysterious subject of debate, and what must be meant is that they discussed the unheard-of idea that the Son of man was to undergo resurrection after a previous death. Yet if this is what Mark meant, it is curious that he was not able to say so unequivocally. An alternative version of the text does make him say this, and is adopted by some commentators, but there can be little doubt that this is a secondary and simplifying reading, and the fact that both Matthew and Luke omit the whole statement indicates that they read in Mark the more difficult reading, and from their later point of view could make little of it. For Mark, at least, it would appear that resurrection itself was still in Judaism a doctrine which could not simply be taken for granted.[59]

This passage may in any case serve to direct attention to a second reason why the centrality of the resurrection in apostolic Christianity, as that Christianity is represented in the New Testament, is puzzling, viz. the fact that very little is said about it by Jesus himself as he is represented in the synoptic gospels, even though these gospels are written from the standpoint of a belief in his resurrection and in resurrection in general. Resurrection is not the only New Testament concept which, while not incompatible with the Old Testament, is not derived directly from it but from the types of Judaism which had developed in the intertestamental period. Such, for example, are the kingdom of God, the Son of man, parables, thaumaturgy and belief in demons. These,

---

[59] The difficulties are well illustrated by E. Lohmeyer, *Das Evangelium des Markus* (1937), pp. 181f., *ad loc.*: 'Mark adds a hardly intelligible sentence; is it possible that the disciples could enquire what resurrection was? The hope was widespread in Judaism after the second century BC, and its acception was vigorously debated by the Pharisees and Sadducees. Hence Mark must, in contradiction of his own text, mean not the resurrection in general, but only that of the Son of man.' He continues that, in the light of Mark 9.31f., where a similar prophecy of the death of the Son of man and his resurrection is followed by the statement that the disciples did not understand what was said, one must suppose a 'not' to have fallen out of the text at 9.10, and render 'they did not take hold of (i.e. understand) the saying'. He further adds that even so, difficulties remain, since the question which is raised immediately is not that of the resurrection, but of the coming of Elijah (9.11f.). Vincent Taylor, *The Gospel according to St Mark* (1952), *ad loc.*, follows Lagrange in choosing the reading 'What does it mean – when he will rise from the dead?', but this choice of what is patently a secondary reading only underlines the difficulty.

however, all differ from resurrection in being very prominent in the synoptic gospels, and taken together cover a good deal of the synoptic material. Resurrection, on the other hand, is notable by its rarity. This is so even if all the references to it in the synoptic gospels are taken as authentic; a critical assessment is likely to reduce them considerably.

The question of resurrection as such comes up for discussion only once, in the somewhat ridiculous conundrum posed by the Sadducees concerning the woman who had had seven husbands in succession and who could not be the wife of all of them in another world (Mark 12.18–27 pars.). A question posed in these terms as a *reductio ad absurdum* is hardly a promising basis for the elucidation of a great matter, and the answer is of necessity confined by the terms of the question to the assertion that resurrection, which is here not argued but simply assumed, involves the creative power of God to transform human life into a non-physical form like that of the angels. To this is added – somewhat awkwardly in the context – either as a further saying of Jesus, possibly from a different context, or as a gloss on what has preceded, what purports to be a proof of resurrection from the Law, whose scriptural authority the Sadducees could not avoid. It appeals to the words spoken by God to Moses: 'I am the God of Abraham and the God of Isaac and the God of Jacob', as evidence that to the God who so speaks the patriarchs are not past and dead figures but are present and alive; their continuance lies in his permanent existence and in their permanent existence in relation to him. This, however, is not a proof of resurrection in general, but rather the opposite. It says of certain special persons, to whom could be added from Jewish tradition such other special figures as Elijah, Enoch and Moses himself, that they are in some sense alive with God apart from and without resurrection.[60] There is a similar ambiguity in the parable of Dives and Lazarus, where we are probably dealing with an adaptation by Jesus of a current tale, and in its closing sentence: 'If they hear not Moses and the prophets, neither will they be persuaded though one rise from the dead', possibly with

----

[60] From its own conception of the resurrection of the Elect as having already taken place but needing to be disclosed, the Epistle to Rheginos (48.3ff.) cites the appearances of Elijah and Moses with Jesus at the Transfiguration as proof of the truth of resurrection, i.e. the disclosure that some have risen.

a Christian adaptation of that. The rich man's request that Lazarus should return from the dead to warn his brethren is interpreted as an instance of resurrection, but this cannot be so by reference to what came to be the normal Jewish doctrine of resurrection, since this concerns all men together at the end, while in the parable the brethren are single individuals still alive on earth.

The injunction in Luke 14.12–14 to invite only those who cannot repay leads to a promise of ultimate repayment in 'the resurrection of the righteous', but a comparison with the similar injunctions in the sermon, Luke 6.32–36 par. Matt. 5.46–48, where they are based on the imitation of God's own generosity, suggests that this semi-technical term may be due to Luke, who alone of New Testament writers has anything like it, viz. in Paul's statement in Acts 24.15 that the hope of Israel is in the resurrection of the righteous and unrighteous. The identification in Matt. 12.39f. of the sign of Jonah with his three-day sojourn in the belly of the whale as a type of the three days of the Son of man in the earth, when compared with the Lukan parallel, appears to be secondary. Finally, the three predictions of the predetermined suffering and death of the Son of man to be followed by his resurrection after three days (or on the third day), which are to be found in Mark, and in Matthew and Luke where they are following Mark, are widely judged to be prophecies after the event. Form-critically they are not units of tradition which could stand up by themselves, nor could they be distinguishable from one another away from their present contexts. They are, rather, punctuations of his narrative provided by Mark in order to relate it dramatically to the passion. They are more precise in detail than is Jesus' manner, and are hardly borne out by the subsequent behaviour of the disciples, or even of Jesus himself in Gethsemane. In face of them it could not be, as is generally maintained, that the resurrection of Jesus came as a surprise. Even those scholars who do not wish to dismiss them as secondary are for the most part prepared to defend only an original form of them in which the prediction, especially that of resurrection, was in less explicit terms.

This notable scarcity in the recorded teaching of Jesus of reference to resurrection, or of any distinctive contribution to the doctrine, presents a problem both in relation to the supposed currency of the doctrine in Judaism and to its dominant place in early Christianity. Is there a straight line here from Judaism to

Jesus, and from Jesus to early Christianity, or is the latter something forced on the gospel of Jesus and with a different emphasis from it? If it is claimed that the preaching of the church is a continuation of Jesus only if it is a repetition of what he said, then the answer to the latter question would probably have to be in the affirmative. If, however, the question is put in the form, 'Was the gospel of Jesus of such kind that the later Christian preaching appears as congruous with it?', then a somewhat different answer is possible. It may be observed that in the one discussion of the subject, arising out of the question of the Sadducees, the emphasis in the reply is on God, on his power to transform the human creature for a non-temporal existence, and on his continuing existence as the God of the living, which guarantees the continuing existence of men. Not to perceive this is said in Mark's account, with some vehemence, to be grievous error and failure to grasp scriptural truth. What men are is what they are to God, and what they are to him will be made evident by his creative action. But what is here enunciated in reply to a question about resurrection is not confined to this limited and rather curious context, but may be said, in one form or another, to be characteristic of a great deal of Jesus' teaching as recorded in the gospels.

One form of this is in the proclamation of the kingdom. As is well known, two kinds of statement about the kingdom lie cheek by jowl in the synoptic gospels and in their sources, that which speaks of the kingdom as having in some sense arrived and as present with men, and that which speaks of it as still in the future, though imminent. A great deal of discussion has been aroused by this fact, and attempts have been made to reduce the material to consistency and order either by taking the futurist statements as authentic, Jesus then being an apocalyptic preacher of an imminent end, and the other kind of statement being an expression of the church's later conviction of having already entered on eternal life, or by taking the present statements as authentic, Jesus then being a preacher of an already realized end, and the future statements being evidence of a relapse of the later church into a more Jewish way of thinking. It could be said, however, with some confidence that neither side has been able to make its point at the expense of the other, and that, whatever judgment may be made on this or that particular saying, it is not possible critically to eliminate one class of statement so as to leave the other class in sole possession of the field. If this is so, it would appear that the nettle has to be grasped, and both kinds of statement have to be taken together, and it has at least to be considered possible that part of the force of Jesus' preaching lies in their juxtaposition. What can hardly be eliminated from the sayings of Jesus, for it governs too much of their form and content, is a sense that a great urgency is attached to the moment at which he is speaking, and that those he is addressing ('this generation') stand at a point of particular crisis; but what creates this urgency and crisis is nothing which can be expressed in terms of the present moment or of this generation itself, but only in terms of an imminent action of God towards them.

In a highly illuminating passage, James M. Robinson draws attention to the way in which this essentially double-sided truth determines the form of Jesus' message.[61] Thus in the Beatitudes, those who are poor, hungry, mourners, etc., are not accounted blessed in virtue of their poverty, hunger, mourning, etc., as such, as though these were virtues to be pursued because they would enable their possessors eventually to arrive somewhere, but because their poverty, hunger, mourning, etc., render them open to the creative and consummating action of God, who will confer on them the opposite in the form of various kinds of satisfaction. This form of speech could be said to be natural to beatitudes and to corresponding woes which go with them, but it is not confined to these. It appears again, for example, in the treatment of the duties of religion, where the same judgment as is passed on the rich and satisfied, 'they have received their reward', is pronounced on those who perform these duties in such a way that their value is humanly assessable. True almsgiving, prayer and fasting are defined as those actions which are so performed that their value is hidden from everyone, the doer included, except God, who sees in secret and confers on them their value. It can appear in certain parables, notably those in Mark 4, where the kingdom is depicted in terms of a contrast between an apparently wasteful sowing or a secret seed and a certain and abundant harvest, or between the smallest seed and the amplest tree, or between a lamp in obscurity and the same no longer in obscurity. These, if they are not to be taken as expressions of the church in the face of missionary disappointment, define the present kingdom as that which is open to,

[61] James M. Robinson, *A New Quest of the Historical Jesus* (1959), pp. 121ff.

and will certainly receive, the proper consummation of what it is from God. A somewhat similar emphasis can be detected in the designation of the disciples as 'little ones', in such statements as that only by becoming as a little child shall a man enter into the kingdom of God, or that the least in the kingdom is greater than the greatest born of woman, or that among disciples the greatest is the one who is small, or that who loses his life now shall find it (i.e. receive it from God), or finally in the compressed formula 'the last shall be first and the first last'. In such statements there is both a contrast and a connection between the present and the future, and the middle term, whether expressly stated or not, is the present will and future action of God.

If the notion of reward plays a considerable part in this teaching, it does so not as motive, but as consequence, and it cannot be dispensed with, for the consequence cannot be stated in terms of what is self-evident and automatic (as, e.g., that virtue is its own reward), or in terms of an abstract and autonomous ethic (as, e.g., that the good is to be done for its own sake), or in terms of some further stage along the line of man's earthly development and achievement, but only in terms of the consummation proper to it, which it lies with the God, whose kingdom it is, whose creatures men are and who is the author of the demand, to confer. There is here a certain definition of human life which, while remaining entirely silent on the subject of resurrection, and while being not at all an ethic of resurrection in, for example, the Pauline sense, is nevertheless not only not incongruous with resurrection, but could be said to be highly congruous with it, once that came to be stated. If the good action is good because, being done in faith and out of non-possession, it leaves the door wide open to God's use and consummation of it, it can be said to be an action which is *capax resurrectionis*, and in the long run it cries out for something like resurrection. On the other hand, a doctrine that virtue is its own reward requires no such antithetical form of expression, in which the present and the future are first set in contrast and are then connected again by the promise of the consummation of God, and it must find the thought of resurrection irrelevant, if not immoral. But in that case, men must either pronounce all things relative and their relativity to be the last word about them, or else must play God from their limited standpoint by conferring on their actions some intrinsic value of their own.

Since, however, it is evident in the gospels that the kingdom is not entirely separable from the person of him who proclaims it, and that the disciple is said to be what he is because he is to be as his master, is to follow him, and is to be involved in his destiny, the question inevitably arises whether, and in what way, Jesus saw himself as involved within his own definition of human life for others. This is a very difficult question to answer, because it is precisely the christology of the gospels, their doctrines of who Jesus was or thought himself to be, which are most likely to be coloured by the church's later and developing conceptions of him which had their origins in a belief in his resurrection. Eduard Schweizer has remarked: 'If Jesus did foresee suffering and rejection for himself and his disciples, then, of course, he saw it not as catastrophe but as a gateway to the glory of the coming kingdom. If he did call himself the Son of man and connected this title with his lowly state on earth as well as with the glory to come, then he must in fact have expected something like his exaltation to the presence of God.'[62] The fact that both these sentences begin with 'if' indicates the difficulty. As is well known, there is the widest possible divergence of view amongst scholars on whether and in what sense Jesus believed himself to be the Messiah, and on the Son of man sayings themselves. This divergence extends from the judgment that all are authentic, and are to be taken together as reflecting Jesus' own conception of himself as the eschatological redeemer, humiliated on earth, rejected by men, but to be exalted by God, to the judgment that only one or the other of the strands is authentic, to the judgment that none are. Even if the first view is taken, that all are authentic, there is room for dispute whether the exaltation or coming on the clouds is simply an expression of vindication at God's hands, or is for the purpose of participating in the final judgment, or is a coming in glory to men. Further, the saying 'whoever denies me before men, the Son of man will deny him' could be held to preserve an original conviction of Jesus that his ministry was indissolubly linked with the functions of the Son of man, but that he was not that figure. Schweizer argues that there was in Judaism an established doctrine of a suffering and righteous one, and that there is evidence in the New Testament that Jesus was so regarded, so that here we have a straight line from the Old Testament to early Christianity by way of 'the Jewish knowledge,

[62] Eduard Schweizer, *Lordship and Discipleship* (1960), p. 36.

as expressed in the Old Testament, of the righteous man's way through humiliation, poverty and suffering to the promised gracious raising up by God',[63] but he is unable to refer to any passages in the synoptic gospels in which Jesus speaks of himself in these terms, and he notes that the word 'exaltation', which is so frequently used in Judaism in this connection, is absent from them.

Apart from the Son of man sayings, there is still, perhaps, enough to indicate that Jesus conceived of himself as involved in a necessary humiliation and in a certain vindication by God which would affect the destiny of God's people, but this is expressed indirectly and in a somewhat fugitive manner rather than directly and systematically, as in the occasional references to his own kingdom, or in such sayings as, 'I have a baptism to undergo, and how am I hampered until the ordeal be over', or, 'today and tomorrow I shall be casting out devils and working cures; on the third day I am perfected' (reach my goal?: Luke 12.50; 13.32).

The position outlined here is a delicately balanced one, and it is not easy to state with confidence that the ministry and teaching of Jesus may not thus be distorted (it could hardly be otherwise in view of the nature of our sources, where that ministry and teaching are presented in the light of a belief in the resurrection). The difficulty is illustrated in an essay by W. Marxsen, in which, in dispute with U. Wilckens, he repudiates a presentation precisely of this kind. A particular strength of Marxsen's essay is his insistence that the word 'resurrection' itself is not a neutral word for an historical description of an event, but an interpretative word which by its use from the beginning imparted to the event to which it refers a particular meaning governed by Jewish apocalyptic and Jewish anthropological thought-forms. He is therefore bound to consider the relation between the eschatological belief that Jesus is the Risen One and the eschatology of the earthly ministry and teaching of Jesus, and he sees two possibilities.

In the first, the resurrection belief is dominant and Jesus is fitted into it as himself the beginning of the new age. The 'earthly Jesus would be, so to speak, merely the precursor of the Risen One, and all that he preached or did would stand, as it were, in a parenthesis, which would disappear only through

[63] *Op. cit.*, p. 15.

the resurrection; or (as Wilckens expresses it): the ministry of Jesus on earth, the claim of the earthly Jesus, needed to be legitimized by eschatology, to be ratified by God. This was then imparted by God through the resurrection of Jesus.'[64] To this he objects, on form-critical grounds, that the material of the gospels originally consisted of independent units which did not convey this sense of themselves, but only when it was imparted to them as they became parts of a single story which moved towards a climax of death and resurrection. Once this secondary motif is removed, the traditions then 'speak only of Jesus' direct claim to sovereignty, to a ministry which *in itself* raised an eschatological claim, but which did not demand ratification'.

The second possibility, which Marxsen considers the only one deserving of consideration, is that what was fundamental was not the resurrection but Jesus himself, who already in his ministry anticipated the end and the judgment, who faced men with God and brought him near, and then through his 'appearance' (understood at that time as 'resurrection') this eschatological ministry and message was renewed in and through the church.

Certainly an interpretation of the tradition which made the ministry of Jesus simply a 'prelude' to, or anticipation of, what was to follow from it would be false (even though a faith orientated in the resurrection would always have difficulty in avoiding this). Nevertheless, Wilckens would seem to be justified and true to the inner content of the tradition in claiming that, while there was nothing purely anticipatory or limited in the teaching of Jesus, he did speak of the kingdom of God and of his own authority in such a way that he drew a distinction between himself and God, and spoke and acted in such a way that a future authentication of his words, promises and actions was the presupposition of what he said and did. This seems to lie too deeply in both the form and the content of the tradition to be a secondary motif.

If the contentions advanced above are not wide of the mark, that is, if the doctrine of resurrection was not firmly fixed in Judaism, and if it is largely absent from the teaching of Jesus, then

[64] W. Marxsen, 'The Resurrection of Jesus as a Historical and Theological Problem', in C. F. D. Moule (ed.), *The Significance of the Resurrection for Faith in Jesus Christ* (1968), pp. 45f.

particular attention is focused on the actual resurrection of Jesus. It may be suggested that only this event, whatever it may have been, could have brought it about that there emerged in Christianity a precise, confident and articulate faith in which resurrection has moved from the circumference to the centre.

II

THE RESURRECTION TRADITION

THE more the resurrection is seen as determinative of the faith, thought and practice of the early church, especially when set alongside both contemporary Judaism and even the contents of the synoptic gospels, the more surprising becomes the state of the tradition concerning the resurrection which that faith caused to be handed on, as that tradition has come down to us in the New Testament. This is so even if the relevant passages are taken just as they stand; it is even more so if they are subjected to criticism; and by criticism is meant here not some dogmatic presupposition about, for example, the relation of matter to spirit, but simply that kind of literary analysis which breaks up the material from its present sequence into component units, so that they are then allowed to speak more for themselves.[1] And it is so from whichever end one starts, whether from the form of the tradition to be found in the early church's profession of faith, or from the form in which it was later incorporated into the gospels as resurrection narratives.

I CORINTHIANS

If we start from the end of the early church's profession, we are met with what has been called the 'fragmentation' of the tradition. It so happens that one of the several matters of dispute in the

[1] H. von Campenhausen, 'The Events of Easter and the Empty Tomb' in *Tradition and Life in the Church* (1968), p. 42, complains that literary criticism, form criticism and tradition-history have led to the neglect of historical enquiry as such, i.e. enquiry into 'the historical core of that to which the tradition gives its historical testimony'. But his own essay affords ample illustration both of the fact that there is no way to the latter except via the former, and also of the guesswork to which the historian is reduced at vital points in the investigation. For a review of criticism up to 1950, written from a Roman Catholic standpoint, see P. de Haes, *La Résurrection de Jesus dans l'apologétique des cinquante dernières années* (1953).

church at Corinth which led to the writing of I Corinthians (*c*. AD 56) to deal with them was resurrection, though precisely what was in dispute is not clear and is itself disputed. The apostle chose to introduce his treatment of it, also for reasons which are not clear, with a rehearsal of the gospel of the cross and resurrection (with a list of witnesses to the resurrection attached), which he had previously proclaimed on the occasion of their conversion (*c*. AD 50):

Now I make known unto you, brethren, the gospel which I preached unto you, which also ye received, wherein also ye stand, by which also ye are saved; in what words I preached it unto you, if ye hold it fast, except ye believed in vain. For I delivered unto you first of all that which I also received, how that Christ died for our sins according to the scriptures; and that he was buried; and that he hath been raised on the third day according to the scriptures; and that he appeared to Cephas; then to the twelve; then he appeared to above five hundred brethren at once, of whom the greater part remain until now, but some are fallen asleep; then he appeared to James; then to all the apostles; and last of all, as unto one born out of due time, he appeared to me also. For I am least of the apostles, that am not meet to be called an apostle, because I persecuted the church of God. But by the grace of God I am what I am; and his grace which was bestowed upon me was not found in vain, but I laboured more abundantly than they all; yet not I, but the grace of God which was in me. Whether then it be I or they, so we preach and so ye believed.

Hence it comes about – and it is a reminder of the indirect and almost casual nature of some of the evidence supplied by the New Testament – that this passage is both the earliest written testimony to the resurrection in the New Testament and, since Paul includes his own experience, probably its only written testimony to come from one who could claim to be himself an 'eye-witness' of the resurrection. Since in the words 'delivered' and 'received' Paul uses the technical language for the handing on of tradition, since the recital of the death, burial and resurrection is said to reflect in its Greek that it had once existed in Aramaic (though this is controverted), and since Paul goes out of his way to emphasize that he was not alone in so preaching, but that 'they' (presumably some, at least, of those listed as witnesses of the resurrection) had said the same thing, this tradition can be taken back early into Paul's life as a Christian, and perhaps beyond that.

For these reasons, the passage becomes the natural starting-point for any consideration of the evidence, and has received special attention.[2] Even when taken on its own, and without reference to other traditions in the New Testament, it raises a number of problems of text, structure and interpretation. Is a rhythmical form to be detected in this passage, and if so, how is it to be set out? Does it consist basically of two parallel statements – that Christ died for our sins and was buried: that he was raised the third day according to the scriptures and appeared? Or is that impossible because 'he appeared' cannot stand alone, but requires to be followed by a statement that he appeared to someone? Does the list of six appearances – to Cephas, the twelve, the more than five hundred, James, the apostles, and Paul – fall into a pattern? Is the pattern one of two triplets, each headed by the name of a single person, the two leaders of the church, Peter and James, or one of three doublets – Peter and the twelve, the more than five hundred and James, the apostles and Paul? If a traditional formula is being quoted, where does it end, and where does Paul begin to add to it? Clearly the reference to himself cannot have belonged to a traditional formula which he had received,[3] nor, probably, does the statement attached to the reference to the more than five hundred that most were still alive but some were dead, for this is too protracted and circumstantial a statement to belong to a formula. This might indicate that the reference to these brethren marks

---

[2] Thus, apart from the commentaries, it is analysed in greater or less detail in: M. Dibelius, *From Tradition to Gospel* (1934), pp. 18ff.; K. H. Rengstorf, *Die Auferstehung Jesu* (1960[4]), pp. 47ff.; E. L. Allen, 'The Lost Kerygma', *NTS* 3 (1956–57), pp. 349ff.; P. Winter, 'I Corinthians xv 3b–7', *NovT* 2 (1958), pp. 142ff.; G. Koch, *Die Auferstehung Jesu Christi* (1959), pp. 25ff., 200ff.; H. Grass, *Ostergeschehen und Osterberichte* (1964[3]), pp. 94ff.; E. Bammel, 'Herkunft und Funktion der Traditionselemente in I Kor. 15.1–11', *TZ* 11 (1955), pp. 401ff.; A. von Harnack, Sitzungbericht der Akademie der Wissenschaften, 1922, pp. 62ff.; W. Michaelis, *Die Erscheinungen des Auferstandenen* (1944), pp. 12ff.; J. Jeremias, *The Eucharistic Words of Jesus* (1966[2]), pp. 129ff.; U. Wilckens, 'The Tradition-history of the Resurrection of Jesus' and G. Delling, 'The Significance of the Resurrection of Jesus for Faith in Jesus Christ', in C. F. D. Moule (ed.), *The Significance of the Message of the Resurrection for Faith in Jesus Christ* (1968), pp. 57ff., 78ff.; J. Kremer, *Das älteste Zeugnis von der Auferstehung Christi* (1967), pp. 12ff.

[3] The suggestion of B. Gerhardsson, *Memory and Manuscript* (1961), p. 299, that, since the other apostles had accepted Paul, his name could have stood in the traditional formula, is scarcely feasible.

the point where the original formula ends, and where Paul begins
to elaborate from his own information. This could be supported
by the fact that at this point the form of the statement changes;
the first four clauses stating that Christ died, was buried, was
raised, and appeared to Cephas and the twelve, are each introduced
by the word ὅτι ('that'), which is proper to a credal formula,
whereas in what follows the verb 'he appeared' is repeated without
any introductory 'that' – 'he appeared to more than five hundred
brethren . . . then he appeared to James; then to all the apostles;
last of all he appeared to me'. If this is so, why does Paul find it
necessary to supplement the traditional formula of appearance to
Cephas (a form of Peter's name confined to Paul in the New
Testament, apart from John 1.43) and the twelve? Is it to gain the
widest possible basis for the witness to the resurrection in view
of what he is going to argue, and so to prepare for the conclusion,
'whether it be I or they, so we preach'? In so doing, is he rehearsing
all the appearances known to him, and if not is there some principle of selection from an even wider field?

Michaelis argued that the traditional formula ended with 'he
appeared', and that the list of names was added by Paul himself,
on the ground that there are three pairs of witnesses with an
individual in each pair, and since Paul must have been responsible for his own name the whole pattern must go back to him.[4]
It is, however, unlikely that 'he appeared' would stand alone
without any mention of those to whom an appearance was
made (cf. Luke 24.34; Acts 9.17; 13.31). The same objection
lies against Rengstorf's arrangement of the verses in such a way
that 'he appeared' stands in exact parallel to 'he was buried'.[5]
Harnack argued that Paul had combined the lists of two rival
parties, the appearances to Peter and the twelve from the Peter
party, and those to James and to all the apostles (= that to the
twelve) from the James party. But this does not account for the
appearance to the brethren, and Paul sets out the appearances
chronologically. These two hypotheses appear in a fresh form
in the articles of Bammel and Winter, who both start from an
independent fourfold traditional formula ending with 'he
appeared', to which Paul has added either (*a*) two originally
independent lists already known to the Corinthians, the first

[4] *Op. cit.*, p. 26. [5] *Op. cit.*, p. 54.

comprising appearances to an individual, a group and a church, and the second appearances to an individual and a group, both once having had some such introduction as 'Christ rose and appeared' (so Bammel); or, (*b*) two lists, both originally three-fold, the second of which once read 'to James, then to the apostles and to all the brethren', but was reduced by Paul through the omission of the last-named (so Winter). This involves a good deal of conjecture, and the present sequence of five appearances does not break up easily into two separate sequences in which one point to be made is that Peter or James in each case was the first to receive an appearance.

Others who postulate a combination of two independent lists are E. Stauffer,[6] the combination already having been made at Antioch, and U. Wilckens:[7] Peter and the twelve; James and the apostles; the appearance to the brethren being added by Paul from oral tradition. Gerhard Koch takes the five appearances as a whole, but sees in the first three the gathering of the church in the persons of those who had already shared in Jesus' earthly ministry (Peter, the twelve, the brethren), and in the last two the symbol of the missionary task of the church towards Israel (James, the apostles = missionaries). Joachim Jeremias deduces from the style and phraseology that the formula originated in Aramaic, pointing to its parallelism, the use of the un-Pauline use of the word 'sins', the presupposition of the use here of the Hebrew text of Isa. 52.13–53.12, καί (and) in the adversative sense (but) before 'he was raised', the passive form 'he was raised' as a semitic way of saying 'God has raised him', a semitic word-order in the expression 'on the third day', and ὤφθη in the sense 'he appeared', reflecting an Aramaic word which can have both the meanings 'he was seen' and 'he appeared'. On the other hand, H. Conzelmann, while agreeing that the language is not Paul's, disputes each of these points, and argues that the wording and syntax at no point require a semitic original but only a semitic way of thinking, and that 'Christ' without an article and the phrase 'according to the scriptures' suggest a Greek original.[8] On the whole, the most

---

[6] E. Stauffer, *Jesus and his Story* (1960), pp. 121ff.

[7] U. Wilckens, *Die Missionsreden der Apostelgeschichte* (1961), pp. 74ff.

[8] H. Conzelmann, 'On the Analysis of the Confessional Formula in I Cor. 15.3–5', *Interpretation*, January 1966, pp. 15ff.

satisfactory analysis would seem to be that which sees a break at the beginning of v. 6 after 'then to the twelve', marking the point at which Paul begins to supplement a traditional formula with reports of other separate appearances.

There are three further questions directly or indirectly connected with the evaluation of this passage:

1. There is the critical-historical question of why Paul penned I Cor. 15 at all, and chose to introduce it in this fashion. Was resurrection one of the subjects raised by the Corinthians themselves in their letter to Paul which he felt bound to deal with (despite the fact that the chapter is not introduced by the words 'now concerning . . .')? Or had he heard from other sources of difficulties over resurrection in the Corinthian church, and felt compelled to deal with the matter before he ended his letter? In either case, what were the difficulties, and why were they appropriately dealt with by beginning from a formula which seems to have little influence on the rest of the chapter?[9]

2. There is the theological-psychological question of how Paul was able to say categorically that the appearance of the risen Lord to himself was 'last of all'. Is this meant to be a factual statement that, as far as he had been able to discover, there had been no appearance of the risen Lord to anyone subsequently to his own – if so, how did he know and how was he to be sure? Or is it an expression of the Pauline 'egoism', and of a dogmatic viewpoint about his own person, that with the appearance to himself and with his call to apostleship the period of revelation was over, and what remained was the mission of the gospel to the world until the parousia?

3. There is the form-critical question of the function which such a traditional formula was designed to perform in the church. Where does its accent lie, and what was it formulated to say and do? If its primary purpose was to assert the resurrection of Jesus with confirmatory evidence of eye-witnesses, why was it preceded by a statement of the saving nature of the death of Christ? If it was a summary statement of the saving nature of the death and resurrection, like similar statements in the New Testament, why was a list of appearances attached? Ulrich

[9] See the discussion in J. C. Hurd, *The Origin of I Corinthians* (1965), pp. 91ff., 195ff., 229ff.

Wilckens interprets the formula from the end backwards. Since Paul, here as elsewhere, refers to the appearance to himself as constituting a call to and authorization of his apostleship, this is how he understood the reference to the appearances to others also, and in doing so he was correctly interpreting the original intention of the formula. It was from the first a legitimation formula concerned with the creation of the Christian community, and grounding the authority of those who were leaders in the church in the fact that they had been recipients of resurrection appearances.[10]

In contrast to the specific mention of individuals and groups, and to Paul's ability to place the appearances in an order, there are no hints in his statement of time or place. It is not said how soon after the third day (which here refers backwards to relate the resurrection to the death and burial, and not forwards to the time of the appearances) the first or any of the appearances took place, nor what periods of time separated them, nor where any of them took place.

That such an early and concise formula should already contain a reference to 'the third day', when it supplies no time reference for the death of Christ to reckon from, and when its other time references ('then', 'after that') are so vague, is striking, and raises the questions of the origin and meaning of this term.

It was already traditional when Paul received it, and appears in formal statements on the lips of Jesus (Matt. 16.21; 17.23; 20.19; cf. 27.63; Luke 9.22; 18.33; 24.7, 46; cf. Acts 10.40); 'after three days' in Mark 8.31; 9.31; 10.34 is probably to be taken as an equivalent expression (cf. Matt. 16.21 with 27.63 and

---

[10] 'The Tradition-history of the Resurrection of Jesus' (see n. 2), pp. 59ff. Also 'Der Ursprung der Überlieferung der Erscheinungen des Auferstandenen' in W. Joest and W. Pannenberg (eds.), *Dogma und Denkstrukturen* (Festschrift für E. Schlink, 1963), pp. 63ff., where he argues that the formula is not a unity, since καὶ ὅτι is not found in such formulas, but a collection of originally independent statements, each one of which legitimized the place or authority of particular individuals or groups in the church. W. Marxsen, *Die Auferstehung Jesu von Nazareth* (1968), pp. 84ff., with reference to I Cor. 15.11: 'So we preach', sees the list as being not one of witnesses to the resurrection as such, but of witnesses to appearances, through which they received the function of preachers of the resurrection. 'Seeing the Lord' and 'mission' were combined from the first; this is how Paul wished to use the formula, whether or not that was its original intention.

12.40), and appears in the form 'in three days' in the reported promise of Jesus to erect a temple made without hands (Mark 14.58; 15.29 pars.).

Why was it thought important to specify the resurrection of Jesus in this way? To suppose that it was a deposit in credal form of an historical reminiscence that it was on the first day of the week, and so on the third day after the crucifixion and burial on a Friday, that the tomb was found empty (Mark 16.2 par.), faces two difficulties. First, this could apply only to Jerusalem traditions, since Galilee was too far away from the scene of burial for appearances on the third day to have any meaning. Secondly, the gospel traditions are statements about the discovery of the tomb as empty (only the legendary Matt. 28.2–4 attempts to connect the emptiness of the tomb with the actual resurrection), whereas the time reference in the kerygmatic formulae is not a statement determining the time of the first resurrection appearances (though Luke 24.21 turns it into this), but is attached to the resurrection itself. But, since the resurrection is represented as the hidden act of God himself, no date could be assigned to it, and no one could tell 'when' it took place, as opposed to 'when' the tomb was found empty or the Lord appeared to men. It would appear, therefore, that 'on the third day' is not intended as a chronological but as a theological statement. It offers an interpretation of the resurrection, and this is suggested by the shape of the formula in I Cor. 15. There, death-resurrection form two inseparable parts of a single gospel. Each is said to be 'according to the scriptures', i.e. according to the divine purposes. The divine purpose of the death is indicated in the statement that it was 'for our sins' (cf. Isa. 53.12?). The corresponding statement 'on the third day' gives the divine purpose of the resurrection (cf. John 2.19–22 for the conjunction of resurrection and believing the scripture). It is thus possible that 'on the third day' and 'according to the scriptures' are not two disjunct statements, but belong together as a single affirmation.

Despite the plural 'according to the scriptures', the clearest scripture to hand was probably Hosea 6.2: 'Come, let us return to the Lord; for he has torn, that he may heal us; he has stricken, and he will bind us up. After two days he will revive us; on the third day he will raise us up, that we may live before him.' This is more likely than the story of Jonah, whose three-day sojourn in the belly of the fish is a probably late, and entirely *ad hoc* application in Matthew's version of the saying about 'the sign of Jonah' (Matt. 12.40).

There is some evidence that Hosea 6.2 was applied by rabbis to the general resurrection,[11] and it is possible that Christians applied it to the resurrection of Jesus, the Messiah, as the embodiment and source of the true Israel (cf. Rom. 4.25: 'who was put to death for our trespasses and raised for our justification'; 6.10: 'the death he died he died to sin, once for all, but the life he lives he lives to God'). G. Delling suggests that the Targum on Hosea here, which reads: 'He will make us live in the days of consolation which are to come; on the day of the resurrection of the dead will he raise us up so that we live before him' has deliberately altered the text by suppressing the reference to two days and the third day in order to contradict the Christian application to the Messiah.[12] That Hosea 6.2 is nowhere cited in the New Testament may indicate that its use had been early, and had left its mark on the tradition at a level deeper than explicit quotation. At a later stage, the prophecies which Jesus himself was believed to have made of the divine necessity of his resurrection after three days (including the mysterious prophecy of the building of a temple made without hands in three days), became the chief basis of the divine intention in the resurrection, rendering appeal to the Old Testament superfluous (the citation of Ps. 16.10, as e.g. in Acts 2.27; 13.35, had the rather different purpose of proving the conquest of death). There is some evidence that 'after two days' and 'on the third day' had the proverbial sense of what is temporary in contrast to what is permanent, and could be the equivalent of 'in a little while' (cf. John 16.16ff.), and that in the context of death could be the equivalent of escaping or surviving death, in contrast to the fourth day when corruption sets in.[13] On the other hand, John

---

[11] Strack-Billerbeck I, p. 747. For a discussion of Hosea 6.2 in this context see B. Lindars, *New Testament Apologetic* (1961), pp. 59ff.

[12] G. Delling, ἡμέρα *TDNT*, ii, 949. See Strack-Billerbeck I, pp. 747, 760, for later rabbinic interpretation of the 'third day' in Hosea 6.2 as the day of the general resurrection.

[13] See the discussion in E. C. Hoskyns, *The Fourth Gospel* (1947)², pp. 199f. For the mystery cults see J. Leipoldt, *Die sterbenden und auferstehenden Götter* (1923), pp. 77ff. H. von Campenhausen, *op. cit.*, p. 46, allows that the expression may be a theological datum, but prefers to see it as a historical datum.

11.39 appears to reflect a belief that death was not complete until the fourth day, so that to express the overcoming of death in numerical symbolism would seem to require 'on the fourth day', unless two parallel conceptions are struggling for expression, the conquest of death and a death which does not see corruption. 'Three days' as expressing the survival of death is certainly attested in the cult myths of the dying and reviving Osiris and Attis. How far this sense lay originally behind the phrases in Hosea, or was still attached to them, or was attached to the early Christian understanding of them before they came to be taken in a strictly chronological sense, can hardly be determined.[14]

Since Paul envisages the whole series as coming to a close only with the appearance of the Lord to himself, it is possible, if this passage is read on its own and not in the light of other New Testament passages, to regard these appearances as intended to cover a considerable period of time, perhaps even a number of years. The questions of time and place are not unconnected with the question of the recipients. If the first two appearances, to Cephas and to the twelve, alone belonged to the traditional formula, a distinction was already drawn in it between Peter as an individual and the twelve of which he was one; and if 'the twelve' is not to be taken here as a loose expression (which has been altered in some manuscripts for the sake of accuracy to 'the eleven'), it might refer to an appearance to the apostolic body after its number had been made up to twelve in the manner described in Acts 1.15ff., that is, subsequent to the period of resurrection appearances as that was reckoned by Lukan standards.

Who the more than five hundred brethren were, and where they were to be found at the time of writing, does not appear. If the reference to them originates from Paul and not from the formula, then it has to be remembered that for Paul, 'brethren' is a regular word for Christian believers, and the large number involved, which

---

Since this cannot have been derived from the resurrection itself, and he thinks it unlikely to have been derived solely from resurrection appearances, he is led to place great emphasis on the empty tomb as giving the 'third day' – or, at least, on Mark's version of it.

[14] See B. Metzger, 'A Suggestion concerning the meaning of I Cor. xv. 4b', *JTS* NS viii (1957), pp. 118ff.

distinguishes this appearance from any others recorded in the New Testament, might suggest a gathering or congregation – hardly the whole Christian community then in existence, but a section of it meeting together – and if the fragmentary picture of the origins of the church in Acts is to be accepted as definitive, a congregation in Jerusalem rather than in Galilee. But if they were already 'brethren', that is Christians, and were gathered as such, they would be so presumably as already believers in the resurrection, and it is difficult to see what purpose such an appearance would serve, or how they would be different after it from before. Nor is it easy to fit this appearance into Wilckens' hypothesis, for to what would such a large number be legitimized?

The mention of an appearance to James has, not unnaturally, been seized upon as a part solution of the problem presented by that puzzling figure. The gospels, so far as they go, give the impression that Jesus' family were not disciples, and therefore potential believers, but were hostile to him; yet in Acts, from ch. 12 onwards, James emerges as a leader of the church in Jerusalem, and Paul himself is a witness that this was already the case by the time of his own visit to Jerusalem some three years after his conversion (Gal. 1.19). Eventually James became the leader of the church in Jerusalem (Acts 12.17; 15.13). When this hostility of his family to Jesus ceased we have no means of knowing. Luke places the family alongside the twelve as already potential believers in the period between the resurrection and the ascension (Acts 1.14), but this may only reflect a more pious attitude towards them on his part. If in the case of James it was a resurrection appearance which was responsible for the change, this could be placed anywhere – in Galilee at his home, or in Jerusalem – and at any time before Paul wrote I Corinthians or Galatians.

It is unlikely that 'all the apostles' is simply a synonym for the twelve, both because this would be a meaningless repetition which added nothing to the witness, and also because for Paul, in distinction from the evangelists and especially from Luke, the word 'apostle' has a wider connotation than the twelve, as when he refers to Andronicus and Junias as 'eminent among the apostles' (Rom. 16.7; cf. I Cor. 12.28; II Cor. 11.5). It would seem to denote leading missionaries, but who they were, so that they could be referred to as constituting a single body, 'all the apostles', at what point in the development of the church they received this appearance, and whether they were apostles before it or were made apostles by it, are not evident.

The force of this passage in I Corinthians, whatever doubts there may be about precise interpretation of its details, lies in its comparatively early date, and in the wide spread of its testimony. It says nothing about the nature of the resurrection, and Paul makes no deductions from it or any further use of it when he is expounding the nature of the resurrection in the rest of the chapter;[15] but it affirms naturally and confidently, with reference both to tradition and to those who could still be appealed to, the varied witness to the event. It is, therefore, remarkable that some ten, twenty, thirty or forty years later, when the gospels came to be written out of the traditions which had been handed down in the meantime, nearly all trace of it, on the evidence of the gospels themselves, had been lost. Some time in the interim it had ceased to exercise any control it may have had.

The method of the form critic has been to start from both ends at once: to ask, on the one hand, what traditions the early Christian communities, in so far as we have evidence about them, would be likely to be concerned to hand on; and to ask, on the other hand, of the gospel material itself how far it reflects the interests and concerns of those communities. He hopes in this way to effect some kind of a juncture. The approach is always in danger of being circular, but there is no other to hand, and it may bring light, as, for example, in the examination of the passion narratives. Here, however, it notably fails through an almost total lack of correspondence. Thus the various narratives of resurrection appearances in the gospels – to the women in Jerusalem and to the eleven in Galilee in Matthew; to the two on the Emmaus road and to the eleven with them in Luke; to Mary Magdalene, to the disciples without Thomas and with him in Jerusalem, and to the seven in Galilee in John – if put into a list do not produce, and can hardly be made to produce, either the constituents of the list in I Cor. 15 or its chronological sequence. Conversely, Paul's list, if it were

---

[15] W. Marxsen, *op. cit.*, pp. 101ff. argues with relation to I Cor. 15, Gal. 1.15–17 and I Cor. 9.1 that, in appealing to the revelation to himself which lay at the basis of his apostleship, Paul is not concerned with the event of the Damascus road, though he can, as in I Cor. 15 and 9, assimilate his language to that of the tradition in referring to the Lord as appearing to him or his seeing the Lord.

written out in the form of narratives of separate appearances, could not be made to produce the narratives found in the gospels.

This is particularly surprising in respect of certain elements in the tradition, notably the appearance to Peter.[16] It stands at the head of the traditional part of Paul's list, and in view of the primacy of Peter in the church, to which more than one strand in the New Testament bears witness, it could have been expected to hold its place there. The one story which *a priori* one would have expected to survive intact would be that of the Lord's appearance to Peter. But it is not so. By the time of the writing of the gospels it had disappeared, leaving behind no more than an echo, and that not in narrative but in credal form ('The Lord is risen indeed, and has appeared to Simon'), which Luke has some difficulty in attaching as an awkward pendant to his Emmaus story. It is particularly surprising that Matthew, with his interest in the primacy of Peter, does not know of it, and even drops the special mention of Peter in his version of Mark 16.7. Scholars have not unnaturally felt moved to enquire whether it may not now lie concealed within a story which had once been a resurrection story, but which had ceased to be recognized as such – as, for example, the story of Peter's call after a miraculous catch of fish (Luke 5.1–10), or his confession of Jesus' messiahship and his blessing as the rock of the church (Matt. 16.13–19), or his walking on the water (Matt. 14.28–33), or his rehabilitation after a miraculous catch of fish (John 21), though in all these stories as they now stand Peter is not alone.

If, as has been suggested, the differences between the tradition in I Cor. 15 and the gospel narratives are partly due to the appearances listed by Paul not finding a place in the gospels because they were held to fall outside a period of resurrection appearances which Luke defines strictly as a period of forty days lying between resurrection and ascension, the conclusion could be drawn that there were at least two differing conceptions abroad in the church of what resurrection was and entailed. To some, it was what it was because the appearances of the risen Lord were confined within the short time required for the purpose of establishing the church on an apostolic basis, while to others it was what it was because appearances continued over a longer period, and were responsible

---

[16] For a discussion of this point, see L. Brun, *Die Auferstehung Christi in der urchristlichen Überlieferung* (1925), pp. 5off.

for decisive moments in the life of the church, including, for Paul, his own conversion.

The discrepancy between the list in I Cor. 15 and the gospel narratives is a reminder to the historian of primitive Christianity of how fortuitous the evidence of the documents can be, and how tendentious they may be. E. L. Allen, while allowing for an element of theological creation in the church in the light of its experience, puts the discrepancy down primarily to the accidents of history.[17] Ulrich Wilckens sees it as an example of the development of early Christianity as a whole, which followed two distinct courses, the first being a tradition in story form of the words and acts of Jesus handed down in the primitive community but unknown to the missionary churches, and the other a tradition of preaching, exhortation and liturgy about the cosmic Christ going back to the Hellenists, the two traditions being brought together for the first time by the evangelists.[18] On the other hand, Ernst Käsemann sees no other hypothesis open to the historian 'than that more detailed narratives which were available were suppressed on dogmatic grounds, because they had ceased to correspond to the views of the second and third generations of Christians.'[19]

This could be so in the case of the appearance to James, who may have been responsible for a certain fixation of the Christian movement at Jerusalem in its early stages, which was later repudiated in the light of the Gentile mission and the eclipse of Jewish Christianity,[20] though we have little evidence of how long Jewish Christianity continued to exercise influence. It could be so in the case of the appearance to the brethren (and 'to all the apostles'), if a tendency towards locating the origin of, and authority in, the church in the twelve apostles ousted lesser figures. It is less easy to suppose in the case of the appearance to Peter, since presumably the views of at least some of the second- and third-generation Christians (though it is not clear who,

[17] E. L. Allen, 'The Lost Kerygma', *NTS* 3 (1956–57), pp. 349ff.

[18] U. Wilckens, 'The Tradition-history of the Resurrection of Jesus', *op. cit.*, pp. 55f.

[19] E. Käsemann, 'Is the Gospel Objective?', in *Essays on New Testament Themes* (1964), p. 49.

[20] An appearance to James is narrated in the Jewish-Christian Gospel of the Hebrews. See E. Hennecke – W. Schneemelcher – R. McL. Wilson, *New Testament Apocrypha* I (1963), p. 165.

when and where) are reflected in Acts, the Gospel of Matthew (esp. Matt. 16.17–19), I and II Peter, and such a passage as John 21, which betray an interest in the primacy of Peter.[21] H. Grass supposes that some appearances disappeared from the tradition (those to the brethren and to all the apostles) because it came to be realized that they belonged, not to the immediate post-resurrection period, but to a later time.[22] If this were so, then, as mentioned above, it might indicate far-reaching differences of perspective in the church. Thus, in Paul there is no hint, when he places the appearance to himself alongside those to others, or when he defends his apostleship on the ground that he has 'seen' the Lord (I Cor. 9.1), that there was any difference in kind between these appearances to others and that to himself; or, conversely, that he understood the appearances to others in any other way than he understood his own. For Luke, however, who is the only New Testament writer to give a description of Paul's 'seeing' the Lord, this is completely ruled out, since in the scheme of Luke-Acts the Lord ceases to appear as the Risen One once the Ascension has taken place, and any subsequent 'appearance' (e.g. to Stephen, Acts 7.55, or to Paul) cannot be a 'substantial' appearance, but only a vision.[23]

Would Paul have recognized the three accounts in Acts as satisfactory versions of what 'seeing' the Lord had meant to him? If so, then presumably he understood the appearances which he lists in I Cor. 15 to have been of the same kind, however those responsible for the formula may have understood them. If not, and if he understood both the appearance to himself and those to others as having more of the 'substantial' character of the appearances in the gospel narrative, then the accounts in Acts of his seeing the Lord in visions must be put

[21] For a full discussion of Matt. 16.17–19, including its possible post-resurrection setting, see O. Cullmann, *Peter: Disciple, Apostle, Martyr* (1962²), Part II, and the literature there cited. W. Marxsen, *op. cit.*, pp. 83–100, sees the appearance to Peter as not only the first, but as the source of any expectation which led to the others, and believes that this can still be discerned, albeit faintly, behind the gospel traditions. He thinks that this is the only hypothesis which can unite the traditions and approach historical fact.

[22] H. Grass, *op. cit.*, pp. 109f.

[23] Acts 9.17: 'Jesus who appeared to you in the way'; 9.27: 'how he had seen the Lord'; 22.14f.: 'to see the Just One . . . witness of what you have seen and heard'; 22.18: 'in a trance I saw him saying to me . . .'; 26.16: 'for this reason I have appeared to thee'; 26.19: 'the heavenly vision'.

down to the dogmatic standpoint of the author of Acts.[24] Unfortunately, Paul nowhere in his letters elaborates on what he means by 'seeing the Lord' (it is not clear that Gal. 1.16 refers to this at all; the meaning may be 'to reveal his Son through me to the Gentiles'), and the argument of I Cor. 15 is not sufficiently precise, nor the two parts of it sufficiently closely linked, to be able to deduce from the exposition of the spiritual body of Christians how Paul thought of the risen body of Christ or of the nature of his appearance. Thus the Pauline evidence hardly provides a fixed point from which the rest of the resurrection tradition may be assessed.[25]

THE GOSPELS

If the evangelists, and those who were responsible for the material which they came to include in their gospels, show little sign of operating with the resurrection tradition reflected in I Corinthians, is it possible to detect what tradition or traditions do lie behind their work? In pursuing this kind of enquiry, there is a preliminary question which form criticism has taught us to ask, and to which Vincent Taylor once drew attention.[26] What would have been the function and purpose of a resurrection story? What had it been handed on to say and do? In distinction from a passion narrative, which by its nature, and in order to say what it had to say, must be a continuous story with one event leading to another (though doubtless much briefer than the present ones), resurrection stories are individual stories, each standing on its own feet, and their present connection in any sequence is plainly the work of the evangelist. In that respect they are like most of the gospel material

[24] W. Pannenberg, *Jesus God and Man* (1968), pp. 92f., lists five elements in the Acts accounts which could be accepted because they correspond with what could follow from Paul's own statements – the identity of the Risen One with Jesus, the appearance of a 'spiritual body', the appearance being from heaven, and the phenomena of light and audition. But the second is absent from Acts, and the last two are not certain in Paul. H. Grass, *op. cit.*, pp. 221f., argues for the reliability of the Acts accounts on the ground that they were so old that they could not be brought by Luke into line with the substantiality of the other resurrection appearances. But for Luke by definition the experience could not be other than a heavenly vision.

[25] So, to some extent, G. W. H. Lampe, in: G. W. H. Lampe and D. M. Mackinnon, *The Resurrection* (1966), pp. 43ff.

[26] Vincent Taylor, *The Formation of the Gospel Tradition* (1933), pp. 59ff.

outside the passion narratives, that is, self-contained units, originally unrelated to anything going before or coming after. This is because their function was not to say a number of separate things, but basically to say one thing – that the Lord is risen, or that Jesus is the Lord.

In their present form and position, the originally independent resurrection stories not only unify the gospel narrative as a whole as the account of the earthly career of him who is now known as the exalted Lord, but they have been unified in relation to one another by each evangelist in his own way and for his own purposes. In Mark the single story of the visit to the tomb ending in terror before divine action is not unconnected with that bare, realistic and awesome character of the passion narrative in Mark, which von Campenhausen finds impressive as evidence of historical trustworthiness,[27] but which may owe not a little to Mark's general theological presentation of Christ and the gospel.

In Matthew, the story is woven into a whole by legendary apologetic material. The resurrection now becomes public, and its reality is vouched for by the presence of soldiers provided by Pilate at the request of the Jewish authorities, who seal the tomb and have it guarded against any possibility of the disciples stealing the body and starting rumours of a resurrection. This purpose is defeated because the soldiers, with the women, become eye-witnesses to the resurrection. After remaining insensible long enough for the angel to give his message to the women and for the women to depart, they recover and convey their report to the authorities, and these have to be bribed to spread the rumour that the body had been stolen while they were asleep. Meanwhile the departing women are met by Jesus, and the return of the eleven to Galilee becomes the result of his express command relayed to them by the women.

In Luke, the links are concerned with 'the apostles and those with them'. The word 'disciple' disappears from Luke's Gospel after 22.45, to reappear in the special form 'the disciples' (= 'the Christians') in Acts 6, and this fact has been held to indicate a special source for Luke's passion and resurrection narratives.[28]

---

[27] H. von Campenhausen, *op. cit.*, pp. 56f.
[28] K. H. Rengstorf, μαθήτης, *TDNT* iv, p. 446.

It could, however, be due to Luke, who would here be preparing for the special position of the apostles in Acts as witnesses to the resurrection and preachers of the gospel of the resurrection. 'The apostles' are introduced at 24.10 as the recipients of the women's news, and it is two 'of them' who walk to Emmaus. These return to tell their story to 'the eleven', the kerygmatic statement 'The Lord has indeed risen and has appeared to Simon' being tucked in at this point. Jesus appears and instructs 'them', leads them to Bethany, blesses and leaves them, and 'they' return to Jerusalem to praise God constantly in the Temple. All this happens in the course of a single day (vv. 13, 33, 36). The Lukan text has suffered interpolation from the Johannine. Verses 12 and 40 should be omitted, as also probably 'and he says to them, Peace be unto you' in v. 36. The end of the gospel has been much discussed in relation to the beginning of Acts and in view of the textual evidence. 'And he was carried up into heaven' with 'worshipping him' in v. 51 could have been omitted to remove the contradiction with the forty days of post-resurrection appearances in Acts 1.3–9, but it is possible that they were added to round off the gospel when it was separated from Acts and had become a book in its own right among the gospels of the canon. If so, the story may have run on into the forty days of Acts 1 and so to the Ascension.

In John, the links are more theological. The part of the women, in the person of Mary Magdalene, is interwoven with that of the apostles in the persons of Peter and the beloved disciple, her witness to the empty tomb being confirmed by them, and her witness to the risen Lord being confirmed by his appearance to them the same day to commission them through the Holy Spirit. The appearance to Thomas does not stand on its own, but is linked to what precedes by an elaborate introduction (20.24f.) which prepares for its theological point.

In principle, one thoroughly well-attested resurrection story was enough to say what had to be said, and so far as witness to the fact of the resurrection is concerned, two or three such stories would not say more than one. Matthew is to all intents and purposes content with a single appearance, which said all that needed to be said, and the congregation which used Matthew's gospel relied on this single story for its grasp of the resurrection. Thus the shape and nature of the stories are related to the function which they were to perform.

Particularly valuable here is Dr C. H. Dodd's form-critical analysis of the resurrection traditions.[29] He seeks to establish a common pattern, appearing, like other gospel material, in two forms, the concise narrative and the longer circumstantial tale. The common pattern consists of:

A. The situation, generally the disciples bereft of their Lord;
B. the appearance of Jesus;
C. his greeting;
D. the recognition;
E. the word of command.

The short, concise version is found in Matt. 28.8–10, 16–20; John 20.19–23; Mark 16.14f., and the longer tale in Luke 24.13–35; John 20.11–17; 21.1–14, with Luke 24.36–49 and John 20.26–29 as highly interpreted and apologetic versions of the first type. Some such pattern may indeed belong to the resurrection traditions, and give indications of the motives which went to their shaping and the purposes they were intended to serve; and Dodd makes the important point that the resurrection stories are lacking in those apocalyptic traits found in the Transfiguration story and in Rev. 1.12–17 (and in the appearance of the angel in Matt. 28.2f.) which would compel immediate recognition of the Lord in glory. However, the following considerations of his thesis suggest themselves:

1. Of the three narratives which are held to establish the pattern of the first form, the concise narrative, Matt. 28.8–10 is hardly a separate pericope. It is likely to have been supplied by the evangelist himself to effect a transition from the story of the empty tomb to the appearance in Galilee, and the words 'Fear not' need not imply doubt, especially when preceded by 'they worshipped him', but rather terror in the presence of the transcendent, a theme carried over from 28.8 and from Mark. In the third, John 20.19–23, the purpose of the words 'he showed them his hands and his side' (the 'side' being dependent

[29] C. H. Dodd, 'The Appearances of the Risen Christ: an Essay in Form-Criticism of the Gospels', in: D. E. Nineham (ed.), *Studies in the Gospels* (1955), pp. 9ff.; reprinted in C. H. Dodd, *More New Testament Studies* (1968), pp. 102ff.

on the special Johannine tradition in John 19.34) may be 'less
to establish His identity in the face of doubt than that their joy
might be fulfilled by the sight of the signs of His victory over the
world (16.33). Since the conquest of the power of the world by
the death and resurrection of the Christ made the Christian mission to the world possible, the exposition of the wounds is at
once followed by the Apostolic commission of the disciples,
secondly by their consecration.'[30]

2. The theme of 'doubt', which is a fairly constant feature of
the narratives, needs careful handling, for it is not undifferentia-
ted. In those stories which hinge on what Dodd calls ἀναγνώρισις
or 'recognition' – the Emmaus story and that in John 21 – the
recognition, once the Lord has made the decisive action, is
immediate and undoubting. In Luke 24.11, 25, however, it is
doubt about the resurrection itself, not about the identity of the
Lord. Gerhard Barth draws attention to these differences.[31] In
Mark 16.14 it is a message of those who had seen the risen Lord
which is disbelieved, and the doubt is overcome by an appearance of the Lord himself. In Luke 24.41 it is an unbelief 'for
joy' accompanied by wonder; in Luke 24.37 it is fear that they
might be seeing a spirit, which is removed by further material
means. In Matt. 28.17 it is the doubt of some contrasted with
the recognition and worship of the majority. Barth sees this
theme of doubt, not as an historical recollection but as a
pragmatic trait with a theological motive. In Matt. 28.17 he
thinks it serves the purpose of underlining the overcoming of
doubt by the authoritative words of the Lord, and agrees with
O. Michel in seeing this as reflecting a problem of the later
church 'which seeks a new certainty about the Risen One
beyond the Easter experience, since the appearance belongs to
the tradition and to an event in the past'. In John 20, the whole
question of doubt becomes a theme in itself, set forth in the
juxtaposition of two separate pericopes in which the doubt of
Thomas is contrasted with the faith of the rest, and a faith is set
forth which can dispense with appearances. H. Grass points to
the intensification of the theme of doubt in the scene in the
Epistula Apostolorum where all the disciples doubt and the Lord

[30] E. C. Hoskyns, *The Fourth Gospel* (1947²), *ad loc.*
[31] G. Barth, 'Matthew's Understanding of the Law', in: G. Bornkamm,
G. Barth, H. J. Held, *Tradition and Interpretation in Matthew* (1963), pp. 132f.

sends first Martha and then Mary, and finally comes himself before they are won to belief. He also concludes that the theme of doubt is not necessarily a sign of authenticity, but could be a device for stressing the wonder and strangeness of the resurrection.[32]

3. In his assessment of John 20.19–23, Dodd judges the insufflation to be a separate incident, and appears to regard the extended form of commission (v. 23) as a 'minimal supplement' of the main pattern. On the other hand, he sees the details of John 21.1–14 as evidence of the story-teller's craft; it is a straightforward uninterrupted dramatic narrative without didactic passages such as are present in Luke 24.13–35. But it is possible to see it otherwise. The gift of the Spirit is in the evangelist's thought integrally related to the apostolic mission and the forgiveness of sins; the commission may also be the main point, as in Matt. 28. In John 21 the details of the apparently artless story are surely intended to convey the truths that the disciples, scattered to their own (cf. 16.32), toil fruitlessly as apostles until the Lord directs operations, when they then make a perfect catch of converts in an undivided church, and the identity of the Lord is significantly first recognized by the beloved disciple. Similarly, are the words of command 'Touch me not . . .' (John 20.17) rightly judged by Dodd to be of 'dramatic value in the story quite independent of their theological import', when the reason for the command is given in Johannine theological terms of the necessary ascent of Jesus to the Father, and are these terms simply an expansion of the story and not its main point? Thus some of the stories at least may be more determined in their shape by the significant sayings to which they lead than by a common pattern.

In one very important respect, resurrection stories differed from the rest of the material outside as well as inside the passion narrative, and it is here that difficulties begin to appear. Resurrection stories are unique in the gospel material in that their intention cannot be to add to an already existing stock of information about the earthly Jesus, nor to tell of an event in a series of events, nor to provide an epilogue to a series, nor to complete a pattern of historical events. What they have to say is directed to all that has

[32] H. Grass, *op. cit.*, p. 29.

been said previously, or that ever could be said, about the earthly Jesus between birth and death, and are intended to place it in a totally new dimension. Like the plus or minus sign in an algebraical formula, they do not belong within the bracket, but outside it, determining anything there may be inside the bracket. But how could truth of this kind be expressed in the form of a narrative, since narrative of event is related to history, and history can know of no event of such a kind as to stand outside the series of events?

The truth is expressed in fact by stories of the man Jesus alive after death making himself known to his friends. This they have in common with a credal formula such as 'died, buried, rose, appeared', but they are less effective for the purpose, for as stories they are unable to contain in themselves three-quarters of the formula ('died, buried, rose'); they can only presuppose it. They can convey the full truth only if, in the continuous narrative of the gospels, they are made to follow on the stories of the passion, burial and discovery of the empty tomb, which together express 'died, buried, rose'. It could thus be possible for independent stories which originally belonged to the post-resurrection period to wander into the main body of the gospel tradition for lack of any clear indication in the story itself that it was the risen Christ and not the earthly Jesus who was speaking or acting. The part of the credal formula which resurrection stories are confined to express-ing is 'he appeared', though even here they are hardly able to convey in narrative form the full force of this statement if 'he appeared' in the credal formula is intended to mean something like 'he came out of the sphere of eternity and invisibility and was made manifest by God'.

The language of the resurrection appearances is predominantly the language of sight,[33] though the significance of what is seen is expressed in terms of what Jesus has to say. When it is said that he 'came' (John 20.19, 24,26; cf. 'drew near': Luke 24.15; 'met': Matt. 28.9), this is simple narrative style without reflec-tion on where he had come from. The statement that 'he stood in their midst' derives its force in John 20.19, 26 from the accompanying circumstance that the doors were shut, and in Luke 24.36, probably, from his having suddenly 'vanished' in

33 For this language see esp. H. Grass, *op. cit.*, pp. 186ff., and K. H. Rengstorf, *op. cit.*, pp. 55ff., 117ff.

the previous story (24.31). Generally some form or other of the verb 'to see' is used. This is so in kergymatic statements in the form 'he appeared' (ὤφθη) – three times in I Cor. 15.5–8, to Simon (Luke 24.34), to those who had accompanied him from Galilee (Acts 13.31). In Acts 26.16 it is on the lips of the Lord himself, and in Acts 9.17, 'he who appeared to you' is on the lips of Ananias describing the appearance to Paul on the Damascus road. Connected with this is the participle in Acts 1.3 'appearing to them over a period of forty days',[34] and the noun in Luke 24.23, where the women see a vision (ὀπτασία) of angels (cf. Acts 26.19, the heavenly vision – ὀπτασία – of the appearance to Paul). It is also found in the gospel narratives of the appearances, where those present 'see' Jesus (Matt. 28.17; Luke 24.24, 39; John 20.14, 18, 20, 25, 27, 29). They fix their eyes on him at the ascension, and will see him return in the same manner as he goes (Acts 1.9–11).

These two usages are related to each other when Paul's 'he appeared also to me' (I Cor. 15.8) is brought together with 'Have I not seen Jesus our Lord?' (I Cor. 9.1), as also in the double statement in Acts 26.16. 'To this end have I appeared to thee, to appoint thee a minister and witness both of the things wherein thou hast seen me and wherein I will appear to thee.' They are not, however, identical, as though 'he appeared to me' was simply another way of saying 'I have seen him'. The passive

---

[34] ὀπτανόμενος, a 'present formed from the aor. passive "I let myself be seen, I appear"', W. Bauer – W.F. Arndt – F. W. Gingrich, *A Greek-English Lexicon of the New Testament* (1957), p. 580. C. F. D. Moule, 'The Ascension – Acts 1.9', *ExpT* lxviii (1956/7), p. 206, n. 1, draws attention to an interesting linguistic parallel in Tobit 12.16–22, where Raphael discloses himself, and announces his departure. The whole passage contains several illustrations of the language in which this kind of story would tend to be couched. Thus, at the angel's self-disclosure the two men ἐταράχθησαν . . . καὶ ἔπεσον ἐπὶ πρόσωπον. ὅτι ἐφοβήθησαν, and the angel replies μὴ φοβεῖσθε. εἰρήνη ὑμῖν ἔσται. He then announces that in all the time he had appeared to them he had not really eaten and drank, but they had seen a vision (πάσας τὰς ἡμέρας ὠπτανόμην ὑμῖν, καὶ οὐκ ἔφαγον οὐδὲ ἔπιον, ἀλλὰ ὅρασιν ὑμεῖς ἐθεωρεῖτε. He then commands them to praise God because he is going to him who sent him (διότι ἀναβαίνω πρὸς τὸν ἀποστείλαντά με). When they get up they see him no more, and they praise the great and wonderful works of God, and how the angel of the Lord had appeared to them (ἐξομολογοῦντο τὰ ἔργα τὰ μεγάλα καὶ θαυμαστὰ αὐτοῦ, ὡς ὤφθη αὐτοῖς ἄγγελος κυρίου). There are parallels in expression here to phrases found in Mark, Luke and John, and one interesting contrast, in that while the angel says that his eating and drinking were apparent only and visionary, Luke intends the eating of Jesus in the presence of his disciples to be real (Luke 24.41–43; Acts 1.4; 10.41).

ὤφθη with the dative of the person to whom the appearance is made cannot be translated 'he was seen by . . .', which would require the preposition 'by' (ὑπό) with the genitive, and if the verb is used as a deponent, the emphasis lies not on the apprehension of the recipient but on the will and initiative of him who appears. It means 'he let himself be seen' (so also in classical usage). Further, both forms of expression have their own nuances and difficulties.

While ὤφθη can be used in a straightforward sense simply to describe the appearance of someone on the scene, it is also, both inside and outside the Bible, used of the earthly manifestation of themselves by supernatural beings who are ordinarily invisible. In connection with the resurrection it is confined to kerygmatic statements, and necessarily so, since it is not simply a factual but also a theological expression. What it intends to say requires some expression of resurrection to precede it (so, 'he has been raised', I Cor. 15.4; 'he was raised', Luke 24.34; 'God raised him', Acts 13.31; 'he manifested himself alive after his death', Acts 1.3). The 'appearance' is the consequence of previous resurrection and is in part a statement of its meaning. Thus 'he was raised and appeared' means that from the state of invisibility, which he occupied as the result of resurrection, Jesus becomes (temporarily) visible before returning back to it. He can only 'appear' in this sense as the Risen One and as a denizen of the eternal world. It is more doubtful whether Rengstorf[35] is right in arguing that as the passive 'he was raised' means 'God raised him', so the passive ὤφθη really means 'God allowed him to become visible'.[36] This sense is explicit in Acts 10.40: 'God raised him up and gave him to be made manifest', but in other places the verb may not be passive but deponent. In Acts 1.3, 'he presented himself alive' and in John 21.1 'he manifested himself' (interpreting 'he was made manifest' in 21.14) make Jesus the agent of his own appearance. Rengstorf further argues that there is a peculiar stress in the repeated ὤφθη of I Cor. 15, and that it reflects an emphasis on the objective nature of the appearances in face of attempts to

---

[35] K. H. Rengstorf, *op. cit.,* p. 57.
[36] See the semantics of this word in the discussions by W. Marxsen and G. Delling in *The Significance of the Message of the Resurrection for Faith in Jesus Christ,* pp. 27f, 83ff.

reduce them to subjective experiences of the disciples. This, however, is a very dubious deduction either from the kerygmatic statement itself, where the repetition is probably rhythmical, or from the context in which Paul has used it. There is no evidence of any such reduction, and to talk in terms of subjective and objective in relation to the early Christians would be an anachronism.

None of the gospel narratives of appearances contains 'he appeared' (the nearest equivalent is the evangelist's comment in John 21.14: 'he was manifested a third time after being raised from the dead'), and what is expressed by way of faith and of the invisible becoming visible had to be conveyed otherwise. This is done in various ways. That it is the beyond which is being made visible, that a special kind of preception is involved in this 'seeing', and that there was something unrecognizable to ordinary sight as well as recognizable in the risen Lord, are indicated by the juxtaposition of sight and doubt (Matt. 28.17, but not v. 9), or by the failure to recognize him until he 'reveals' himself by a word (John 20.16), or by an action (Luke 24.30; John 21.6) or more crudely by a demonstration (John 20.27; Luke 24.42f. is rather different, being aimed against a phantom theory of the resurrection), as also by his sudden appearance in circumstances which would ordinarily render it impossible (John 20.19, 26) and his sudden disappearance (Luke 24.31). There is also something of the revelatory character of ὤφθη in statements about 'seeing'. Thus 'I (we) have seen the Lord' is a different kind of statement from 'I (we) have seen Jesus', since it is not simply a statement of visible fact but involves a christological confession of that which Jesus had become through the resurrection – the Lord. The one who is visibly seen is the invisible heavenly one, and the difference between seeing the earthly Jesus and seeing the risen Jesus lies in his lordship, which is not the object of ordinary sight. Thus something of what was to belong to that 'seeing' which was to take place at the parousia (cf. Mark 14.62) is transferred to the resurrection appearances. This may have been intended by 'there ye shall see him' in Mark 16.7 and may have been reproduced by Matthew in an appearance in which the risen Jesus is worshipped as the universal Lord (Matt. 28.9, 17ff.).

Neither 'he appeared' nor 'I have seen the Lord' yield

information about the nature of the risen Lord or of his 'body'. The only New Testament writer who could say both in relation to himself is Paul (I Cor. 15.8 and 9.1), and it so happens that he nowhere spells out in his letters what this means. If the argument in I Cor. 15.35–49 on the necessity for putting on the spiritual body of immortality which is the result of a resurrection in glory is in any way based on a parallel with the resurrection body of Christ, it does not appear likely that Paul thought of this body as the object of earthly sight. In the three accounts in Acts of the 'appearance' of the Lord to Paul on the Damascus road, the emphasis is on what is spoken and heard, and there is no 'seeing' except of a light which blinds. It cannot, however, be assumed that these are the kind of accounts which Paul would himself have given of the occurrence, or that he would recognize himself in the narratives of Acts. For the author of Acts, the occurrence cannot have been of the same kind as he had narrated in his gospel or as are found in the other gospels, since it is part of his scheme that such appearances ceased at the Ascension. Thus for Luke, as in a different manner for John, the resurrection form of Jesus was a temporary state and not one in which he exercises his permanent lordship, and the resurrection, for all its importance, falls short of what is final.

The new dimension of the 'appearance' is not expressed by the frankly supernatural – the stories are noticeably reserved, and Jesus is not depicted, as at the Transfiguration, in a body of glory – but is rather suggested by the sudden presence and sudden removal of Jesus, and by emphasis on the fact that some or all doubted who he was, which in various forms is a fairly constant theme. What, however, distinguishes the gospel stories from the credal formula, and where they are strong and it is weak, is that in all of them the risen Lord does not just 'appear', but speaks, and in what he says interprets the resurrection and its consequences. As stories, they are for the most part shaped so that their main weight falls, not on the nature of the appearance but on what is spoken, and the reason for there being more than one story lies, not, as in the formula, in the need for more than one attestation of the event ('whether it be I or they'), but in the various truths which the Lord has to utter. But here there is encountered a second form of the fragmentation of the tradition, which may be stated as follows, that not only does the Lord not say the same things in any two gospels, but that it is hardly the same Lord who speaks. In Matthew it is evidently a Matthaean Lord who speaks, in Luke a Lukan Lord and in John a Johannine Lord.

(a) Mark

In the case of books like the gospels, ends, like beginnings, are likely to exhibit variation and complexity, since with reference to the person whom the church came to believe Jesus to be it is the origin of his life and the issue of it which will be most difficult to state. So Mark traces the origin to the Baptist as the fulfilment of Scripture, Luke to a supernatural birth within the pious in Israel, Matthew to the beginning of sacred history in Abraham, and John to the eternity of the divine Word. In their endings, the gospels are at their maximum of variation, and the matter is now further complicated by the extraordinary riddle of the ending of Mark's gospel.

So long as this gospel was taken simply·as one of the four, and vv. 9–20 of its final chapter as the true text, then its information about the risen Lord, looking no it was in pictorial detail and reading like a bare summary, was nevertheless taken as part of the stock of tradition and as corroborative of what was to be found in more detail elsewhere. When, however, it was established on textual and linguistic grounds that these verses were a later, probably second-century, addition, and that the most reliable manuscripts ended with the words of the young man to the women, 'but go, tell his disciples and Peter, He goeth before you into Galilee: there ye shall see him, as he said unto you', and with the statement 'and they went out and fled from the tomb; for trembling and astonishment had come upon them: and they said nothing to anyone; for they were afraid' (Mark 16.7f.); and when also it was shown that Mark was the earliest of the gospels, and that Matthew and Luke had written theirs by reference to his, then the situation was vastly changed. At the heart of the resurrection tradition appeared a vacuum, the nature and meaning of which scholars continue to debate.

Is this a puzzle simply, or a mystery? Is the gospel a torso? This was for a long time the generally held opinion. For some reason, whether because the end was suppressed, or because through some accident of history it was never written, or because the end of the original manuscript had suffered damage and loss, the gospel breaks off in the middle of a sentence. Attempts were then made to extrapolate from the gospel, and particularly from the words 'he goes before you into Galilee; there ye shall see him', as to what the original ending must have been, and sometimes to look for hidden traces of this ending elsewhere in the New Testament. This is a very natural view, is still widely held, and may well be right, but it is not without formidable difficulties. Is it to be supposed that the community for which Mark wrote was quite incapable of making good the lacuna from its knowledge of the resurrection tradition by which it lived, especially if that community was an important church, and if there was a close relation between the evangelist and the community, whose tradition he was expressing in writing? If, as seems likely on the evidence, the copy of Mark used by Matthew and Luke also broke off at this point – they diverge sharply here both from each other and from anything which is likely to have stood in Mark – is it to be supposed that there was only one manuscript of Mark in existence, and that a mutilated one, or that if there were more than one they were reproductions of a mutilated copy which had never been made good? This is indeed a great puzzle.

On the other hand, there are some who maintain that it is incorrect to say that the text breaks off in the middle of a sentence. Rather does Mark deliberately end in a highly abrupt and staccato way, which is admittedly an extreme example of his manner, but which is also eloquent of how he understands the resurrection. The story of the visit to the tomb would not then be a mutilated fragment which was intended to have a rounded conclusion and sequel, but a unit complete in itself. It was a way of preaching the resurrection, however surprising that may be to us who have been brought up on Matthew's, Luke's or John's view of the matter, or on a harmony of all three. Mark brings his gospel to an end on a note of silence enforced by terror and awe, and puts down his pen because the rest is silence, and cannot be told. The end of the gospel would not then be a puzzle, to be resolved tentatively by guesswork, but a genuine mystery, bringing men to the threshold of the supernatural and leaving them there. This view also is not without formidable difficulties.

What was it that Mark thought was to follow, and that could not be expressed, since other evangelists and the traditions they used had undertaken to express it? Can it be, as Lohmeyer suggested, that it was the parousia? But Mark knew well enough that this had not taken place. Can it be that for Mark resurrection belonged within the wider concept of exaltation to God, which could not be depicted in terms of a man, even a risen man, appearing among and alongside men? Do we on either view of the gospel's ending know for certain the meaning of the words on which the issue of the gospel now comes to hinge, 'he goes before you into Galilee', which refer back to previous words of Jesus himself, 'after I am raised up, I will go before you into Galilee' (Mark 14.28)? Does 'go before', which is as ambiguous in the Greek as it is in the English, mean 'go on in advance of you with a view to a reunion in Galilee', or 'go at your head, like a shepherd leading his flock, to Galilee'? And in either case, for what purpose is the journey to Galilee, since a gospel can hardly come to an end simply on a note of reunion? We have to reconcile ourselves to the fact that there is this curious hiatus, call it puzzle or mystery, at the heart of the resurrection tradition of the gospels, and that it is likely to remain there.[37]

The problem had been discussed by Eusebius and Jerome. How it appeared once textual criticism had shown that in the most reliable ancient witnesses the gospel ended at 16.8 can be seen from F. J. Hort's argument for the spuriousness of 16.9–20 on grounds of intrinsic evidence:[38] 'It is incredible that the evangelist deliberately concluded either a paragraph with ἐφοβοῦντο γάρ, or the Gospel with a petty detail of a secondary event, leaving his narrative hanging in the air. Each of these points of intrinsic evidence is of very great weight: but the first admits, as we shall see, a two-sided application; and such support as either of them lends to the genuineness of vv. 9–20 is dependent on the assumption that nothing but a deliberate intention of the evangelist to close the Gospel at v. 8 could have caused its termination at that point in the most original text transmitted to us. The assumption fails, however, for two other contingencies have to be taken into account: either the Gospel may never have been finished, or it may have lost its last leaf before it was

[37] For the text in Greek and English of the various endings of Mark and discussions of them, see Vincent Taylor, *The Gospel according to St Mark*, and D. E. Nineham, *Saint Mark* (1963), *ad loc*.
[38] F. J. Hort, *The New Testament in Greek*, vol. ii (1882), appendix, pp. 46f.

multiplied by transcription . . . though the presence of these verses (9–20) furnishes a sufficient conclusion to the Gospel, it furnishes none to the equally mutilated sentence and paragraph.' Westcott and Hort therefore ended their text of Mark's gospel not with a full stop but with a colon followed by asterisks. So later F. C. Burkitt,[39] in discussing the textual evidence, wrote: 'That the Gospel was originally intended to finish at verse 8 is quite inconceivable. Not only the narrative, the paragraph and the sentence are each left incomplete, but even the subordinate clause seems to hang in the air. Greek sentences do not usually finish off with a particle, and the two last words ἐφοβοῦντο γάρ . . . may well have meant 'for they were afraid of' *something* now lost, whether it was the chief Priests or the fanatical mob or the incredulous and mournful scorn of St. Peter and his companions. The Gospel as we have it is accidentally imperfect, not intentionally curtailed; in other words, the MS from which all our copies are derived must have lost one or more leaves at the end.' Earlier, after asserting that 'in no case could the Gospel have originally ended with γάρ', Burkitt raises the question whether the text should not be printed with a grave accent on γὰρ to indicate that the sentence had once run on.[40]

This view has continued to be held to the present time, perhaps by most scholars, though not always with the same confidence. Thus H. B. Swete thought it 'perhaps improbable that the Evangelist deliberately concluded a paragraph with ἐφοβοῦντο γάρ'.[41] B. H. Streeter, who devoted a whole chapter to the problem,[42] concluded that the author cannot have meant to end without an account of appearances to the apostles in Galilee, which are twice mentioned in the text (14.28; 16.7), and that either he did not live to finish his book, or, more probably, that the last leaf was torn off before any copies of it got into circulation. In the conviction that it is highly improbable that the earliest account of the resurrection appearances had vanished without trace, he then speculated that the original ending of the gospel was to be seen underlying John's account of the appearances to Mary and the disciples at the sea of Galilee, and to do so

[39] F. C. Burkitt, *Two Lectures on the Gospels* (1901), pp. 25ff.
[40] F. C. Burkitt, *The Old Latin and the Itala* (1896), p. 49, n.1.
[41] H. B. Swete, *The Gospel according to St Mark* (1898), p. 399.
[42] B. H. Streeter, *The Four Gospels* (1924), ch. xii.

had to postulate than an unmutilated copy of the gospel had been sent by Mark from Rome to Ephesus immediately on completion.

A. E. J. Rawlinson preferred to put the matter in the form of a series of questions:[43] 'Could the sentence "for they were *afraid*", on any reasonable view, be originally meant as the conclusion of a book? Are the words even the conclusion of a sentence? . . . It appears in any case to be virtually certain that Mark must have intended to chronicle an appearance of the Risen Lord to S. Peter, and probably other appearances as well. . . . The author broke off in the middle of a sentence and never resumed. Did he die? Was he suddenly arrested and martyred? Or did he leave Rome where he was working, and for some reason never return? We have no data for answering these questions, but at least it is probable that even if the original autograph of the Gospel were damaged or torn, the missing portion would surely have been restored by the author himself, had he been living and accessible.' Vincent Taylor, after considering alternatives, finds it incredible that Mark intended such a conclusion, and for him, 'The view that ἐφοβοῦντο γάρ is not the intended ending stands'.[44] He refers to Rudolf Bultmann,[45] who holds that this cannot have been the original ending on the grounds that the other evangelists did not regard it so, that in giving only a promise and not an account of an appearance it would contradict the character of the resurrection tradition as we have it in the other gospels, and that 'for they were afraid' is manifestly apologetic in tone and does not make a good end. C. E. B. Cranfield is more hesitant.[46] He rejects as unlikely that the original ending was suppressed,[47] and as not very likely that the ending was lost or destroyed by some mischance since 'it involves assuming both that Mark himself was dead or otherwise unavailable to rewrite the ending and at the same time that the gospel had not been in use long enough for

[43] A. E. J. Rawlinson, *The Gospel according to St Mark* (1925), p. 268ff.
[44] Vincent Taylor, *op. cit.*, p. 609.
[45] R. Bultmann, *The History of the Synoptic Tradition* (1968²), p. 285, n.2.
[46] C. E. B. Cranfield, *St Mark* (1959), pp. 470f.; cf. also his discussion of the whole passage, 'St Mark 16.1–8', *SJT* 5 (1952), pp. 282ff., 398ff.
[47] Suppression of appearances in Galilee because they conflicted with the narratives in Luke and John was supposed by B. W. Bacon, *The Beginnings of the Gospel Story* (1909), p. 227, and by others.

someone else to restore it from memory'. The view that Mark intended to end so 'should surely be rejected' on the ground that resurrection appearances belonged to the tradition, and his conclusion is that 'while absolute certainty is impossible, the most likely alternative is that Mark intended to include at least one such narrative, but for some reason never finished his work.'[48]

There were, however, dissentient voices, and each of Hort's points has been controverted. In 1903, Wellhausen, while remarking that the majority of exegetes regarded 16.8 as an impossible ending, complained that they had not understood the force of 16.4, which supplied all that was needed, so that it would be a pity to add anything to it.[49] He argued that while a resurrection appearance could have stood in the place of 16.1–8, it could not follow after it, since such an appearance was already anticipated in 16.7 and would lose its point if the resurrection had already been announced to the disciples. E. P. Gould was content simply to state that 'the brevity of this ending is quite parallel to the beginning of the Gospel, the beginning and ending being both alike outside the main purpose of the evangelist. It is not strange, therefore, but rather consonant with Mark's manner',[50] and W. C. Allen that 'the dramatic and abrupt ending is quite in accordance with the vividness which characterises the whole Gospel. The fear is not the fear of doubt, but the awe of proximity to the supernatural.'[51] W. G. Kümmel could write in 1963 that 'scholarship in increasing measure is inclining toward the view that Mark reached his intended end with 16.8', quoting in support W. Michaelis, R. H. Lightfoot, E. Lohmeyer, F. C. Grant, W. Grundmann, P. Carrington, A. M. Farrer, A. F. J. Klijn, W. Marxsen, R. C. Heard, J. Schreiber, H. A. Guy, J. B. Tyson, W. C. Allen, L. J. D. Richardson and others.[52]

Negatively, attention has been drawn to the weakness of the hypotheses advanced to account for an early mutilation of the

[48] Similar judgments are to be found in the commentaries of C. H. Turner, in *A New Commentary on Holy Scripture* (1928), B. H. Branscomb, Moffatt Commentaries (1937), and J. Schniewind, Das Neue Testament Deutsch (1947).
[49] *Das Evangelium Marci* (1903), p. 146.
[50] E. P. Gould, *The Gospel according to Saint Mark* (1896), p. 304.
[51] W. C. Allen, *The Gospel according to Saint Mark* (1915), p. 191.
[52] W. G. Kümmel, *Introduction to the New Testament* (1966), pp. 71f.

gospel which could not have been made good – the martyrdom of the evangelist, the loss of a final page, etc. P. Carrington dubs these 'melodramatic hypotheses', which involve the 'impossible inference that Mark's Gospel passed through a long period of neglect while there was still only one copy of it' (the view of Burkitt), whereas its use by Matthew and Luke point in the opposite direction that 'it was early disseminated and eagerly received',[53] while E. Trocmé refers to them as 'suppositions romanesques d'un genre naïf'.[54] A. M. Farrer observes that such accidents could happen but are not at all likely, and that 'history would become a field for uncontrolled fantasy, if historians allowed themselves the free use of such suppositions'.[55] As noted above, Cranfield feels the force of these objections, but his conjecture that 'for some reason' Mark never finished his work still leaves the difficulty of explaining how an unfinished work so established itself as to become the basis of the gospels of Matthew and Luke, and these difficulties are the greater the more Mark's gospel is seen as giving expression to the tradition of the community within which it was written, and less as the individual work of a particular author who was the only one who could finish it.

Positively, it has been argued that 16.8 is not impossible as an ending of a sentence, a paragraph or even a book. Wilamowitz had already denied that it was impossible Greek usage, and instances have been adduced in Greek literature and the papyri of short sentences ending with γάρ to form the conclusion of a paragraph, a letter or a section of a book.[56] R. H. Lightfoot worked carefully over these instances and added others;[57] note should be taken of the LXX examples Gen. 18.15 and 45.3, and especially of the latter, where the situation is that of Joseph

---

[53] P. Carrington, *According to Mark* (1960), p. 335. F. C. Burkitt, *The Gospel History and its Transmission* (1906), p. 261, had maintained that it was evident 'that at one time no more than a single mutilated copy was in existence, or at least available. The work had dropped out of circulation, it had lost its public, and we can only guess at the reasons which led to its resuscitation.'

[54] E. Trocmé, *La Formation de l'Evangile selon Marc* (1963), p. 52.

[55] A. M. Farrer, *St Matthew and St Mark* (1954), p. 144.

[56] So R. R. Ottley, 'ἐφοβοῦντο γάρ', *JTS* xxvii (1926), pp. 407–9; C. H. Kraeling, 'Mark 16.8', *JBL* 45 (1926), pp. 357f; H. J. Cadbury, 'Mark 16.8', *JBL* 46 (1927), pp. 344ff.

[57] R. H. Lightfoot, *Locality and Doctrine in the Gospels* (1938), ch. 1.

disclosing himself to his brethren who believed him dead. He
further examined the place of fear in the Gospel of Mark and
the absolute use of the verb 'to fear' without an object or
following clause, and he also pointed to short sentences with
γάρ as a feature of Mark's style. A. M. Farrer, who had argued
for the effectiveness of 16.1–8 as a conclusion of the gospel on
poetic grounds,[58] and as corresponding to structural rhythms
discernible elsewhere in the gospel,[59] came to modify his opinion
to the extent of postulating not an additional pericope or
pericopes but a single sentence such as 'But Jesus sent forth
his disciples to preach the gospel among all nations', which could
easily have been removed to make room for the longer spurious
ending when that was thought necessary, and in this way lost.[60]
His reason for this supposition is his understanding of the way
in which Matthew builds up his narrative by amplification of
Mark, and his desire to find a basis in Mark of Matthew's concluding paragraph. It cannot, of course, be shown that this
paragraph grew out of anything more in Mark than the words
'I will go before you into Galilee', together with the necessity
of providing a missing conclusion, and the sentence proposed
by Farrer will strike some as banal, and as hardly what Mark
is likely to have written to conclude what Farrer himself describes as 'a carefully composed book'. While it could easily
have been removed to make room for a longer ending, this
could hardly be so in the case of the shorter ending,[61] since this
says little more than what is now postulated as the original
conclusion.

J. M. Creed argued forcefully that in itself the unit is complete;[62] it says that the women were so overwhelmed that 'they
kept their experience to themselves'. Only if something is thought
to follow does the latent incoherence between the message of the
angel and the fear and silence of the women become intoler-
able. H. A. Guy thought that the gospel ended so because

---

[58] A. M. Farrer, *The Glass of Vision* (1948), ch. viii.
[59] A. M. Farrer, *A Study in St Mark* (1951), ch. vii.
[60] A. M. Farrer, *St Matthew and St Mark*, ch. ix.
[61] 'But they reported briefly to Peter and those with him all that they had been told. And after that, Jesus himself sent out by means of them from east and west the sacred and imperishable proclamation of eternal salvation'.
[62] J. M. Creed, 'The Conclusion of the Gospel according to Saint Mark', *JTS* xxxi (1930), pp. 175ff.

Mark was an unpolished writer;[63] E. Trocmé that the unit was of this kind because it was liturgical;[64] while P. Carrington thought of it as leading into the liturgy as the Gospel lection.[65]

If 16.1–8 is to be treated as a unit complete in itself and as a possible ending of the gospel, how is it to be estimated and interpreted? The question raises considerable difficulties. In the first place, it belongs to the tradition, not of the resurrection appearances, but of the empty tomb. It may, indeed, be the only representative of that tradition, for the authority of Mark for Matthew and Luke is nowhere more evident than that they felt compelled to reproduce such an awkward paragraph, and to build their own versions round three of the distinctive features of the Markan account, fear, 'you seek Jesus . . . he is not here, he is risen', and the angelic reference to Galilee (Luke's awkward 'while he was in Galilee . . .' is plainly dictated by the Markan original), and the differences – the earthquake, descent and appearance of the angel and the guards in Matthew, and the two men in shining garments, the women's worship and the kerygmatic statement in Luke – are readily explicable as editorial work of the evangelists concerned. It is less clear whether John's account is an independent tradition or a radical version of Mark's, designed to bring the empty tomb into connection with an appearance to the women[66] and to bring the apostles, in the persons of the distinctively Johannine pair, Peter and the beloved disciple, into connection with it.

The status of this tradition in Mark is not easy to discern. The empty tomb does not seem to have belonged to the earliest kerygma of the resurrection, and should probably not be read out of either the references to the burial (I Cor. 15.4; Rom. 6.4; Col. 2.12), which are meant to emphasize the reality of the death,[67] or the mention of the 'third day', which probably had its origin in the application of the scriptures rather than in the

---

[63] H. A. Guy, *The Origin of the Gospel of Mark* (1954), pp. 162f.

[64] E. Trocmé, *op. cit.*, p. 51.

[65] P. Carrington, *According to Mark*, pp. 335ff.

[66] Or one of them; note 'We know not . . .' in John 20.2. But this probably means 'I'.

[67] Or that, as a notable figure, he had a grave; so K. H. Rengstorf, *op. cit.*, pp. 51ff. See H. von Campenhausen's change of mind on this (*op. cit.*, pp. 54f. and n.52 and n.53). '"Dead and buried" – this expression may simply be used to underline the reality and apparent finality of the death itself, and say nothing beyond this.'

visit of the women. This may, however, be due to the fact that
reference to the tomb being found empty could hardly be made
in a statement which was kerygmatic in form. It is argued that
the tradition is a relatively late addition to the resurrection faith,
but the grounds of the argument, viz. that the earliest Easter
faith presented Jesus as exalted to heaven straight from death,[68]
or that 'what is certainly the oldest view held by the church
made no distinction between the resurrection of Christ and his
elevation to the right hand of the Father',[69] are not very firmly
based, since it can be held that the very idea of resurrection
contained within itself the idea of exaltation, and the passages
referred to may be understood as reflecting developed theologies
of the writers concerned rather than survivals of an original
conception.[70] On the other hand, attempts to establish an historical kernel of the empty tomb story are not very convincing.
Mark's story is not a simple naturalistic account, but rather a
proclamation of divine miracle and power in the face of death
and human incapacity. It is in the other gospels that, under the
pressure of polemic and apologetic, the story becomes more
naturalistic, the silence of the women is removed, and the empty
tomb acts as a sign pointing forward to the appearances. In
Mark it is in itself the proclamation of the resurrection, and is
made so by the non-naturalistic elements, i.e. the contradiction
in the women setting out with the question, 'Who will roll away
the stone?', and the presence of the interpreting angel, who, in
place of the Lord, utters the vital statements. It is difficult to see
what historical nucleus would be left if these were removed.[71]
And the very basis of the narrative, a visit for a delayed embalming

[68] M. Goguel, *La Foi à la Resurrection de Jesus dans le christianisme primitif*
(1933), pp. 213ff.
[69] G. Bornkamm, *Jesus of Nazareth* (1960), p. 183.
[70] Goguel: Matt. 27.51–53; Bornkamm: John 3.14; 12.32, 34; Acts 2.33;
5.30f; Phil. 2.9; Heb. 1.3–13; 8.1.
[71] The most notable example of an attempt to arrive at an historical nucleus
is, of course, H. von Campenhausen's essay. Mark's story he regards as basic,
and to be followed exclusively. It also has legendary features, but he believes
that it can be so dissected that 'what remains over and above this narrator's
artifice – a journey to the tomb that is found opened and empty – is something
quite simple and not at all incredible'. The grounds for this are said to be that
the wish to anoint the body serves to give some concrete motive to the journey
to the tomb, and the concern about the stone was only brought in 'to prepare
the miracle and heighten its effect', and the angel's action 'is confined within
narrow and modest bounds', *op. cit.*, p. 59.

of a body already buried, is itself improbable, and is dropped by Matthew and John. The crux of the story involves the legendary element of the angel.

In the second place, it is difficult to decide how far Mark's story may be ascribed to reliable tradition, or is the construction of the evangelist. The introduction of women rather than disciples as the first to receive any intimation of the resurrection comes as a surprise, and may point to old tradition, though the motive for their visit in a delayed embalming which accounts for their presence at all is dubious. The story begins from their reflection, which is absent from the other gospels, 'Who will roll away the stone for us from the door of the tomb? . . . for it was very large'. These words presuppose the previous account of the burial of Jesus, about which there had been no hint that it had been incomplete, and taken literally should have caused the women to stay at home, as they could not rely on assistance being available when they arrived. The words serve rather to set the scene, and to hint at the greatness of the miracle. The women enter the tomb (so in Mark only), and see a young man clad in a white robe sitting on the right side – 'sitting' may denote majesty and authority, and 'on the right side' the side of good fortune. In this verse (v. 5) 'apparently Mark is writing freely, for every word belongs to his vocabulary'.[72] The young man is presumably an angel. He is certainly written up as such by Matthew, while Luke has two men in flashing apparel, and sees in this 'a vision of angels' (Luke 24.4, 23), and so does John (20.12), though there they are seen only by Mary and not by the two disciples.

There are parallels to angels appearing as young men (νεανίσκοι) in Hellenistic Jewish literature (II Macc. 3.26; Jos. *Ant.* 5.277), though not in scripture, and the clothing is that conventional for heavenly beings. Nevertheless, this would be the only angel to appear in Mark, and his description by the diminutive νεανίσκος is curious, though it is hardly curious enough to provide the starting-point for A. M. Farrer's typological elaboration here, whereby this young man is connected with the young man (νεανίσκος) who fled at the arrest (Mark 14.51), leaving, like Joseph with Potiphar's wife, the 'linen cloth' (σινδόνα) as his only clothing in the hands of his pursuers;

---

[72] Vincent Taylor, *op. cit., ad loc.*

and whereby both are connected with Joseph of Arimathea, who, like the patriarch Joseph, performed, the pious rite of burial, here with a 'linen cloth' (σινδόνι, Mark 15.46), so that the young man at the tomb is to be seen as the heavenly representative of the new Joseph, Jesus, who is to reveal himself to his brethren, and who is met, as was the patriarch, with no response, 'for they were terrified' (Gen. 45.3).[73] The words of the young man have a kerygmatic sound: 'Jesus you seek, the Nazarene, the crucified one; he has been raised; he is not here; see the place where they placed him'. They constitute a divine announcement of the resurrection ('He has been raised', i.e. by God; 'he is not here', i.e. he has left the tomb – cf. Matt. 27.53 – and is in heaven?); and they assert both the overcoming of the cross by resurrection and the identity of the risen one with the human Jesus. There is no particular emphasis on the emptiness of the tomb. The empty tomb interprets the message of the resurrection, not *vice versa* – contrast the versions of Matthew, where it is the earthquake and the appearance of the angel which are decisive, of Luke, where the message about the empty tomb is regarded as idle chatter (Luke 24.3–11), and of John, where the empty tomb as such is the basis of belief (John 20.2–9). Thus in Mark, the visit to the tomb is the means by which the resurrection itself is declared, and not a prelude to, or presupposition of, appearances of the risen Lord to follow. It is only when in the other gospels it lies side by side with such appearances, with which awkward connections have then to be made, that it takes on the note of apologetic.

But having announced the resurrection, why does the young man not stop there? As it stands, the story, and with it the whole gospel, reaches its climax not with the resurrection and the women, but with the command to tell the disciples and Peter that, 'He goes before you into Galilee – there you will see him – as he said unto you'. This is without doubt a Markan construction to the extent that it presupposes in 'as he said unto you' a knowledge of the passage Mark 14.27–31, and in particular of 14.28, which in itself may be an isolated logion, since in the context it breaks the connection between 14.27 and 14.29, and is plainly a preparation for 16.7 – perhaps to the extent that the separate mention of Peter in 16.7 reflects the isolation of Peter

[73] *A Study in St Mark*, pp. 141, 174, 334.

amongst the 'all' who will be made to stumble in 14.27–29. A curious feature in 14.28, that the resurrection is referred to in a subordinate clause and is used as a time indication ('after I am raised up . . .'), recurs in the juxtaposition of 16.6 and 16.7, in that the fact of the resurrection, to which 'St Mark has given full expression',[74] is relegated to second place by the announcement of what is to follow as the climax. For this reason, and because v. 8 seems to preclude the all-important message being delivered, there has been much discussion of the status of v. 7 and v. 8.[75] There can be little doubt, however, that both come from Mark. 16.7 is prepared for by 14.28 (despite the absence of the latter in the Fâyum fragment). 16.8 is clearly Markan redactional language, is to be related to Mark's theology as a whole, and if so probably governs the whole story. The fear and silence are hardly to be explained as a depreciation of the women, or as something temporary to be later removed, or as an addition to sever any connection of the disciples with the empty tomb and to secure that their experience of the risen Lord was totally independent of it. For in Mark there are no appearances of the Lord to disciples to be safeguarded in this way. 16.8 rather emphasizes the event as divine through a reaction to it of human disobedience, and perhaps recalls Mark 10.32.

Thus Mark will nowhere have betrayed the standpoint from which he writes his gospel more than here, in this final instance of his two motifs of fear and silence. What, then, does the statement of the young man mean, 'He goes before you into Galilee; there you will see him (as he said unto you)'? It is a statement, since there is no express command to the disciples to go to Galilee. Why does Galilee reappear here in the gospel, if it is not to indicate simply a retrogression to something left behind? What is the meaning of 'go before'? And what is the meaning of the words 'there you shall see him', which are added by the young man to the original statement of Jesus (14.28) in explication of the 'going before'?

[74] R. H. Lightfoot, *The Gospel Message of St Mark* (1950), p. 93.
[75] See the discussion in W. Marxsen, *Der Evangelist Markus* (1956), pp. 47ff. The possibility that 16.7 (and 14.28) were later additions to Mark's text is raised by R. Bultmann, *The History of the Synoptic Tradition*, p. 267 n.1, and by others (A. Loisy, A. Meyer, J. M. Creed) before him. It is discussed by L. Schenke, *Auferstehungsverkündigung und leeres Grab* (1968). Against the removal of 16.7 see H. von Campenhausen, *op. cit.*, p. 71 n.129.

It was the strength of the thesis of E. Lohmeyer,[76] which was developed by R. H. Lightfoot[77] and by others, that the only 'event' to which the resurrection could be subordinate is the parousia. In that case, 'there you will see him' refers to the sight, not of the risen Lord in the sense of a resurrection appearance, but of the risen Lord in his parousia glory and activity as the Son of man (Mark 13.26; 14.62), and Galilee as the necessary location for this belongs with the emphasis in Mark's gospel on Galilee as the land of revelation. Mark would then be a witness to the expectation of the parousia as still vital, and as the only proper climax of a εὐαγγέλιον. The weakness of this thesis is that Mark should write in this way when he knew that the parousia had not taken place for Peter and his companions, and this difficulty can hardly be said to be removed by Lightfoot's observation that 'this was the form in which his (the reader's) conviction of the triumph and supremacy of his Master expressed itself'.[78] W. Marxsen gives the thesis some additional precision by his view of the gospel as written for a specific purpose at a particular time; the advance of the Romans on Jerusalem from AD 66 initiates the events of the end referred to in 13.14ff., and so presages an imminent parousia, and the Christians are to leave Jerusalem for Galilee, where the risen and exalted Lord, who is living a concealed existence, will manifest himself. In 16.7, this is made a divine command, and evokes terror at the proximity of the parousia. It would seem to be a consequence of this view that the Christian community addressed in Mark's Gospel must be a Palestinian community, for whom the attack on Jerusalem is a personal concern and the journey to Galilee feasible; the remainder of the Christians are presumably the elect who will be gathered from the four winds (13.27).[79] However, 16.7 is only very indirectly a command to go to Galilee, and 14.28, on which it is based, is hardly a command at all. It is primarily concerned, not with the disciples but with the Lord and his 'preceding', and this word 'precede' does not itself evoke the thought of the parousia. Lightfoot maintains that 14.28 must be interpreted in the light of 16.7 and not

76 E. Lohmeyer, *Galiläa und Jerusalem* (1936), passim; *Das Evangelium des Markus* (1937), pp. 355ff.
77 R. H. Lightfoot, *Locality and Doctrine in the Gospels, passim.*
78 R. H. Lightfoot, *op. cit.*, p. 44 n.2.
79 W. Marxsen, *Der Evangelist Markus*, pp. 73ff.

vice versa;[80] but is this necessarily so? The former, if it is firmly in the text, is the previous statement in the gospel, however much it may have been glossed in 16.7 by 'there you will see him', and the context of 14.28 is the apostasy of the twelve, Peter included (this is picked up in 'his disciples and Peter'), which is prophesied in terms of the scattering of a shepherd's flock. The reversal of this is more likely to be the re-assembly of the flock under the shepherd than a parousia manifestation to them in their scattered condition (that the disciples actually scattered to Galilee has no basis in the tradition except John 21.1ff. interpreted in the light of John 16.32).

I have therefore argued elsewhere[81] that προάγειν should here be given what is its most common meaning, 'to lead', which is the meaning in all the instances of προάγειν governing an object cited from the papyri by F. Preisigke, and which is the only possible meaning in 14.28 if the shepherd-sheep metaphor is being continued from 14.27. If this is the meaning of προάγειν, then Galilee in conjunction with it is likely to mean not the land of revelation and parousia, but the land of the Gentiles, which is symbolic of the world wide mission. In this mission, Jesus is known as the universal Lord. In that case, Mark 16.7 hardly implies two appearances, one to Peter and one to the disciples.[82] It may be noted that of the two references in Mark's gospel to the proclamation of the gospel subsequent to Jesus' death, one links it with his burial and tomb (14.8f.), and the other places it among the end-events which precede the parousia (13.10). In his own way, Matthew would seem to have read something like this out of Mark, and may have done so without a concluding sentence in Mark such as Farrer postulates. At this point of the universal mission, the gospel of Jesus Christ which Mark sets out to write catches up with his readers who are themselves part of it.

(b) Matthew

It is a surprising fact, to which perhaps insufficient attention has been given, that Matthew has so little to add to the framework

[80] R. H. Lightfoot, *op. cit.*, p. 52 n.2.
[81] C. F. Evans, 'I will go before you into Galilee', *JTS* NS v (1954), pp. 3–18.
[82] So R. Branton, 'The Resurrection in the Early Church', in: A. Wikgren (ed.), *Early Christian Origins* (1961), pp. 37f.

supplied to him by Mark when he comes to the passion and resurrection. As the synopsis shows, his passion narrative is a writing out of Mark's almost word for word, and his few additions are either legendary and apologetic, as in the suicide of Judas, the dream of Pilate's wife and Pilate's washing of his hands, and the setting of the guard at the tomb, or they interpret the events by a crudely literal version of the supernatural, as in the statement that at the moment of the death of Jesus there was an earthquake, tombs were opened, and many bodies of the saintly dead were raised so as to be able after his resurrection to visit Jerusalem as apparitions. Can it really be the case that the church at Antioch or Jerusalem, with which scholars have connected this gospel, did not possess a passion narrative of its own, nor traditions of greater worth than these?

The same characteristics are to be found in Matthew's resurrection chapter. He comes as near as he can to describing the indescribable, the divine act of resurrection itself, by use of the biblical device of an earthquake and a descent of the angel of the Lord to unseal the tomb; and the fear which in Mark is the result of the mysterious hinting words of the young man is now translated into terror at the aspect of the angel. The guards at the sealed tomb, who are found only in Matthew's version, together with the women, who because of the sealing of the tomb can now come only to visit it and not to anoint the body, become spectators of a divine miracle. The bribing of the guards to spread the report that the disciples had stolen the body is plainly apologetic, invented in the course of Jewish-Christian controversy which the evangelist testifies as continuing to the time of his writing (Matt. 28.15). Mark's abrupt ending had, as it were, laid a stymie for Matthew, for if the command of the young man is not obeyed and the message not delivered to the disciples, how shall the story proceed and the gospel of the resurrection become known?

To surmount this difficulty, and to forge a connection between the scene at the tomb and the one announcement of the gospel of the resurrection which he intends to give, Matthew edits. The words of the angel become more definite, 'Go quickly, and tell his disciples, He is risen from the dead', and the promise, 'He goes before you into Galilee; there you shall see him', is no longer qualified, as in Mark, by 'as he said unto you' – words which were ambiguous, in that they could be taken to mean that Jesus had said

this previously to the women and not to the disciples – but become
words spoken on the angel's own authority, 'Lo, I have told you'.
While the element of fear is retained from Mark, it is now combined
with joy as the women hasten to do what they are told. They are
met on the way by Jesus himself, who becomes the object of their
worship, and who reiterates in his own person the words of the
angel in such a way as to leave no doubt that 'he goes before you
into Galilee' means that the disciples are to rendezvous with the
Lord there. Matthew's is thus the only gospel with an appearance
to the group of women associated with the visit to the tomb, and it
is difficult to resist the view that this owes its origin to the necessity
of connecting the two traditions of the empty tomb and of the
appearances, and of overcoming the impasse presented by Mark's
story to one who is using Mark's gospel as closely as Matthew
does, but who wishes to go on to say more than Mark. It does
nothing to change the locale, and Matthew does not become a
witness to Jerusalem appearances.

The appearance in Galilee, with which Matthew's gospel closes,
is as impressive a passage as any in the New Testament. H. von
Campenhausen refers to it as 'this monumental closing scene' and
as 'the one ideal, concluding tableau'.[83] 'Resurrection appearance',
in the sense which is generally attached to that phrase in the light
of other stories, is a misnomer. It is an exaltation scene, and
becomes a resurrection appearance only by its present position
after the death and grave scenes. It is a christophany, and manifestation of Jesus as King-Messiah and universal ruler, who has been
given the uttermost parts of the earth for his possession. There is
nothing temporary about it, and an ascension to an exalted state
after it in the Lukan or even the Johannine sense, or any subsequent
movement from Galilee to Jerusalem, would be unthinkable.[84]
The scene is appointed by Jesus himself. It is 'the mountain', which
recalls in this gospel the 'exceeding high mountain' from which
Jesus had been shown in his temptations the kingdoms of the
world (Matt. 4.8), 'the mountain' from which the sermon had been
preached (Matt. 5.20ff.), to which Jesus had retired for prayer
(Matt. 14.23), where he had healed the sick (Matt. 15.29), and
where he had been transfigured (Matt. 17.1). It is the mountain of

[83] *Op. cit.,* p. 51.
[84] Contrary to C. F. D. Moule, 'The Ascension – Acts 1.9', *ExpT* lxviii
(1956/7), p. 207.

revelation, which is nowhere in particular, except that it must be in Galilee, the land of revelation and of the Gentiles (4.12ff.).

The element of resurrection is passed over briefly with the words, 'and seeing him they worshipped, but some doubted'. The words which Jesus speaks fall into the threefold pattern of the coronation ritual of the divine king which had belonged to oriental cult, and which has left its mark on the Old and New Testaments. First is the announcement (here by the king himself) that God has conferred on him total and universal rule ('all power has been given to me in heaven and on earth'); then the proclamation of his kingship (here to be carried out by the king's own messengers), which itself falls into three parts, the commands to make Christian disciples of the whole world, to baptize in God's threefold name, and to instruct it in the observance of Jesus' commandments; finally comes the assertion of his enthronement, here in the form of the promise of his divine assistance and protection until the consummation of the age. That this is a Matthaean construction is suggested by the high proportion of words in it which belong to Matthew's vocabulary, and by the concentration in a single sentence of precisely those aspects which make it a climax and conclusion of Matthew's particular presentation of the gospel material and of the figure of Christ, and which would make it as out of place at the end of any other gospel as it is completely in place here.

In Matthew's gospel alone it has been emphasized that during the days of his flesh, both Jesus and his disciples have been confined in their mission to Israel (Matt. 10.5f.; 15.24); so it is emphasized that through his exaltation his scope and theirs have become universal and stretch to the end of time. As in this gospel particularly the body of disciples begins to appear as a church under the discipline of the apostles, and the material is arranged for church use, so now the resurrection commission is in terms of church order – to make disciples, to baptize and to instruct. As this gospel is a gospel of the new divine law and its Christ the supreme teacher, so here the accent lies on the observance of the commandments of one who rules over the universe; and as it is peculiar to this gospel that even the earthly Jesus promises that where two or three are gathered together in his name he will be in their midst (Matt. 18.20), so he promises his perpetual presence with them.

Matthew's slavish dependence on Mark in the passion and resurrection narratives and his lack of any authentic tradition here is a puzzle. It certainly points against the common attribution of this gospel to Antioch, which would surely have had a passion narrative of its own, or against the common location of the resurrection traditions of I Cor. 15 at Antioch. It is plain that Matthew's final chapter furnishes neither reliable historical information nor early Christian tradition about the resurrection, but only an example of later christological belief as it had developed in one area of the church, and of the apologetic which had been conducted in that area in the face of Jewish attacks. The apologetic becomes patent in the statement that the Jewish story of the theft of the body of Jesus by the disciples was still current at the time of the evangelist's writing (28.15); but it extends back to 27.62, where Matthew begins to edit the Markan account, and it governs the whole presentation. The controversy reflected here between Christians and Jews has its starting-point in the Christian proclamation of the resurrection (27.64: 'lest they say to the people, He has been raised from the dead'), which undoes the action of Pilate and the Jewish authorities in the crucifixion; but it is not conducted over any claims to have seen the Lord which formed the original basis of the proclamation, but over the empty tomb, and thus over what can be presented as public fact. Matthew attaches special importance to the tomb for he surrounds it with a guard; his apologetic is about the tomb and the body, not about the resurrection.

Hence the story begins with the public officials concerned, the Jewish authorities and Pilate (the apocryphal tendency here was eventually to lead to the invention of the so-called Acts of Pilate), though their reference to Jesus having said 'After three days I shall rise' cannot be to any public statement of his, and reflects again the later Christian preaching of the resurrection. The tomb is now officially sealed by a Roman guard lent to the Jewish authorities by Pilate for a three-day period, and when some of them report back its unsealing by divine agency (not, as might be expected, to Pilate, but to the Jewish authorities, thus showing that this was a Christian-Jewish controversy), they have to be bribed to say that the disciples stole the body while they were asleep in duty (though how it was then to be known that it was the disciples who had done this is not allowed for in the story). The Jewish authorities undertake to make it good with Pilate if their negligence reaches his ears, as surely it must. How these machinations had become public property and had reached the ears of Christians does not appear, unless the evangelist intends to leave this possibility open by the statement that it was only 'some of the guard' who participated in them. This Matthaean apologetic is probably evidence that some Jewish opponents had taken the tradition of the empty tomb seriously, and had set out to combat it, but it is hardly possible to deduce from Matthew's account where the controversy had begun, and at what time, and whether by the time it began any possibility of investigation into facts and historical details had disappeared.[85] This Matthaean type apologetic is reproduced and further developed in the Gospel of Peter, where it moves even more into the centre of the picture, with the result that the testimony of faith in the resurrection is replaced by an attempt at direct proof.[86]

This tissue of improbabilities of Matthew's story[87] has left its stamp on his rewriting of the Markan original. Since the tomb is officially sealed and guarded, there is now no question of the two women (here Matthew depends on Mark 15.47 rather than Mark 16.1) coming for the purpose of embalming the body; they come for an unmotivated visit to the tomb. They do not, as in Mark, enter the tomb to see a young man in a white robe there. They see outside the official angel of God ($\mathring{\alpha}\gamma\gamma\epsilon\lambda\text{o}\varsigma\ \kappa\nu\rho\acute{\iota}o\nu$: LXX *passim*, cf. Matt. 1.20, 24; 2.13, 19), whose appearance and dress recall those of the angel in Dan. 10.6 and of God in Dan. 7.9 (Theodotion; cf. also I Enoch 71.1). He has descended from heaven to open the tomb – it is not clear whether this means that he effected the resurrection, or that he revealed that Jesus had risen from a sealed tomb. He causes an earthquake (a familiar, apocalyptic feature – cf. Mark 13.8; Rev. 8.5; Isa. 29.6, etc.) and sits enthroned on the stone. But the angel is seen not, as in

---

[85] See some wise remarks by R. R. Bater, 'Towards a More Biblical View of the Resurrection', *Interpretation*, January 1969, pp. 5off. on the dubiousness of the assumption that the career of Christ was from the first a conspicuous affair, or that, even if the disciples began to preach in Jerusalem as soon after the crucifixion as Acts says they did, anyone took much notice.

[86] See Chr. Maurer, 'The Gospel of Peter', in *New Testament Apocrypha* I (1963), p. 181.

[87] Cf. the remarks of H. von Campenhausen, *op. cit.*, p. 63.

the other gospels, by the women alone (or, in John, by the disciples), but also by the guard, who, as often in scenes of this kind, become as dead men. Thus the resurrection, or its immediate effects, are objectified, and become public facts observable to outsiders. The Markan motif of fear is taken up, but now becomes fear at the terrible aspect of the angel, and is shared by guards and women. The latter are told that they, in contrast to the guards, are not to fear, for the angel knows that they are seeking Jesus the crucified (Mark's 'the Nazarene' is omitted). They are invited to inspect the tomb (δεῦτε, ἴδετε), and are told that his resurrection is the reason for his not being there ('he is not here, for he has been raised'). The resurrection is referred back to Jesus' previous prophecy, but the message they are to deliver 'quickly' to the disciples (there is no special mention of Peter, as there is to be no special appearance to him), is not, as in Mark, referred back to previous words of Jesus, but is altered so as to be spoken by the angel on his own divine authority as angel of the Lord. This removes an ambiguity in Mark's 'as he said unto you', which could apply to 'he goes before you into Galilee,' or to 'there ye shall see him' (for which there had been no preparation in Mark), and leaves the way open for a subsequent elucidation of the angel's message by Jesus himself (v.10).

The purpose of the appearance of Jesus himself to the women, which now follows, is obscure. Perhaps it was to forge a connection between the tradition of the empty tomb and that of the resurrection appearances. Only a remnant of the 'fear' in the Markan original is retained, in that the women leave the tomb with fear and also great joy, and with the intention of delivering the message. They have no doubt who he is, and though taking hold of the feet (cf. John 20.17) of one who has a body, they worship him (as the exalted Lord? – vv. 9 and 17 are the only references to worship in the resurrection tradition); Jesus has no more to say than to repeat in his own person the message of the angel in such a way as to leave no doubt that the disciples, his brethren (cf. John 20.17, and the emphasis in Matthew on God as the Father of the disciples), are to go to Galilee, where they will see him. The appearance there to the eleven is also briefly told and is relatively colourless. In contrast to the splendour of the angel and the majestic words which follow, there is no epiphany of the Lord in glorious apparel, and no record of his disappearance or ascension, as there is no wonder on the part of the disciples, though there is worship. Jesus appears and is recognized, though some doubt. The narrative is really an introduction to the majestic words that follow.

Matthew 28.18–20 has been the subject of considerable discussion,[88] not only because of the remarkable content of the verses, but also because as a conclusion of the gospel of Matthew they come as something of a surprise, reversing at the last moment the severe limitation of the mission both of Jesus and of the disciples imposed in 15.24 and 10.5f. They are unlikely to have had any basis in Mark; the narrative introducing them is vague and not like Mark's, and, surprisingly in view of the place of Peter in Matthew's gospel, the detail of Mark's special mention of Peter in the angel's message is not taken up. It is doubtful whether the location of the appearance in Galilee was given Matthew by the tradition; he may simply have interpreted the message to mean a journey to Galilee and an appearance there, and may have supplied 'the mountain' as a suitable venue for revelation.

In themselves, vv. 18–20 are universalist (note the repeated emphasis on 'all'), and situationless. They divide into three statements (18b, 19–20a, 20b). Do these belong together as a single whole, reflecting some existing pattern of thought, or were they originally independent statements brought together by Matthew (so Michel), and if so, what governed the evangelist in combining them? The wording of v. 18b is thought by some to be based on Dan. 7.14, the granting of power, glory and a

---

[88] On Matt. 28.18–20, see esp. G. Barth, 'Matthew's Understanding of the Law' in G. Bornkamm, G. Barth and H. J. Held, *Tradition and Interpretation in Matthew* (1960), pp. 131ff. and the references there; G. Bornkamm, 'Der Auferstandene und der Irdische. Mt. 28.16–20', in *Zeit und Geschichte* (Bultmann Festschrift, 1964), pp. 171ff.; K. H. Rengstorf, 'A Formula of the Judaean Royal Ritual', *NovT* 5 (1961), pp. 283ff.; O. Michel, 'Der Abschluss des Mätthäusevangeliums; *EvTh* 10 (1950/51), pp. 16ff; E. Lohmeyer, *Das Evangelium des Matthäus* (1956), *ad loc.*, and 'Mir ist gegeben alle Gewalt', in *In Memoriam Ernst Lohmeyer* (1951), pp. 22ff.; A. Vögtle, 'Das christologische und ekklesiologische Anliegen von Mt. 28.18–20' in *Studia Evangelica*, Vol. II (1964), pp. 266ff., who stresses the relation with Dan. 7.13; H. W. Bartsch, *Das Auferstehungszeugnis* (1965), p. 12, who supposes from a comparison of the description of the angel in Matt. 28.2–4 with that of Christ in Rev. 1.13ff.; 8.5, that Matthew originally had a story of the appearance of the Lord as the Son of man, which has now been combined with the empty tomb story.

kingdom to the one like a son of man. What follows in Daniel – 'that all peoples, nations and languages should serve him: his dominion is an everlasting dominion, which shall not pass away, and his kingdom one that shall not be destroyed' – could stand behind 19–20a, though less clearly behind 20b. But the term Son of man is not introduced by Matthew here, and in his gospel, when it is not being used of the earthly Jesus, it is closely connected with the parousia and judgment (e.g. 24.27–44), which are precisely not in view in 28.18–20.

K. H. Rengstorf sees the background in Ps. 2, an Israelite version of the near-eastern enthronement ritual and adoption of the king as God's son, in which God invites the king with the words: 'Ask of me and I will give thee the nations for thine inheritance, and the uttermost parts of the earth for thy possession', and he points to other traces of the same conception of Jesus in the Gospel of Matthew, notably in the genealogy and in the temptation narrative, 4.8f. 'The final self-revelation of Jesus in the Gospel of Matthew stands exclusively under the sign of the revelation of his universal royal prerogative. Here Jesus is not the judge, but the anointed king of God, his everlasting Messiah, who is about to assume dominion over the world. God himself, fulfilling his promise, has given him this universal kingship. For this reason, the task of Jesus' apostles as his royal messengers is to work for the general acknowledgement of his universal royal right, and to gather all nations into his kindgom.' Again, however, the actual term Son of God is missing, and would have been more clearly indicated had the text run, 'All power has been given me by my Father . . .', as in 11.27. The title most clearly suggested by New Testament parallels would be 'Lord' (Kyrios), especially by Phil. 2.11, which speaks, as here, of a Lordship of Jesus over heaven and earth, whereas both Dan. 7 and Ps. 2 speak only of dominion over the earth. But, as G. Bornkamm observes,[89] lordship is not connected with the Gentile mission, and he points to another scheme, to be found in the epistles, of the μυστήριον or divine plan of salvation, which has been hidden but is now revealed through the divine messengers in the mission to the world. None of these patterns, however, provides an exact parallel to vv. 18–20, which may

---

[89] G. Bornkamm, 'Der Auferstandene und der Irdische', p. 77.

thus be a Christian creation (cf. Matt. 11.27f. for a somewhat similar triple sequence).

In 19–20a the vocabulary, when it is not unique, as in the clause about baptism, is so thoroughly Matthaean that the composition of these verses must be ascribed to the evangelist. Each of the three parts into which they fall is notable. Verse 19a is as explicit a statement of the universal mission of the church as anywhere in the New Testament, and, as already observed, this comes as a surprise in view of the severe restriction of the mission in 15.24 and 10.5f., and in view of the strongly Jewish tone of the gospel. On the other hand, there are other indications in the gospel of a universal scope (e.g. 13.38, 'the field is the world'; 12.18–21, 'on his name shall the Gentiles hope'; and 24.14 as a rephrasing of Mark 13.10), and recent studies of this gospel have drawn attention to these, and have suggested that the gospel should be located in Hellenistic rather than in Jewish Christianity.[90] The question then arises whether the evangelist wishes to portray a mission previously limited to the Jews as bursting its bounds through the death and resurrection of Jesus to become a mission to the Gentiles which now goes on side by side with the mission to the Jews; or whether he sees the mission to the Jews as already over in the earthly mission of Jesus and of the apostles during his lifetime, and as having resulted in its rejection by Israel and in Israel's rejection by God (cf. 8.11f.; 21.43).

The apostolic commission in Matthew also contains the only statement in the New Testament of baptism as an institution and command of Jesus himself (contrast Luke 24.46–49, where it is absent from the instructions, and Acts 2.38, where it is simply assumed). Baptism in the threefold name presumably reflects the developed practice of Matthew's church; its next mention is in the Didache (if that work is to be given an early date), which elsewhere shows the influence of Matthew's gospel or of its tradition. But the most distinctive feature of the commission is the command to 'make disciples' (μαθητεύσατε), and to teach them to observe everything which Jesus had commanded. This verb 'to make (be) a disciple' is found in

[90] See K. W. Clark, 'The Gentile Bias in Matthew', *JBL* lxvi (1947), pp. 165ff.; W. Trilling, *Das Wahre Israel* (1959); P. Nepper-Christensen, *Das Matthäusevangelium; ein judenchristliches Evangelium?*.

Matt. 13.52; 27.57 and elsewhere in the New Testament only in Acts 14.21 of making Christian converts; in Acts also from 6.1 onwards, 'the disciples' appears as a regular term for Christian believers. Its correlative is διδάσκαλος (teacher, cf. Matt. 10.24), which is found in conjunction with κύριος (master or lord) in John 13.13f. (cf. Matt. 7.21f., where the hailing of Jesus as 'Lord' is of no avail without the doing of the Father's will). Thus in Matthew, the enthroned Lord remains teacher and rabbi, and the gospel which is to be preached throughout the world (Matt. 24.14) is not, as in Luke, that of repentance unto remission of sins in virtue of the passion and resurrection of the Christ (Luke 24.46f.; Acts 2.38), nor, as in John, the forgiveness of sins and the interpretation of the truth of Christ through the Spirit (John 20.2f.), but instruction in the observance of the commandments which Jesus had given in the past, and of which Matthew's gospel is particularly the repository. Thus the bridge between the past and the present is made by the permanence of the words of Jesus, and there is no reference to any gift of the Spirit or any mighty works which the author of the longer ending of Mark called 'the accompanying signs'. Nevertheless, the commission, and the gospel itself, close with the most explicit statement in the New Testament of the permanent presence of the exalted Lord with his disciples until 'the consummation of the age' (a technical term found, apart from Heb. 9.26, only in Matthew in the New Testament). The manner of his presence is not specified, and the resurrection existence of Jesus is left a permanently open one. O. Michel observes that the presence is expressed in terms which denote divine succour, referring to such passages as Ex. 3.12; Josh. 1.5, 9, and that it has been prepared for earlier in this gospel, not only by the saying peculiar to Matthew, 'Where two or three are gathered together in my name, there am I in the midst' (18.20), but by the prophecy of the angel that Jesus will be called Emmanuel, which means 'God with us' (1.23). Thus the concluding verses of this gospel provide a confessional statement for the reader of what it means to become a Christian and to be a Christian in the present, and of the apostolic commission which lies at the basis of present Christian faith and existence.[91]

[91] Cf. W. Marxsen, *Die Auferstehung Jesu von Nazareth*, p. 51.

(c) Luke

On turning to Luke, we find a picture which is almost as different as it could be. Luke also uses Mark, and has to overcome the impasse presented by Mark's ending, especially as he either knows of no Galilean appearances, or chooses to disregard them. This he does by having instead of a young man who says 'he goes before you into Galilee', two angels who say in kerygmatic fashion, 'Remember how he spake unto you when he was yet in Galilee, saying that the Son of man must be delivered up into the hands of sinful men and be crucified, and the third day rise again.' The women so addressed are, as in Mark, from among those who had followed Jesus from Galilee to Jerusalem (Luke 23.49; 24.10 = Mark 15.40f., 47; 16.1ff.), but only in Luke's gospel does it appear natural for them to be reminded of what had been said to disciples previously in Galilee, since he alone refers to them, and particularly to two here mentioned, Mary Magdalene and Joanna, as the constant companions of Jesus and the twelve on their preaching missions (Luke 8.1–3). The women recall the words and report to the apostles, to whom this seems as idle talk. Thus Luke turns the awkward corner. Galilee is a thing of the past to be remembered; Jerusalem is the centre from which the gospel is in Acts to go to the whole world, and Jerusalem in Luke's gospel and in Acts is the scene of the Lord's appearances.

The story which follows of the walk to Emmaus is also one of the most remarkable in the New Testament, but for different reasons. In two respects it is similar to Matthew's story. It also is concerned with the church; not, however, as in Matthew, with its mission, baptism and apostolic instruction, but with its doctrine of the crucified and glorified Messiah and the scriptural basis for this, and with the knowledge of this Christ in the sacrament of the eucharist. Like Matthew's, it is also a story which could be said 'to have almost everything'. In other respects the two could hardly be more different. The Matthaean story is formal, impersonal, hieratic, with the rounded shape of a doctrinal statement; the Lukan is informal, personal, human, with the marks of an artistic literary creation. Whereas the Matthaean says what has to be said by means of a single, compact and highly concentrated sentence, the Lukan does this in leisurely fashion and by means of the technique of the 'flash-back'. Two of them (in the context in which

Luke has placed the story, 'them' refers to the eleven and 'all the rest': Luke 24.9f.), one named Cleopas and the other unnamed, are on the road to Emmaus engaged in earnest discussion. What is being discussed is the events of the passion and the empty tomb; in this way the story is tied back to what has gone before. They are joined by a travelling companion to whom, on his enquiry, they communicate the subjects of their conversation and their bewilderment about them. He rebukes their unbelief, declares the meaning of the events and interprets them from scripture. When on arrival at their destination he makes to go on further, they prevail on him to stay, and when in the course of a meal he breaks bread, they recognize him as Jesus, and he thereupon becomes invisible. They recall the warming of their hearts at his previous scriptural exposition, and they return to Jerusalem to recount to the eleven what had happened on the journey and their recognition of him in the breaking of the bread. Here the link is with what is to follow.

These are the bare outlines of the story. Its language has been described as a 'treasury of Luke's Septuagintal style and vocabulary', and the exquisite story telling and the vivid human touches are what the reader has come to expect from Luke's gospel in particular, as he will also find them in its continuation in Acts. So also is the extreme objectification of the supernatural provided in the picture of a risen one who spends several hours in the company of others, engaged in entirely human occupations, and who then becomes invisible. But the force of the story lies in the conversation. In reply to the stranger's enquiry, Cleopas is made to rehearse the subject of their conversation in terms which might have been taken from one of the apostolic sermons in Acts. It had been about, 'the things concerning Jesus of Nazareth, who was a prophet mighty in deed and word before God and all people and how the chief priests and our rulers handed him over to the judgment of death, and crucified him'. Cleopas cannot go on, as the apostolic sermon was later to go on, with the proclamation of the resurrection, since it is not yet known to the apostles, but he is made to come as near to it as he can in the circumstances when he proceeds with 'and we hoped that it was he who was to redeem Israel; what is more, this is the third day since these things happened; moreover some women of our company have astounded us; going early to the tomb, and failing to find his body they came saying they had seen a vision of angels, who said he was alive; and some of our people went to the tomb, and found things as the women had said, but him they saw not.' There is here no hint of the women's witness not being accepted. Cleopas is made in the circumstances to supply in advance all the ingredients of the resurrection faith except the resurrection itself. This Jesus himself, in face of their faithless failure to draw the right conclusions, now provides, and in credal form. 'Was it not divinely ordained that the Messiah should through suffering thus enter into his glory?' From the whole of scripture he shows this to be so. By the time the story has reached this point, it has succeeded in doing what no other resurrection story was able to do; it has presented in the form of a narrative the whole later credal formula 'died for our sins according to the scriptures, and was buried, and was raised the third day according to the scriptures and appeared'; and it has traced back to Jesus himself, as something normal and to be expected, both the Christian doctrine of a suffering and exalted Messiah at which the church eventually arrived, and also the scriptural research which, on the evidence of the New Testament as a whole and of the speeches in Acts in particular, was to lie behind the church's interpretation of its gospel. There is here no Markan awe and terror in the presence of the mystery, and no Pauline stumbling-block of the cross, for all is now presented as natural, to be comprehended as the divine will.

Complete as it is, however, the Emmaus story lacks one vital element, the command and commission to the apostles, and this Luke supplies in his second story. In its first part it contains the most literal identification of the risen form of the Lord with a human body; he is no ghost, but has flesh and bones, and eats to show his humanity. This may be intended to contradict docetism, and if so, presumably belongs not to the time of Jesus but to that stage in the development of the tradition when the church had to grapple with that problem as it arose in a Hellenistic milieu. But it may be due to Luke's tendency towards a realistic description of the supernatural. The main argument, however, lies in the second part of the story. The Lord imparts to the whole apostolic body and others what he had previously conveyed to the two on the road, and now declares it as a reiteration of what he had said to them during the period of the earthy ministry, and of what the angels had reminded the women that he had said (Luke 24.6f.), viz. that the whole Old Testament, properly understood, speaks of him, and in particular speaks of the gospel of the suffering Christ who rises on the third day, of the proclamation to the whole world, beginning at Jerusalem, and of repentance and remission of sins in his name. They are to bear witness of this, and to enable them to do so they are to wait in the city for the Father's promise, the power from on high, the Spirit which Jesus will send to them. All this is spoken, not as in Matthew from beyond exaltation by a Lord already exalted, but with exaltation still in prospect. Hence in Luke the period of resurrection appearances is temporary, being brought to an end by a separate act of ascension, which is itself the prelude to the era of the Spirit. It is, once more, impossible that all this should stand anywhere else than at the end of Luke's gospel, for it contains in advance and in a nutshell, and from the Lord's own mouth, that particular account of Christian origins which Luke is to give in his second volume.[92]

As the most coherent account, written like much else in this gospel in an orderly fashion or in sequence (καθεξῆς Luke 1.3), the Lukan resurrection narrative has exercised the greater influence on the Christian mind. Significantly D. P. Fuller, in seeking a New Testament counterpart to the modern approach to the relation of Easter faith and history, concentrates entirely on the presentation to be found in Luke–Acts.

Luke's account in ch. 24 is a carefully constructed unity, even though the traditions which compose it are not completely harmonized. There is first a unity of place. There is no reference to the flight of the disciples, and all happens in and around Jerusalem (though Emmaus defies exact identification), whither the gospel narrative has been directed from 9.51 onwards (cf. 13.22, 33; 17.11; 18.31; 19.11, 28), and which is the base from which the Christian message with its heritage from Judaism is to proceed to the world (24.47; Acts. 1.4ff., etc.). There is a unity of time, as the journey to Emmaus is said to take place on the same day, the first day of the week, as the visit to the tomb (24.1,13), and the

---

[92] On the Lukan account see esp.: P. Schubert, 'The Structure and Significance of Luke 24', in W. Eltester (ed.), *Neutestamentliche Studien für R. Bultmann* (1954), pp. 165ff.; P. Menoud, 'Remarques sur les textes de l'ascension dans Luc-Actes', *ibid.*, pp. 158ff.; E. Lohse, *Die Auferstehung Jesu Christ im Zeugnis des Lukasevangeliums* (1961); A. N. Wilder, 'Variant Traditions of the Resurrection in Acts', *JBL* 62 (1943), pp. 347ff.; A. R. C. Leaney, 'The Resurrection Narratives in Luke xxiv. 12–53', *NTS* 2 (1955–56), pp. 110ff.; D. P. Fuller, *Easter Faith and History* (1965), chs. vii–viii.

return from Emmaus is 'at the same hour' (24.33), the reference to the appearance to Peter being tucked into the story at this point (v. 34); and on the most natural reading of the text the journey to Bethany follows immediately, though this would seem to involve an appearance and journey at night, since the meal at Emmaus had been in the evening. There is a unity of material, since 24.22f. is the only place where the visit to the tomb is referred to in a story of a resurrection appearance. There is also a unity of theme, as the interpretative kernel of the three very different component units is the same, viz., the necessity of the death and resurrection ('must', v. 7; 'necessary', v. 26; 'must', v. 44). In the two latter this necessity is said to lie in the Old Testament scriptures (vv. 25–27, 32, 44–47), while in the first it lies in previous prophecies by Jesus himself in Galilee, to the last of which (18.31), though it was not made in Galilee, Luke had himself added the fulfilment of Old Testament prophecy to his Markan original.

What most distinguishes Luke's account from those of the other gospels is that the resurrection is not an end in itself or a symbol of exaltation or parousia, but a point of transition. It both looks forward to what is to follow from it, the gift of the Spirit and the mission of the church, which are to be the subject of historical description, and is also looked back upon as the firm historical base for what is to follow. This is the result of Luke's purpose of writing two volumes, or a single volume in two parts, and of the differences of perspective which this involved.

This purpose, and what eventually happened to these two volumes when they were separated in the arrangement of the canon, may also have been responsible in the long run for the unusually large number of textual variants which complicate any analysis of ch.24 as a whole and any judgment on particular facets of it. Thus in most modern editions the following are either omitted from the text or bracketed as very doubtful: 'of the Lord Jesus' (v. 3); 'He is not here but has risen' (v. 6); the whole of v. 12; 'And he says to them, "Peace be to you"' (v. 36); the whole of v. 40; 'and he was carried up into heaven' and 'worshipped him and' (vv. 51f.). These are all omitted by the Western text, and are thus part of the wider problem of the variations in the text of Luke–Acts which Dibelius wished to

account for by the original destination of the work for, and its
currency in, the secular world rather than in the Church.[93] But
they are not suspect on this ground alone (the Western text has
readings in this chapter which are not acceptable, and P[75] has
all these disputed readings), but also on the ground that most of
them have the appearance of assimilations to the text of other
gospels (in v. 5, cf. Matt. 28.6; for v. 12 cf. John 20.3–10; in
v. 36 cf. John 20.19). A. R. C. Leaney argues for the retention of
the last three of these variants, and sees them as evidence for
the use of a common source by Luke and John, which each
evangelist has developed in his own way.[94] Judgment on v. 12
is difficult. On neither supposition, that it is a later insertion, or
that it is from Luke's use of a common source with John, does a
visit by Peter alone to the tomb supply an adequate basis for the
words 'certain of our company went to the tomb' in v. 24,
whereas there is undoubtedly some connection between v. 12
and John 20.3–10. The word for 'stooping down' ($\pi\alpha\rho\alpha\kappa\acute{\upsilon}\psi\alpha\varsigma$)
is repeated in John 20.5, 11, and may be John's word rather
than that of a source, and the same may apply to the word for
'graveclothes' ($\mathring{o}\theta\acute{o}\nu\iota\alpha$) which apart from here is found only in
John's account of the empty tomb in the New Testament, and
which John has in his story of the burial (19.40), the repetition
of the word in John 20.5–7 emphasizing that the body had not
been snatched. 'The graveclothes alone' (or, 'by themselves',
$\mu\acute{o}\nu\alpha$) reads like a summary of John 20.7, especially as there has
been no reference to them when the women enter the tomb
(Luke 24.3). Luke would probably have used the verb 'to
wonder' ($\theta\alpha\upsilon\mu\acute{a}\zeta\epsilon\iota\nu$) with a preposition rather than with a direct
object to follow (as in 2.33; 4.22; 9.43; 20.26; but cf. 7.9; Acts
7.31). The participial 'what had happened' ($\tau\grave{o}\ \gamma\epsilon\gamma\upsilon\upsilon\acute{o}\varsigma$) is
thoroughly Lukan. If v. 12 is an interpolation, it reflects the
tendency to bring apostles into relation with the empty tomb,
which is found in John 20, and in a more general sense in Luke
24.24, but is here confined to Peter, perhaps with reference to
Luke 24.34. The variants in vv. 36–40 are more clearly inter-

[93] M. Dibelius, 'The Text of Acts', *Studies in the Acts of the Apostles* (1956),
pp. 89f. On the textual problem of 24.51 see B. M. Metzger, *Historical and
Literary Studies* (1968), pp. 77f; C. F. D. Moule, 'The Ascension-Acts 1.9',
ExpT lxviii (1956–57), p. 16 n.1.
[94] A. R. C. Leaney, 'The Resurrection Narratives in Luke xxiv. 12–53',
NTS 2 (1955–56), pp. 110ff.

polations, since they disturb the story. 'He says to them, "Peace be to you" ' includes a verb in the historic present, which is very rare in Luke, while the salutation 'Peace' has particular force in John 20.19, 26, where it picks up the promise of peace to the disciples in John 16.33. Moreover, the terror of the disciples at seeing a ghost is more plausible if the text had simply 'he stood in the midst of them', and Jesus had not already reassured them with the words, 'It is I: be not afraid'. Verse 40, 'having said this he showed them his hands and his feet' (so some MSS) comes as an awkward repetition after 'behold my hands and feet' in v. 39, whereas the similar words in John 20.20 have real force, and are taken up in John 20.27.

The last case, 'and was carried up into heaven', raises a larger issue, for the mention of an ascension here introduces a very abbreviated and formal duplicate of Acts 1.9–11, which is then in Acts 1.2 referred to as already in the past, and also introduces a contradiction with Acts 1.3–11, where ascension takes place after a forty-day period of resurrection appearance. A possible explanation might be that Luke was somehow responsible for the contradiction, and that it was subsequently removed by excision, leaving the gospel to end with a (temporary?) withdrawal of Jesus ('he parted from them'). On the other hand, Acts 1.1–5 is an extraordinary sentence, of which it is impossible to establish either the syntax or the translation of the text as usually printed.[95] It opens with a μέν clause ('on the one hand') which has no corresponding δέ clause ('on the other hand'), and while this has parallels elsewhere, it is hardly what was to be expected in the correct Greek of which prefaces where composed. It is overloaded with participles, some of which are awkwardly connected with the verbs (e.g. in vv. 2 and 4), and at v. 5 it changes abruptly from indirect to direct speech. P. Menoud[96] sees certain words and phrases as indications of a later hand ('to do and to teach' as a description of Jesus' mission, the four hapax legomena in 'proofs', 'appearing', 'staying with' and 'wait', and the clumsy Greek of 'not after these many days'), which he also finds in Luke 24.50–53 in 'raising his hands he

[95] See F. J. Foakes-Jackson and Kirsopp Lake, etc., *The Beginnings of Christianity* Vol. V (1933), pp. 1ff.; Vol. III (1926), pp. 256ff.; and the punctuation of RV and the breaking up of the sentence in RSV and NEB.

[96] P. Menoud, 'Remarques sur les textes de l'ascension dans Luc-Actes', pp. 152ff.

blessed them'.[97] To these may perhaps be added 'he led them out', the Greek word used generally meaning in Luke–Acts 'to deliver (from prison)'. Menoud would thus see these two passages as later insertions into a text in which originally Acts 1.6 followed directly after Luke 24.49.[98] In that case, while Luke will have believed in an extended period of resurrection appearances, or in an extended period during which the risen Lord companied continuously in human form with disciples (if Acts 13.31 means this), the specification of this period as a 'biblical' period of forty days, which is not mentioned in the speeches in Acts,[99] will have been the work of a redactor who provided a secondary preface to summarize the contents of the gospel as a separate book now ending with an ascension, to elaborate the post-resurrection period as being occupied with 'the things concerning the kingdom of God' (another expression without parallel in the New Testament), to repeat the command of Luke 24.49, and to introduce in direct speech what in Acts 11.16 appears as a saying of the Lord. The occasion for such a massive reconstruction of the text could have been when Luke's volume was divided into two to conform to the requirements of the canon. The first volume, being now a work on its own included among the books called gospels, needed to be retouched to give it an ending which would make it complete in itself, and the second volume, also now on its own, needed an introduction.

Hugh Anderson, in his study of the Easter witness of the evangelists, seeks a solution along different lines:[100] 'So long as Luke was regarded as an accurate historian or chronicler in the unqualified sense of the Harnack era, the incongruity of his two accounts of the Ascension constituted a grave offence to the critics, who frequently succumbed to the harmonizing tendency

[97] This is denied by P. Schubert, 'The Structure and Significance of Luke 24', pp. 168f.
[98] For similar, though not identical suggestions, see P. Menoud, *op. cit.,* p. 151, n.13; H. Sählin, *Der Messias und das Gottesvolk* (1945), pp. 11ff.
[99] On this phrase see H. Sählin, *op. cit.,* pp. 343ff; V. Larrãnaga, *L'Ascension de Notre-Seigneur dans le Nouveau Testament* (1938), pp. 603ff.; and on the lack of reference to it before Tertullian, M. S. Enslin, 'The Ascension Story', *JBL* 47 (1928), pp. 66ff.; P. H. Menoud, 'Pendant quarante jours, Actes 1.3', in *Neotestamentica et Patristica* (1962), pp. 148ff.
[100] See H. Anderson, 'The Easter Witness of the Evangelists', in H. Anderson and W. Barclay (eds.), *The New Testament in Historical and Contemporary Perspective; Essays in Memory of G. H. C. Macgregor* (1965), pp. 49ff.

of numerous ancient manuscripts by choosing to reject either Luke 24.50–53 in whole or in part, or Acts 1.1–11 in whole or in such parts as v. 3 and vv. 9–11. However, with the dramatic shift that has taken place of late in Lukan studies, whereby Luke "the historian" has had to yield to Luke "the theologian of sacred history", there has been an increasing readiness in some quarters to accept the integrity both of the longer text of Luke 24.50–53 and of Acts 1.1–11, and to seek a "theological" explanation for the apparent discrepancy in Luke's two reports of the Ascension.' This 'theological' explanation is that in Luke 24.50–53 Luke has reproduced the earlier tradition that the resurrection and the ascension coincided (and the argument of Acts 2.32f. is compared), whereas in Acts 1.9–11 he interprets the resurrection 'realistically' and historically as marking the transition from the time of Jesus, which reaches its climax in the resurrection, and the time of the Spirit and the church, or, alternatively, as itself marking 'the close of the history of Jesus and the inauguration of the new era of the Church and the Spirit'. Luke would thus not have felt any contradiction in a forty days interval period in which the apostles were prepared for their task of witness.

But apart from the general questions whether the shift in Lukan studies is justified, and whether the historian is released from any feeling of contradiction once he turns theologian and his history is sacred, 24.50–53 can hardly be said to reproduce the older tradition. This would not seem to have been that the resurrection and the ascension 'coincided' by being 'closely combined', but that the resurrection was itself the ascension, whereas here, however closely adjacent, they are distinguished, and in Acts 2.24–33 they are separately argued for. If by Luke's realism is meant that in Acts 1.9–11 material expression is given to the truth of Christ's lordship by a physical act of ascent after instructing his disciples in the necessary truth and bidding them to wait for the Spirit who will empower them to be his witnesses to the end of the earth, is the Acts account more realistic than Luke 24.36–53?

D. P. Fuller has a somewhat different explanation.[101] The account of the ascension is reiterated because the two accounts perform different functions: that in Luke 24 represents the

101 D. P. Fuller, *Easter Faith and History*, pp. 196ff.

ascension as the great climax to the resurrection, while that in Acts functions as a basis for the subsequent narrative in Acts, and appearances over forty days accompanied by instruction stress the foundational function of the resurrection for what is to follow. 'Thus the three accounts of the ascension in Luke 24.50–Acts 1.9 are not the result of clumsy editing, for each has its distinctive function. Luke 24.51 provides the climax to the Gospel of Luke. Acts 1.2 reiterates this climax so that the reader will not forget the point of the Gospel while proceeding with Acts. Acts 1.9–11 sets forth the ascension as terminating the resurrection appearances so they can function as the basis of what follows.'[102] But this interpretation is linked with Fuller's understanding of Luke–Acts as a whole, whereby the words in Luke's prologue to the gospel 'the things which have been fulfilled amongst us' (Luke 1.1) are taken to mean the events of Acts occurring in fulfilment of the Christ event recorded in the gospel. But this expression may be no more than a solemn way of saying 'the things which happened amongst us', and even if 'fulfilled' is to be stressed, it surely in a prologue refers to the events of both the gospel and Acts. Further, the last words of Luke 24.51, 'and he was carried up into heaven', are as jejune a description as possible of the ascension, and hardly form a climax to a process which Luke had already described in 9.51 as an ἀνάλημψις or assumption. Both by its wording and content the account of the ascension in Acts 1.9–11 serves better as a climax.[103]

Luke's version of the women's visit to the tomb gives the impression of having been written from an established belief in the empty tomb, and its factual basis for faith in the resurrection, and is an illustration of how this story was developed to

[102] D. P. Fuller, *op. cit.*, p. 198.
[103] P. A. van Stempvoort, 'The Interpretation of the Ascension in Luke and Acts', *NTS* 5 (1958), pp. 30ff., argues for the retention of the longer readings, and accounts for the divergencies on the supposition that Luke himself had two views of the Ascension. The first, represented in the longer text of the gospel, was doxological; it depicts Christ as departing from the disciples with the priestly act of blessing, and their worship. The second, in Acts, is ecclesiastical and historical, and leads into the future and the growth of the church. It is doubtful, however, whether such a procedure is plausible, or that the two interpretations can be held to be complementary. At the least, if they exist, they must imply a very considerable disjunction in Luke's mind between his first and second volumes.

serve different purposes. The women still come with spices (as in Mark), but there is no questioning about how they will roll away the stone. It is simply said without comment that they found the stone (which has not been mentioned previously by Luke) rolled away, and then explicitly, in contrast to Mark and Matthew, that on entering the tomb themselves they failed to find the body ('of the Lord Jesus' is almost certainly a later addition; this later christological expression is never found in the gospels, except, perhaps, in the spurious ending to Mark, 16.19). It is only after this discovery by the women that in Luke there is an angelic appearance; in Mark the invitation to the tomb follows the proclamation of the resurrection. The duplication of Mark's one 'young man in a white robe' to two men in shining apparel (they reappear in Acts 1.10 as two men in white apparel), who nevertheless speak as one, is probably to be explained as a trait of popular writing (cf. Acts 9.38). The view that this is a further instance of Luke's concern with the Jewish requisite of a twofold or threefold witness to an event is hardly necessary here,[104] since it is the women or the disciples who are witnesses to the resurrection; while the identification of the two with Moses and Elijah, on the ground that in Luke's version of the Transfiguration story these are described as 'two men' who appear in glory,[105] is surely implausible. As Acts 10.31 shows, this is a normal way for the evangelist to describe an angel, and Luke 24.23 indicates what he meant by them ('a vision of angels'). Mark's motif of fear is retained (the word used by Luke, ἔμφοβος, occurs, apart from Rev. 11.13, only in Luke–Acts in the New Testament; cf. Acts 10.4), but becomes reverence for the angels (cf. Luke 1.12f., 30; 2.9f. – for 'bowing to the ground' cf. Gen. 18.2; Josh. 5.14, etc.; but Luke's expression is distinctive). The Markan 'You seek Jesus the Nazarene, the crucified one; he has been raised, he is not here', is replaced by the effective question, 'Why do you seek the living one among the dead?' (cf. the not dissimilar question in the face of misunderstanding in Acts 1.11). 'The living one' is almost a title here (cf. Rev. 1.18), and may be compared with Luke's emphatic use of the verb 'to live' (ζῆν) in 10.28; 15.32, the addition to Mark's story in 20.38; 24.23;

104 L. Morgenthaler, *Die lukanische Geschichtsschreibung als Zeugnis* ii (1949), p. 9.
105 So A. R. C. Leaney, *The Gospel according to St Luke* (1958), p. 71.

Acts 1.3; 25.19, and the description of Jesus in Acts as 'the pioneer of life' (Acts 3.15). The reason for this alteration is that what they are to be given is not a message for the disciples with reference to a previous promise of Jesus to go before them into Galilee after the resurrection, but a reminder of a previous prophecy by Jesus of his necessary resurrection as the Son of man after delivery into the hands of sinful men and crucifixion. This appears to be a loose combination of the three previous prophecies – 'must' coming from that in 9.22 ,'into the hands of men' from that in 9.44, and ἀναστῆναι from that in 18.33. 'Sinful' appears only here, but it is a favourite word with Luke, and prepares for the appeal in the speeches in Acts for repentance from Israel on the basis of the resurrection. Since this prophecy is said to have been spoken to them, it has to be supposed that the women were among 'the disciples' to whom the prophecies had been spoken (9.18, 43; cf. 23.55, where they are expressly said to have followed with the disciples from Galilee), but that like them had not believed, as is shown by their coming to the tomb; hence the angelic rebuke. Luke is here almost certainly operating solely on the basis of the Markan text with its mention of Galilee, and he here gives some indication of the extent to which he was prepared to rewrite his Markan original if this was required. In this case he begins to rewrite from the beginning of the pericope, and upon the authority of angelic beings swings the location of the resurrection appearances from Galilee to Jerusalem. For Luke Galilee is now in the past and something to be remembered. He has brought the tomb, the women and the message into immediate touch with the disciples, whereas in Mark and Matthew there is a hiatus between them. Into the story of the empty tomb the kerygma of the cross and resurrection on the third day is introduced, and is to be taken up in the appearances and in the speeches in Acts, in the form that the resurrection is not so much the reversal of the cross as its natural, because foreordained, consequence (for the 'must' of 24.7, cf. Luke 9.22; 13.33; 17.25; 22.37; 24.26, 44; and the frequent references to the divine preordination in Acts).

The ending of the story is somewhat confused; both text and punctuation are obscure. The women have been hitherto unspecified except that they have followed from Galilee and had seen the tomb beforehand, and were therefore in a position to know where it was and to recall a previous prophecy in Galilee. They do remember, and presumably believe, and they go and recount their experiences to the 'eleven and all the rest' (24.8f.). Three women are then named as, along with 'the rest' of the women (cf. Luke 8.3), telling these things to the apostles (24.10). Of these three, two are identical with those named by Mark, while the other, Joanna, replacing Mark's Salome, is one of those previously named in Luke 8.3 as travelling with and ministering to Jesus in Galilee. 'The eleven and all the rest' appear again in 24.33 as 'the eleven and those with them', and are named in Acts 1.13f. as companying with others (cf. Acts 1.15, 21). On the other hand, 'the apostles' means for Luke the twelve (here the eleven), who are in Acts the principal witnesses of the resurrection. Luke thus not only links the resurrection backwards to the previous earthly ministry in Galilee, with which it is in continuity, and forwards to the preaching of the resurrection in Jerusalem, but also prepares for the picture of a wider and a narrower circle which he gives in Acts. The women's message is met with incredulity, and dismissed as nonsense. This should probably not be taken to indicate that Luke attached little importance to the empty tomb.[106] On the contrary, he lays greater stress on the emptiness of the tomb and the absence of the body as being discovered by the women themselves, and this is the presupposition for the statement of the angels that Jesus as the living one is not to be sought among the dead, and hence of the reiteration to the women and by the women to the disciples of Jesus' own prophecy of his resurrection. The same point is rehearsed in 24.23, 'and not finding his body they came saying that they had seen a vision of angels who said he was alive'. The physical fact of the empty tomb is a basis of Luke's thoroughly physical presentation of the appearances of the risen Lord. Its dismissal as nonsense through incredulity performs the same function as the references to doubt in other accounts, or as such a statement as 'their eyes were holden not to recognize him' (24.16). It underlines the greatness and marvel of what human beings fail to grasp until it is revealed.

The Emmaus story (24.13ff.) is linked with what precedes,

---

[106] As by P. Schubert, *op. cit.*, pp. 167f.; H. Anderson, *Jesus and Christian Origins* (1964), p. 227. Luke expressly contradicts Matthew and John in denying that any women had seen Jesus at the tomb (Luke 24.24).

not only because it is two 'of them', sc. of the eleven and those
with them, who make the journey on the same day as the visit
to the tomb, but also because the subject of their conversation
is the events so far related by Luke, and the queries to which
they have given rise (vv. 14f.). The story is unique in two respects, which may be connected. In the first place, it is the only
account of a resurrection appearance which may be called a
'legend' in the technical sense of a story of a supernatural being
who companies naturally as a man with mortals and converses
for a considerable time with men who entertain him unawares.[107]
This accords with the Lukan emphasis in Acts on Jesus as a
man even in resurrection (e.g. Acts 2.22ff., 'Jesus of Nazareth, a
man approved by God . . .' whose flesh did not see corruption
and was raised by God; 3.14, 'you asked for a murderous man
to be given you and killed the prince of life, whom God raised';
17.31, 'God has set a day in which he will judge the world by
a man whom he has determined . . . raising him from the dead').
As a result, the story is the furthest possible remove from the
category of heavenly vision of the Lord in glory. In the second
place, only here is the mode of the risen Jesus' departure from
his disciples before the ascension described at all in the form of
'vanishing from sight' or becoming invisible. Schubert thinks
that there may have been a shorter version of the story. In its
present form the legend has become a highly artificial vehicle
for a statement of the apostolic preaching as it is found later in
Acts, which is here according to the requirements of narrative
distributed between the participants. In reply to an enquiry
as to the subject of their conversation they state 'the things
concerning Jesus of Nazareth, who was a prophetic man,
mighty in deed and word before God and all the people'
(cf. Acts 2.22; 3.22f.; 10.38f.), and whom they had hoped
would be the redeemer of Israel (cf. Acts 5.31; 13.23; Luke
1.68; Acts 1.6). The recital includes, somewhat awkwardly
(21b, ἀλλά γε καί followed in 22 by ἀλλά καί, 'moreover'),
the most recent events, so that the story of the empty tomb
is tied into the kerygma; 'him they did not see' (24b) presupposes a knowledge that an empty tomb means resurrection and is expected to be followed by appearances of the risen

---

[107] Cf. Gen. 18.1ff. E. Lohse, *op. cit.*, compares the legend of Philemon and
Baucis, who entertained Juppiter and Minerva.

Lord. The unknown stranger then provides proof from the whole scope of the Old Testament scriptures of the necessity of the Messiah's suffering and his entrance by this route into his glory (cf. Acts 3.13 for glory, and *passim* in the Acts speeches for the use of the Old Testament to expound the resurrection, esp. 2.25ff.), and it is this scriptural interpretation that they subsequently dwell upon (v. 32; in v. 27, with 'the things concerning himself', the narrative temporarily breaks down, as though the two already knew that the one talking to them was Jesus the Messiah). But another powerful theme is combined with that of the fulfilment of scripture. In language recalling both the Feeding of the Five Thousand and the action of the Last Supper, the stranger takes, blesses, breaks and distributes bread, and this is the moment both of their recognition and of his vanishing. Naturalistic explanations, e.g. that Jesus had a particular way of blessing or of breaking bread which made him recognizable, or that the blessed bread restored their wearied mental and physical faculties[108] are surely beside the point. One half of the whole story is later summed up in the statement of 35b, 'how he was made known to them in the breaking of the bread', which is Luke's distinctive expression for the Christian common meal in Acts 2.42, and would be a proper summary of his version of the last supper if the shorter text is to be read. Together with the first part, it becomes a powerful statement of the believer's knowledge of the risen Lord, human and supernatural, in both word and sacrament. It is probably fortuitous that here and in the next incident there are possible parallels in wording to the Markan story of the Walking on the Water, an incident omitted by Luke, such as the intention to go on further (Luke 24.28; cf. Mark 6.48), fear at seeing an apparition (Luke 24.37; cf. Mark 6.49), and the verb 'terrified' (ταράσσεσθαι Luke 24.38; cf. Mark 6.50).

Verse 34 is both revealing and baffling. It shows that Luke was aware of a statement kerygmatic in form and language ('The Lord has risen and has appeared to . . .'), and similar to that in I Cor. 15.3 (Cephas as a name of Peter is, apart from John 1.42, confined to Paul in the New Testament; Simon, apart from John 1.41f.; 21.15ff., is confined to the synoptists). Even if it was not extracted from the head of a list of appearances designed

108 So A. R. C. Leaney, *The Gospel according to St Luke*, p. 293.

to mark Peter as the first person to whom the risen Lord appeared, it makes this point here, and so prepares for the prominence of Peter in Acts. In its form it would appear to ground the whole resurrection faith and its emergence in the belief and consciousness of the apostles ('The Lord has been raised') upon the appearance to Peter ('and has appeared to Simon'). Marxsen argues from this verse, and its wording, as well as from the other faint indications of a primacy of Peter connected with the resurrection, that this was indeed the case, that the appearance to Peter was not only first but constitutive of faith for others, for whom appearances were not the origin of faith as for Peter. This, Marxsen believes, is the only possible way in which the traditions as they now stand can make sense, and bring us anywhere near historical fact.[109] To the extent that this is a correct deduction from the fugitive evidence, it underlines how far down the stream of development the gospel traditions as we have them are. For well-nigh all traces of this constitutive character of the appearance to Peter have been lost, and the story which would have expressed it has disappeared. Luke is only able to make the point by an awkward insertion at the tail end of another story, which now assumes the prominence, and at the price of following it with a story of an appearance to those who already believe, though the story itself does not fit this situation. Luke was presumably unaware of any story of an appearance to Peter alone, and no such is referred to in the speeches in Acts, even when Peter is the spokesman of the Twelve. If Luke 5.1–10 was originally this story, Luke has failed to recognize it as such, and it would in any case be ruled out for him since it takes place in Galilee, and as a fishing story can only take place there.

The appearance to the eleven and those with them (Luke 24.36–49) is plainly an independent story, and reflects different concerns and a different milieu from vv. 13–33. Though connected with it by 'as they were talking of these things' (v. 36), the appearance is not such as might have been expected from the previous story, i.e. one of a man mixing naturally among men and needing no explanation; it is rather of such a kind as to give the impression of a ghost. The fright and terror it occasions follow awkwardly after the previous assured statements that the

[109] See W. Marxsen, *Die Auferstehung Jesu von Nazareth*, esp. pp. 86ff.

Lord had risen and appeared to Peter, and that he had travelled with two on the road and had been known to them in the breaking of the bread. Nor, if 'peace be unto you' in v. 36 and the whole of v. 40 are omitted, could it be called a variant version of the appearance in John 20.19–23. Although there are common elements in the joy, the Spirit and the apostolic witness, they are all used quite differently and distinctively. In John the joy is joy at the resurrection itself and at recognition, in Luke it is a joy which hardly allows belief and needs a further act of eating to confirm it; in John, the Spirit is given there and then by insufflation, in Luke it is promised for the future as the promise of the Father; in John the sending is of the disciples into the world, in Luke it is the sending of the Spirit. When allowance has been made for both the Lukan and the Johannine traits in each case, it is difficult to envisage what an original common substratum might have been.

Like the Emmaus story, the appearance to the eleven and others falls into two parts, the significant event itself and the instruction on the kerygma, though here in reverse order. The first part, the event (vv. 36–39), seems to be intended to serve two purposes at once. The showing of the hands and feet (v. 39a) is meant to answer doubt and to establish the identity of Jesus, presumably because his hands and feet bear the marks of wounds (though this is not said), while the command to 'feel me and see that a spirit does not have flesh and bones as you see me having' answers not doubt but terror at the possibility of a ghost, and is the 'crudest' description of the glory (v. 26) of the risen Lord in terms of an earthly body. This corporeality is even more stressed if, with Marcion, Tertullian and Hilary, the reading 'bones' in place of 'flesh and bones' is adopted, for then it would appear to be stated in the most literalistic form of Jewish resurrection belief, whereby the bones, of which the flesh and skin are only the covering, were the essential things, whose destruction meant the loss of all hope of resurrection.[110] Ignatius has a passage which may stand in some relation to this one when he says (Smyrn. 3.2f.), 'And when he came to Peter and his

---

[110] See K. Bornhauser, *Die Gebeine der Töten* (1921). In that case the argument in Acts 2.29 might be that David cannot have risen because his bones are still in the grave, and Luke 24.39 might be prepared for by the statement in 24.3 that they did not find the body.

company he says to them, "Lay hold and handle me and see that
I am not a demon without a body". And at once they touched
him and believed, being united to his flesh and spirit . . .
Moreover after the resurrection he ate and drank with them as
fleshly, although spiritually united to the Father.' Ignatius'
words 'handle and see that . . .' are identical in Greek with
those in Luke 24.39, but his striking phrase 'demon without a
body' is not. Helmut Koester[111] reaches the tentative conclusion
that Ignatius is not dependent on Luke's gospel here but on a
variant of Luke's story. The context of the passage in Ignatius
is an attack on docetism: 'He genuinely suffered as even he
genuinely raised himself. It is not as some unbelievers say, that
his passion was a sham. It is they who are a sham. Yes, and
their fate will fit their fancies – they will be ghosts and apparitions. For myself, I am convinced and believe that even after
the resurrection he was in the flesh' (Smyrn. 2–3.1). The same
intention is probably to be seen in Luke, who is not afraid to
materialize the supernatural (cf. 3.21), and who may be here
drawing out what is implied in the risen Lord being a man. It
is not said that the disciples ate and drank with him, as in Acts
10.41, but Jesus' eating here, and the meal in 24.30, where,
however, he only gives the food, could supply the basis for it.

In the second part, vv. 44–49, which is solemnly introduced
by an echo of the opening words of Deuteronomy, 'These are
my words which I spoke to you while I was yet with you', v.
44a (cf. 'These are the words which Moses spake unto all Israel
beyond Jordan in the wilderness', Deut. 1.1), the two previous
kerygmatic statements are combined, the words of Jesus on the
one hand which he had uttered while still with them (44a = 6),
and on the other hand the fulfilment of all the scriptures (here
expressed in a possibly liturgical phrase as 'Moses, the prophets
and the psalms') concerning him, and the opening of their
minds to understand the scriptures so (44b = 27; 45 = 32).
What is to be found in the scriptures is that the Christ must
suffer (46a = 26a) and rise from the dead (46b = 7b). But in
view of the fact that it is apostolic missionaries who are now
being addressed, there is added, also as the fulfilment of scripture, the proclamation from now on in the name of the risen

[111] H. Koester, *Synoptische Überlieferung bei den Apostolischen Vätern* (1957),
pp. 45 ff.

Messiah to all nations of repentance unto remission of sins. Thus there is to be extended to all nations what had been the Baptist's message to Israel (3.3). This corresponds with Luke's emphasis in his gospel on repentance, which also appears at the climax of Peter's first preaching of the gospel (Acts 2.38). 'Beginning from Jerusalem' (the grammar is somewhat awkward here owing to a Lukan participial usage with the verb 'to begin'), the disciples are to be those who bear witness of these things, and they are to remain there until they are clothed from above with power, which is further specified as the promise of the Father which Jesus sends forth. This designation of the Spirit as the promise (of God), which is also found in Acts 2.33, 39 (cf. 1.4), is peculiar to Luke, who also connects it with the resurrection (Acts 13.32; 26.6f.). The word does not belong to the vocabulary of the gospels, and could hardly do so since it is a Hellenistic word without Aramaic equivalent. The idea found in Paul and elsewhere in the New Testament that the Old Testament is a book of promise is a Christian creation.

These same themes are recapitulated in the opening of Acts. The reception of power in the coming of the Spirit, and the universal witness of the disciples are repeated (Acts 1.8) in the context of a question from them implying the limitation of the kingdom to Israel, of their necessary ignorance of the final events which remain under the disposition of the Father, and of their assurance of the return of Jesus in the same manner as they have seen him depart; and his ascension as the risen man into heaven, which brings the resurrection period to an end, is depicted as a physical event. These themes are then developed theologically by Peter in the first proclamation of the gospel. In the context of the gift of a universal language he interprets the Spirit through a citation of Joel as a promise of the last days, and bears witness to Jesus as a man approved by God, who is first raised from the dead without corruption, and then ascends to receive the promise of the Spirit from the Father and to pour it out. But two significant additions are made, whether by the hand of Luke or that of a redactor. First, the risen Lord is said to have been 'visible' (the verb occurs here only in the New Testament, the corresponding noun, with the meaning of 'vision', being confined to Luke in the New Testament, except for II Cor. 12.1) to the disciples, either now and then over a period of forty days or continuously throughout that period (depending on the force of the preposition διά here). This is a most remarkable statement in view of the fact that it would provide the strongest possible basis for apostolic preaching of the resurrection, and yet no details of any kind are given to substantiate it – the appearances referred to cannot be simply those mentioned in Luke 24. It could be meant to be taken up by (or if from the hand of a redactor, be derived from) Peter's statement in his preaching to Cornelius (Acts 10.41) that God made Jesus manifest 'not to all the people, but unto witnesses that were chosen before of God, to us, who did eat and drink with him after he rose from the dead', and Paul's statement in his preaching at Antioch (Acts 13.531) that 'he was seen for many days by them who came up with him from Galilee to Jerusalem, who are now his witnesses to the people', especially if the obscure participle in Acts 1.4, συναλιζόμενος, is to be translated 'eating with',[112] or if the variant reading συναυλιζόμενος ('companying with') is to be adopted.

In complete contrast to the lack of any details about these forty-day appearances, they are here designated as many 'proofs' (τεκμηρίοις), a word found only here in the New Testament, and in the rest of the Greek Bible only in Wisdom 5.11; 19.13; III Macc. 3.24, but which has the precise sense of 'demonstrative evidence' or 'incontrovertible proof'. The expression with which they are introduced, 'he presented himself alive after his passion', is unique in the New Testament in its emphasis on Jesus as the agent of his own appearances (for this expression cf. Acts 9.41, 'He presented her alive (to them)'; the closest parallel is John 21.1, 'he manifested himself'). Secondly, the topic of these forty-day appearances is said to be instruction in 'the things concerning the kingdom of God', but again no details are given on this vital matter, and it is difficult to determine what the expression is intended to mean. Does it refer to further teaching about the kingdom of God of the same kind as Jesus had given during his earthly ministry and as had been recorded in the gospel, or does it place under this head the kerygma which was to be preached by the apostles as recorded in Acts? Luke can describe the preaching of Philip as

[112] The verb is rare, and occurs only here in the New Testament. For the problem, see Bauer's *Lexicon*, and the literature cited there.

'gospelling concerning the kingdom of God and the name of Jesus Christ' (Acts 8.12, a hendiadys?), which is presumably the same as 'preaching Christ' (Acts 8.5), and he can describe the preaching of Paul as 'preaching', 'persuading concerning', and 'attesting' the kingdom of God (Acts 19.8; 20.25; 28.23, 31), which is also combined with, or identical with, preaching and teaching about Jesus (Acts 28.23, 31). If this is the coverage of the phrase, then it could include all the subsequent christology of the preaching in Acts, including, as expressly derived from the risen Lord himself, the doctrine that he is the coming judge of all (Acts 10.42). Thus while in Matthew the continuity between past and present is secured by the permanent presence of the exalted Lord with his disciples, who instruct converts baptized into the threefold name in obedience to his commandments spoken on earth, in Luke–Acts it is secured by the Spirit which the Lord pours out from the Father, and by the proclamation of the apostolic message of the suffering and risen Messiah, of repentance and forgiveness, as the truth of scripture. This message is not represented as the conclusions to which the apostles had come in the light of events, but simply, and improbably, as the repetition of what the Lord himself had told them in advance and in detail between his resurrection and ascension.

C. F. D. Moule offers as a suggestion which would make room both for Galilean and Jerusalem appearances that the movements of the disciples were governed by attendance at the festivals, and the appearances of Jesus were accommodated to this.[113] The message of the young man in Mark (Matthew) means that when they return to Galilee after the Passover they will find the risen Lord there; he appears to them in Galilee (and perhaps to the more than five hundred brethren of I Cor. 15.6 who are now presumably believers through such an appearance), and, perhaps, leads them back to Jerusalem for Pentecost (if the 'follow me' of John 21.19 means this), or they return to Jerusalem as pious pilgrims for Pentecost and there the Lord companies with them and commands them not to go back to Galilee this time but to stay where they are. Some such movement might account at some stage for the diversity of the traditions, and might be discernible behind them as in a palimp-

113 C. F. D. Moule, 'The Post-Resurrection Appearances in the Light of Festival Pilgrimages', *NTS* 4 (1957–58), pp. 58ff.

sest. It cannot account for them as we now have them, for as Moule admits, these cannot be harmonized fully. The Matthaean (and Markan?) versions envisage no further manifestations, and 'Follow me' in John 21.19 cannot have had the meaning suggested in the present context in John's gospel, or hardly in any context. On this view Luke 24.36–53 has to be divided into two incidents, one just after Passover and one just before Pentecost, and the forty days of Acts 1.3 cannot be brought into connection with the fifty days between Passover and Pentecost, as this would involve the improbabilities of a return to Jerusalem immediately after getting back to Galilee from Passover (if that), and a festival sojourn at Jerusalem for nearly six weeks before the festival itself. The hypothesis involves taking seriously the forty-days sojourn of the risen Lord with the disciples, which, if it had taken place, would surely have left some mark on the tradition in detail. And if it did take place, without leaving any such mark, then that would seem to argue that the traditions are hardly of such a kind as to allow this sort of historical reconstruction, however tentative.

D. P. Fuller[114] argues that Luke's whole treatment of the resurrection is the key to Luke–Acts, and that it has an important bearing on the modern problem of Easter faith and history. The prologue Luke 1.1–4, which is a prologue to Luke–Acts, states that the intention of the whole work is to provide verification of the instruction which Theophilus and the reader have already received, and 'the things which have been fulfilled amongst us' refer to the events of Acts in which Luke had himself participated and to which the Christ-event recorded in the first volume had led as its consequence. From these events the historical certainty of the resurrection was to be deduced as alone capable of producing them. This fulfilment consisted primarily in the Gentile mission, from whose success as an undeniable fact of history the resurrection was to be deduced as the only adequate cause. The apostles would not have committed themselves to such a mission at the apostolic council but for the resurrection appearances they had received, and its chief protagonist, Paul, can only be accounted for on the basis of an appearance of, and command from, the risen Christ. This Gentile mission reaches its climax at Ephesus in Acts 19, and

114 D. P. Fuller, *Easter Faith and History, passim.*

the rest of the book, chs. 20–28, is a series of arguments between Paul and the Jews, at the centre of which is the theme of the resurrection as both the hope of Judaism and as the sole adequate explanation of Paul's behaviour. Thus for Luke, faith in the resurrection is historically based and at the centre of Christianity. For the apostles it arose from a combination of irrefutable empirical evidence and the power of grace to recognize the necessary inferences from it; for others it arises from the irrefutable evidence of the Gentile mission and the inference that only the resurrection of Jesus could have brought Jews to commit themselves to it, and from the changes brought about in human character.

There are specific points in this reconstruction which are open to question, notably the interpretation put upon the words 'the things fulfilled amongst us', of which others, presumably evangelists, have already by Luke's time drawn up a narrative. This surely refers to the events of both volumes, the Christ-event and the happenings in the early church, and the word 'fulfilled' here is either a solemn word for 'happened', or indicates that the events of both volumes were the fulfilment of divine purpose, not that the events of the second volume were the 'fulfilment' of those in the first volume. Further, the argument that the resurrection and ascension in Luke's gospel form a climax from which Acts then proceeds by way of fulfilment is not altogether convincing, since Luke's arrangement of his material, especially in putting the substance of the apostolic kerygma on the lips of the Lord in Luke 24, emphasizes the element of continuation. Fuller is undoubtedly right in stressing the centrality of the resurrection in Luke–Acts and its relation to the mission of the church. Whatever its explanation, the theme of success story is strong in Acts, and accounts in part for the incorporation of Paul into the narrative. The question is, however, how far historical facts as distinct from religious or theological interpretations may be deduced from it.

Fuller does not enter into a critical examination of the Lukan resurrection traditions, but takes them as they stand; consequently he does not face this question in its full force, and his argument from Christian experience in this Lukan form tends in the direction of placing the maximum weight on the weakest points. Thus the overwhelming evidence of the 'many irrefutable proofs' of Acts1.3, upon which Luke bases the apostolic witness, is the least satisfactory of all the evidence for the resurrection Indeed, is it not negligible? That 'Theophilus could know from the Gentile mission . . . that the apostles had been entrusted with a teaching office whereby they became the inspired organs of divine revelation'[115] ignores the strong possibility that the whole picture of 'the apostles' and the apostolic office in Luke–Acts does not correspond with the historical facts of Christian origins, but is a figment of Luke read back from his own day. Likewise, that the substance of the apostolic teaching, including the interpretation of the passion and resurrection from the Old Testament, was simply a repetition of what the risen Lord had already imparted to the apostles is historically less likely than that the kerygma represents a form of preaching familiar in Luke's own day, which is put back into the mouth of the Lord. The weakness of this deductive mode of argument may be seen in the following passage where Fuller extends it: 'It should be noted in passing that such a line of argument makes it possible for one to arrive at the truth of Scripture from the resurrection of Christ, without having to set up as an a priori that the Scriptures are inspired and true. From the Gentile mission comes the argument not only for the resurrection of Christ but also for the divine origin of the teaching office of the apostles, or, in other words, their inspiration. Thus it follows that the apostolic writings of the New Testament are inspired. Other New Testament writings (Mark, Luke–Acts, Hebrews and Jude) find their authority by virtue of the fact that their authors, who were close associates of the apostles, wrote in such a way that both their message and the spirit in which they spoke qualify them to speak alongside of the apostles. The Old Testament's inspiration, then, becomes certain because the New Testament apostles taught it (cf. II Tim. 3.16f.) and constantly implied it by their quotation of it as the word of God.'[115a] Here almost all the questions are begged – the existence of a teaching office of the 'apostles', its divine origin, if by that is meant its institution by the risen Christ, the permanence of inspiration to cover all their writings, the close association of the other New Testament writers with the apostles and what in any case that would mean, and the impossibility of mistake in the use of the Old Testament.

[115] D. P. Fuller, *op. cit.*, p. 224.   [115a] *Op. cit.*, p. 228.

(*d*) *John*

With the Fourth Gospel, matters are rather different, for here there is something of a tension between the resurrection stories and the rest of the Gospel, and the tension is reflected within the stories themselves. The attentive reader of this Gospel will have been made aware that it is 'ascent' rather than 'resurrection' which is the key word to describe the issue of Jesus' life and ministry. In John 3, it is stated that no one has ascended into heaven except he who has come down from heaven, the Son of man, and in John 6 the question intended to resolve the disciples' difficulty about eating the flesh of Jesus is: 'What if you see the Son of man ascending where he was before?' This is not, however, ascent as Luke understood it, for by his subtle double use of the word 'lift up' to mean both physical elevation in space and spiritual exaltation to the Father – as in the statement, 'I, if I be lifted up, will draw all men unto me' (John 12.32), and in the insistence that Jesus suffers the Roman punishment of death through hoisting up on a cross, and not the Jewish one of stoning (John 18.30ff., referring back to 12.33) – the evangelist indicates that this spiritual ascent takes place at the cross and by means of it, and through the love and obedience which lie within it. Strictly speaking, there is no place in the Fourth Gospel for resurrection stories, since the ascent or exaltation has already taken place. Nevertheless, and doubtless in deference to Christian tradition, the evangelist supplies three, to which a fourth has been added, whether by himself, or by another hand, and in all of them traditional elements lie side by side with what is characteristically Johannine.

The first appearance is to one woman alone from amongst those associated with the empty tomb, in contrast to Matthew's version, where the Lord appears to all of them, and to Luke's, where he appears to none of them. To her the angels at the tomb do not give any command, but only ask the question, 'Why weepest thou? Whom seekest thou?' The command is given by the Lord himself, whom she does not recognize until he calls her by name, as it had been said earlier in this gospel that the good shepherd calls his sheep by name, and they hear his voice, and that he knows them and they him (John 10.3, 14f.). The command is to tell the Lord's brethren not, as in Mark and Matthew, that he goes before them into Galilee, but that he is on the way of ascent to his and their

God and Father, as it has been said earlier in this gospel that it is expedient that he goes on a journey to the Father so that he may return to them, and the Spirit may come to them (John 16.7). Here there is a tension between his ascent having taken place at the cross and the words to Mary Magdalene, 'Touch me not, for I have not yet ascended'. It is the logical consequence of this message having been delivered that the disciples are now prepared to receive the Spirit, and that when Jesus appears to them it will be from the other side of his ascent.

Hence John's second story is both like and unlike Luke's second. Like Luke's, it is to a band of disciples (apparently the apostolic band without Thomas) gathered on the first day of the week, and the Lord stresses the reality of his body as a proof of identity (though the mention of the side refers back to the spear-thrust, which is itself peculiar to John's passion narrative and would appear there to have a symbolic aspect in the flow of blood and water). There is a commissioning of the disciples, though formulated in Johannine idiom ('As my Father has apostled me, so I apostle you'), and with it the power to forgive sins. Yet at its heart it is very different, because, in a symbolic act recalling the breathing of life into a man by God at the first creation in Genesis, the Lord inaugurates the new creation by himself breathing on them the Holy Spirit. Here there is no place for ascension as an event closing a period of forty days of appearances, nor for a Pentecost to follow. Rather, there is here an alternative version to Like's of the origin of the Spirit in the church.

The appearance to the disciples with Thomas in their company includes, like Luke's story, the strongest possible emphasis upon the physical reality of the Lord's risen body, and this is more certainly in contradiction of the docetism which is specially combated in this gospel and in the First Epistle of John which goes with it. In the person of Thomas, a special issue is made of the theme of doubt, which is a fairly constant element in all the resurrection stories, but the story is unique among them in that the result of the appearances is to elicit a christological confession, a confession indeed, 'my Lord and my God', which goes beyond any other in the New Testament, and which is hardly intelligible except on the background of the statement in the evangelist's own theological prologue, 'the Word was God'. The comment of Jesus with which the pericope closes, 'because thou hast seen me thou

hast believed; blessed are those who have not seen and yet have
believed', as well as the request to Thomas to touch and believe,
pick up the theme of the relation between seeing and believing
and between flesh and spirit which is a particular concern of this
gospel.

The appearance which occupies the whole of John 21, whatever
its origin and status, has some resemblances to Luke's Emmaus
story, even though it is concerned with Galilee and not Jerusalem
– the mention of seven disciples, two of them unnamed, the human
details of the disciples' fishing, the fire and the breakfast, the extended and leisurely form of the narrative. But intertwined with
this is the symbolism typical of this gospel, and no story is heavier
with it. The apostolic mission to the world, so long as it is self-
directed ('I go a fishing; we also come with thee') is barren; when
directed by the risen Lord it makes the perfect catch of men (the
hundred and fifty-three species of fish in the sea), and yet the net
of the church remains unbroken under the leadership of the
apostolic shepherd, Peter, now restored after his fall, and with the
abiding of the beloved disciples, until the Lord comes.

John also weaves separate traditions into a scheme, which consists of two sections of two episodes each, with a further episode
intercalated in the first section,[116] and is 'a carefully constructed
literary whole'.[117] This scheme is different from Luke's. There
is unity of time ('the first day of the week', 20.1, 19, followed
by 'eight days later', 20.26), and a unity of place in that the doors
being shut for fear of the Jews indicates Jerusalem. Some
attempt is made to interlock the episodes. Thus Mary's report
of the removal of the body brings about the visit of the two
disciples to the tomb, and the resumption of the story about
Mary leads to an announcement to be delivered to the disciples
that the Lord has appeared to her and is ascending. The appearance to the disciples occasions neither surprise nor doubt, but
only joy; the theme of doubt is reserved for the story about
Thomas, which is prepared for by their announcement to him
that they have seen the Lord and by the previous mention of
the showing of the hands and side. Thomas's confession is
followed by the blessing of those who believe without sight,

[116] Barnabas Lindars, 'The Composition of John XX', *NTS* 7 (1960–61),
pp. 142ff.
[117] E. C. Hoskyns, *The Fourth Gospel*, p. 549.

and the book concludes with the statement that it has been written to evoke in its readers faith in Jesus as the Christ and Son of God. But the force of the chapter does not lie here, but in the juxtaposition of episodes, each complete in itself, and each containing one aspect of the resurrection. 'The general impression of a narrative sequence conceals the absence of a logical connection between the episodes. Thus, the central point of the first episode, which is seen in the words, 'and he saw and believed', has no connection with what happens to Mary Magdalene in the next episode. Similarly, no link is offered between the message given to Mary and any possible effect of the message upon the disciples gathered behind closed doors in the next episode. So in the fourth episode the lack of logical connection is even more apparent. The third episode clearly supposes that all the eleven are gathered in the place where Jesus appears to them, and that all recognize him, and are recipients of the Spirit. It is obvious, therefore, that the fourth episode is complete in itself and that Thomas is selected, as the beloved disciple and Mary have been selected, to be the vehicle of a particular aspect of the resurrection and its consequences'.[118] Thus not only can the separate appearances not be harmonized but also the several attitudes of disciples, and Hooke notes that this same lack of logical connection obtains both between chs. 21 and 20 and between the separate episodes in ch. 21.

It is difficult to decide in what form these separate traditions were available to the evangelist, whether in a source,[119] or in the synoptic gospels themselves, or in traditions which also underlie the synoptic gospels. The nearest parallel is with Luke in 20.19–23, though if Luke 24.36b and 40 are omitted on textual grounds this is reduced to 'he stood in the midst'. There is a mixture of what is and is not distinctively Johannine both in thought and language. Johannine are the association of Peter and the beloved disciple, which is continued in ch. 21 (cf. 13.23f.; 18.15?), the theme of seeing and believing (20.8, 25; cf. 4.48; 6.30), the calling of Mary by name (cf. 10.3, 14), the 'ascent' to the Father (20.17; cf. 3.13; 6.62; 14.12, 28; 16.28), the fear of the Jews (cf. 7.13; 19.38), peace (20.19, 21, 26; cf. 14.27; 16.33),

[118] S. H. Hooke, *The Resurrection of Christ* (1967), p. 84.
[119] Continuous with the passion; so, on stylistic grounds, R. Bultmann, *Das Evangelium des Johannes* (1962[17]), pp. 491ff.

the hands and side (20.20, 25, 27; cf. 19.34, where it may be due to the evangelist rather than his source), the mission based upon the sending of the Son by the Father (20.21; cf. 17.18). Surprising on the other hand are the massive realism of the appearances when compared with their interpretation in advance in chs. 13–17 as spiritual ascent to the Father, and the absence of the words 'glory' and 'glorify' which belong to that interpretation (7.39; 12.16–28; 13.31f.; 16.14; 17.1–5), the insufflation of the Spirit for the sending of the Paraclete, and the specification of the gift of the forgiveness and retention of sins. A great deal, though not all, of the language is Johannine,[120] especially in the dramatic stories of Mary and Thomas, which may thus be constructions of the evangelist on the basis of a brief tradition or saying.

John 20.1–10 would seem to represent an end-product of the development of the story of the empty tomb. So far as any visit of women to the tomb is concerned, it has become colourless. Only one of the women is now left to it. 'We know not' (20.2) could possibly be a relic of a story in which more than one woman was involved, but the use of plural for singular is found in this gospel elsewhere (John 3.2, 11; 9.31). Mary Magdalene is perhaps borrowed from the independent story about her in vv. 11ff. She knows where the tomb is, although in this gospel neither she nor any other women have anything to do with anointing (John 19.38–42). No reason is given for the visit, and the stone is introduced for the first time at her arrival. Although she must have looked into the tomb to be able to report the absence of the body, this is not stated, and would have involved her seeing the special condition of the graveclothes and perhaps the two angels. The former for John concerns the two disciples, and the latter is not germane to the narrative at this point; the angels and their message belong to the separate story in 20.11–18. Thus the purpose of 20.1f. is strictly limited and apologetic. It allows the view of the unbeliever to be stated (and to be reiterated in 20.13, 15), that the basis of the whole resurrection faith was a human removal of the body, or grave robbery (this is similar to Matt. 27.63f.), and is put into the mouth of a believer. It thus provides the background for vv. 3–10, where the empty tomb becomes the basis of belief. John's version of this episode

120 Cf. B. Lindars, *op. cit.*, pp. 144ff.

is very different from that of any of the synoptics, and its spiritual significance is removed from the women and attached to disciples.[121]

That only Peter and the beloved disciple, and not all the disciples, are sought out by Mary, and that these two alone go to the tomb, is connected with whatever purpose the evangelist had in mind in combining and contrasting Peter and this other mysterious figure in his gospel.[122] Despite the plural 'they did not know . . .' (v. 9) in the evangelist's account, it is probably to be understood that only the beloved disciple, who arrives before Peter, but at the climax of the story enters the tomb after him, believed, and that he is the type of those who believe without seeing (20.29). Though it is not said here, or in vv. 27–29, what was believed, the verb being used absolutely as elsewhere in the gospel, it is probable that belief in the resurrection as such is meant. If so, the primary apostolic belief in the resurrection is represented as being independent of appearances either of angels or of the Lord, or of subsequent interpretation of the resurrection of the Messiah by reference to the Old Testament (contrast Luke, and for v. 9 cf. the comment of the evangelist in the related context, 2.22). Since it is based on observation of the graveclothes, for which the description of Lazarus emerging from the tomb with graveclothes and face cloth still on him (11.44) prepares, it gives the lie to the polemical statement already uttered by Mary that the tomb had been robbed, and hints at the possibility of divine agency. The empty tomb thus becomes a 'sign' of the Johannine type; it is a sign of resurrection, a means of grasping a heavenly truth not previously known from scripture and independent of it.

The story in John 20.11–18 stands on its own, and begins

[121] The attempt of P. Benoit, 'Marie-Madeleine et les Disciples au Tombeau selon Joh. 20.1–10' in W. Eltester (ed.), *Judentum, Urchristentum, Kirche* (Jeremias Festschrift, 1964), pp. 141ff., to uncover from this passage, Luke 24.12 and Matt. 28.9f. an original story of the discovery of the empty tomb by Mary and Peter, is hardly convincing.

[122] R. Bultmann, *Das Evangelium des Johannes*, pp. 369f., 531, suggests that they are symbols of Jewish and Gentile Christianity; H. Grass, *op. cit.*, p. 57, that they represent rivalry between Petrine and Johannine circles in the church. W. Marxsen, *Die Auferstehung Jesu von Nazareth*, pp. 86, 92, sees the story as indirect evidence in Johannine form of the knowledge of the primacy of Peter in connection with the resurrection. But it is not clear that the evangelist intends to denote a primacy by Peter's entry first into the tomb, and not rather a primacy of the beloved disciple as the first to believe.

abruptly. If it is from a source, it must have had some such introduction as 20.1, though even so the difficulty would remain that, whereas in the synoptic tradition of the visit of the women the tomb and angel(s) are immediately connected, here there have to be two inspections of the tomb, the first to bring Mary to tears and only the second vouchsafing a vision of angels (who were not there for the two disciples to see). Other differences are the highly affective character of the story, which requires that only one person shall be involved to be addressed personally by name, and the reduction of the role of the angels to a question about tears, which in any case is repeated by the Lord himself, who adds the question, reminiscent of the question of the angels in the synoptic tradition, 'Whom do you seek?'. The displacement of angels by the Lord himself, evident in Matt. 28.9f., is here carried further.

The polemical view of the resurrection faith as based on grave robbery, which is reiterated (vv. 13, 15), is now contradicted in Mary's case by an appearance of the Lord himself. Her supposition that he is the gardener depends on the special Johannine tradition that the grave was located in a garden near enough to the scene of the crucifixion to permit a burial before the sabbath (19.38–42). Her recognition of the Lord when he utters her name can hardly be explained naturalistically by the tone of voice, since he had spoken to her already. It is, rather, a dramatization of the truth uttered in 10.3f., 14, that the good shepherd calls his own sheep by name, and they hear his voice and know him. Her response ῥαββουνί ('Master') stands in some contrast to Thomas's 'My Lord and my God', though τὸν κύριον in 20.2, 13 probably means not 'the Master' but 'the Lord', as generally in resurrection contexts. If ῥαββουνί indicates a presumption that Jesus has returned to his former life with men, it may be the immediate occasion for the next words, 'Do not touch me' (or, 'Cease touching me'). This would then be a further instance of what is a regular feature of the Fourth Gospel, the crude misunderstanding which provides the basis of an exposition of spiritual truth, and Mary would be a type, like Nicodemus and others, in that she understands resurrection as a restoration to a previous life. What had been meant by Jesus 'coming again' to his disciples (14.3, 18, 23) had been misunderstood, and must be given its true explanation.

The exact force of v. 17a is not clear. It could indicate that since Jesus is already in the process of a metamorphosis into the exalted Lord which is not complete, he is no longer the object of human touch. Or, if the 'not yet' is stressed, that there will indeed be a 'touching' of him when he has ascended, and that Mary's action is not so much improper as premature. Only on the latter interpretation is the injunction compatible with the later command to Thomas to touch, and then only if Jesus is presumed to have ascended in the meantime. Since this is not indicated, the resultant picture would be very confused. To avoid these difficulties W. Marxsen suggests a sense which he brings out by the translation 'Touch me not. I am, to be sure, not yet ascended to my Father (i.e. you can touch me at present; but I would prefer you now did something else namely) Go and tell my brethren. . . .' This is itself forced.[123]

Verse 17b is plainly of the greatest importance. It resembles the synoptic tradition in that a crucial message, involving the particular evangelist's whole understanding of the resurrection, is to be conveyed by a woman to the disciples. On the other hand, the message is altogether different in content, and is closely related to the thought of the Fourth Gospel as a whole. It is neither Mark's (and Matthew's) message that Jesus goes before them into Galilee, nor Luke's reminder of what he had said in Galilee about the necessary crucifixion and resurrection of the Son of man, but rather that he is ascending to their common Father and God. With the word 'ascend' ($\dot{a}\nu\alpha\beta\alpha\acute{i}\nu\epsilon\iota\nu$ in this theological sense is found only in John's Gospel, cf. 3.13; 6.62), the accent is laid on exaltation to the Father as the meaning of resurrection. It is further notable that here alone in the Fourth Gospel the disciples to whom the message is to be delivered are called by Jesus his brethren, and that God is called his and their Father and his and their God. This picks up a dominant theme of the whole gospel.[124] Already in the prologue a distinction is made amongst those to whom the Logos came between those who did not receive him and those who did receive him, and to whom, as the only Son, he gave the right to become sons of God. This distinction divides the Gospel into

[123] W. Marxsen, *Die Auferstehung Jesu von Nazareth*, p. 64.
[124] See W. Grundmann, 'Zur Rede vom Vater im Johannes-Evangelium', *ZNTW* (1961), pp. 213ff.

two parts, the first (chs. 2–12) being concerned with rejection by the Jews who refuse the new birth of the Spirit and falsely call God their Father (3.3; 5.37f.; 8.19ff.), and the second (chs. 13–20) being concerned with Jesus and those who are really his own, whose mutual relationship is parallel to that between the Father and the Son (14.20). Their future entry into the relation of sonship to the Father is one of the subjects of the last discourses, and is represented as soon to be realized after the 'little while' of Jesus' return to the Father whence he had come (14.1–4, 12, 20–28; 16.5–23, 28). It is also a subject of the high-priestly prayer that those who belong to the God who is addressed throughout as Father may be with Jesus where he is. It is thus the fulfilment of the whole gospel of divine sonship in the Son through Christ's exaltation to the Father that the message of 20.17b is to convey.

It is part of the lack of logical connection between the separate episodes that no indication is given of the effect of the delivery of this message to the disciples (v. 18), whoever may be meant by 'disciples' in this chapter. Are they led by it to expect, and do they receive, a bodily appearance of an already ascended Lord, and if so, is the evangelist's understanding of the incarnation that in some form it persists in the exalted state of a heavenly man? The mention of the closed doors is to indicate the miracle, for it is a risen Jesus who can be touched who enters despite them; that they were closed for fear of the Jews is a Johannine touch, 'the Jews' remaining the enemies in this Gospel even in the context of the resurrection. In this context is it suggested that the previous message had not removed the fear? The reaction of the disciples to Jesus 'coming to them' (cf. 14.28), to his greeting 'Peace', and to the showing of tokens of identification (or symbols of the passion) is joy at seeing him. This is in fulfilment of the words in 14.27f.: 'Peace I leave to you, my peace I give to you . . . you have heard that I said to you, "I go away and come to you". If you loved me you would have rejoiced because I am going to the Father,' and of the words in 16.19–33.[125] As with Matthew and Luke (and possibly Mark), the immediate issue of the resurrection is the mission to the world, which is here stated very succinctly by the ascended

---

[125] For joy and peace as designations of eschatological salvation, see R. Bultmann, *Das Evangelium des Johannes,* pp. 386f.

Lord in Johannine form and terminology as grounded upon the mission of the Son into the world by the Father (cf. 17.18, 8, 25; 5.36; 6.57). As the ascended Lord he also, after repeating the announcement of peace, confers the eschatological gift of the Spirit (cf. 16.7; 14.16f., 26; 15.26; 7.39), not, however, by an act of sending (15.26; 16.7), but by an inbreathing like that of God at creation when he breathed into Adam the breath of life (Gen. 2.7; Wisdom 15.11), which the disciples 'receive' as the world is not able to do (14.17–19). With it is conferred the power to forgive and to retain sins. This is itself a divine prerogative, but its selection here as the only consequence of the reception of the Spirit to be specified is surprising, since the forgiveness of sins is not otherwise mentioned in this gospel (contrast I John 1.9; 2.12). It is true that the work of the Spirit has already been said to consist in the conviction of the world in respect of sin, righteousness and judgment (16.8ff.), in continuation of the function of Jesus himself (5.27; 9.39), and this pertains to the disciples' mission to the world, but the language of 20.23 (κρατεῖν, to retain, or refuse to remit cf. Matt. 16.19; 18.18) fits better a limited disciplinary function within the Christian community than a power exercised towards the world in the apostolic mission. There is no mention of the Lord's departure from the disciples, and the story ends with his words, which thus stand out as the spiritual truths which have to be uttered.

What follows (vv. 24f.) as a connecting link is a fairly detailed account of the reaction of Thomas to the report of the disciples that they had seen the Lord, in which the previous statement 'he showed them his hands and his side' is picked up. Compared with this, the account of the appearance to the disciples and Thomas is formal and brief, v. 26b being a repetition of v. 19. Though Thomas is not said to have responded to the invitation to touch, the realism of the Johannine narrative is at its greatest here and goes beyond what is required, since in v. 29 it is faith with sight and faith without sight which are contrasted, and not faith with or without touch, and for this contrast it would have been sufficient for Thomas to have 'seen' the Lord like the rest. The confession 'My Lord and my God' may have in mind the title of Caesar in the imperial cult,[126] especially in

[126] Cf. 'Dominus et deus noster', applied to Domitian, Suetonius, *Domitian* 13.

view of the dominance of the theme 'Christ or Caesar' in the Johannine passion narrative. In this context it makes the end of the gospel match its beginning, where the Logos is God. The fact that nevertheless the confession does not bring the gospel to a close, but leads on to a blessing of those who believe without sight, and then to vv. 30f. as the conclusion, suggests that the evangelist is here grappling with a theological problem of how the resurrection can become the basis of the faith of subsequent believers (cf. I Peter 1.8). For the evangelist, the link between the present and the past is, at least in part, the preservation for faith of some account of the acts of Jesus (and of his words that transform those acts into signs), though elsewhere in the gospel emphasis is laid on the future interpretative work of the Spirit.

Chapter 21 is exceedingly difficult to assess. In its present position it depicts a scene of complete desertion in fulfilment of 16.32, if 'each to his own' there refers to their homes in Galilee. But it comes too late, since 16.32, like Mark 14.50, indicates a flight at the arrest of Jesus, and can hardly refer to apostasy from a resurrection faith established by the events of ch. 20. For the writer, whether the evangelist or a redactor, it becomes a third manifestation of the risen Lord to his disciples (21.1, 14); but taken by itself, it gives the impression of a single appearance, unconnected with any other, and perhaps the first and only one. While in its present position it can be interpreted of the fruits of the apostolic mission referred to in 20.20f., by itself it gives the impression that the disciples concerned have not yet received any such commission. It thus opens up a vista of floating tradition, in this case a resurrection tradition attached to Galilee, to which has been added a further tradition of the rehabilitation of Peter, but the original shape and unity of these traditions are impossible to discern in face of the layers of interwoven symbolical motifs in them. Such are, the number of the disciples made up to seven by the addition of two unnamed; although it is only Peter and the beloved disciple who play any part in the story and its sequel, and the combination of this pair is a Johannine trait; Peter as the head (is there a relic of 'his disciples and Peter' of Mark 16.7?), who 'goes fishing' (cf. 15.16: 'that you may go and bring forth fruit'); the unknown stranger on the shore, who knows in advance that they have caught nothing, and who is automatically obeyed when he tells them to fish on the right (or favourable) side of the boat (cf. 15.5: 'without me ye can do nothing'); the perfect catch of fish;[127] the recognition of the Lord by the beloved disciple; the fact that the net is not broken by the number of the fish; the reference to the fish as 'something to eat' (v. 5) or as 'fish to eat' (v. 10), which nevertheless cannot be used for this purpose because they represent the converts; the (eucharistic?) meal prepared and distributed by the Lord himself. The whole story is a dramatization of the apostolic mission. This symbolism continues into the appendix to the story. The statements made to Peter, both the statement about himself (21.18) and that made to him about the beloved disciple (21.22), are such as to need interpretation, which is given in Johannine style. Verse 18 may represent a particular application to Peter of a proverbial saying contrasting the activity of youth with the helplessness of old age (so, Bultmann *ad loc.*). Marxsen thinks that at an earlier stage in the tradition it meant that while in his youth Peter had followed his own will, in his old age he was to be completely devoted to the service of another. Whatever its meaning, it is here, in Johannine manner (cf. 13.36), interpreted of his death. The statement about the beloved disciple, v. 22, is a final instance in the gospel of a saying of the Lord of a Johannine type ('If I will that he abides till I come . . .') being taken in a literal sense and so misunderstood.

The similarity of the whole story to that in Luke 5.1–10 raises the question whether the latter, and possibly all stories of the call of disciples to become fishers of men, may not be post-resurrection stories; or, contrariwise, whether John's story was originally a story of the earthly ministry, and was transmuted into a post-resurrection story. The argument of E. C. Hoskyns, that the chapter should not be taken as an epilogue or appendix, since a gospel properly ends not with appearances of the risen Lord but with a confident statement that the mission to the world will be the means by which many will be saved,[128] is not compelling in view of the reference to the mission to the world in 20.21, which is to be interpreted by 17.18–21 and 15.16.

[127] For possible explanations of the number, see E. C. Hoskyns, *op. cit.*, *ad loc.*; J. A. Emerton, 'The Hundred and Fifty-three Fishes in John xxi. 11', *JTS* NS ix (1958), pp. 86ff.

[128] E. C. Hoskyns, *op. cit.*, pp. 550, 561f.

Linguistic considerations are not decisive. It can be maintained that vocabulary and style are sufficiently Johannine for the chapter to have been written by the evangelist himself, any differences in vocabulary being put down to the special subject matter. If, on the other hand, the differences are held to indicate a later editor,[129] the similarities are such that he must be presumed to have belonged to a Johannine school of thought. The main argument for its being an appendix is that the evangelist is hardly likely to have destroyed the ending in 20.30–31.

CONCLUSION

The analysis of the resurrection traditions in this chapter has not been as detailed as it could be; but it is likely that however detailed the analysis, it would not diminish the impression that it is not simply difficult to harmonize these traditions, but quite impossible. Attempts to combine them by means of inspired guesses and hypotheses, of which F. F. Morrison's *Who Moved the Stone?* has been for so long known as an outstanding and brilliant example, are really defeated from the start. For what have to be combined are not a number of scattered pieces from an originally single matrix, but separate expressions of the Easter faith. Each of these is complete in itself; each has developed along its own line so as to serve in the end as a proper conclusion for an evangelist of his own particular version of the gospel. Behind and within all the traditions, of course, is the conviction that Jesus of Nazareth continues to be and to operate, and that in him past, present and future are somehow related; but the mode of this continuation is differently conceived in the four gospels, and in each case is closely related to the theology of the particular gospel concerned. Each evangelist gives his own version as a total version, which was not intended to stand up only if it stood alongside another, or was supplemented by another.

Nor is it sufficient to say, with G. Bornkamm, that we have to reckon with gaps,[130] unless we go on to say that the gaps are not such as could be filled in by additional facts. They are not gaps in a whole, but gaps between wholes. Nor is it sufficient to say, for example, of the empty tomb traditions that the differences are

[129] So R. Bultmann, *Das Evangelium des Johannes*, pp. 542f.
[130] G. Bornkamm, *Jesus of Nazareth*, p. 182.

'relatively minor legendary accretions' and 'what one would look for in genuine accounts of so confused and confusing a scene',[131] for in this tradition differences can so often be accounted for in terms of conscious editorial modification which governs the whole version. It is not natural confusion but rather the lack of it, and the influence of rational reflection and apologetic, which have given rise to the contradictions. Nor can one set of facts be convincingly shown to be a development from another, as, for instance, in the much-discussed contradiction between Galilee and Jerusalem as the scene of the appearances. The case for Galilee was put with admirable clarity by Kirsopp Lake.[132] The disciples fled to Galilee; there the appearances took place; but since ultimately the church was centred on Jerusalem, traditions arose to place the appearances there, and made necessary the story of the empty tomb. But there is no certainty that the words in the passion narrative, 'they all forsook him and fled' denote a flight back to Galilee (von Campenhausen regards this interpretation of the words as a 'Legend of the Critics'), nor that 'I will go before you into Galilee' and 'he goes before you into Galilee' mean a rendezvous there, and not that Jesus will lead them into Galilee (whatever that may mean), while the two Galilean appearances, those in Matthew and John, are so theological or symbolical that they supply the flimsiest basis for reconstructing a historical course of subsequent developments. Nor is the case much better if, with von Campenhausen, 'we resolve to set aside altogether the demonstrably later accounts, one and all, and to follow exclusively the Marcan tradition, which was used by the other evangelists as their source, and by them, elaborated and developed', since, as he himself admits, the Marcan account already shows 'the inconsistencies of the different traditions', and some will think that in his own essay he deduces too confidently historical facts and sequences from theologically coloured statements. W. Marxsen's attempt to bring order by the hypothesis of a first appearance to Peter, which is the source of the resurrection faith of all others, is, on his own showing, tentative, and the evidence for it is at best faintly discernible as in a palimpsest.

Deeper than differences of geographical location are those of

[131] J. A. T. Robinson, 'The Resurrection in the New Testament', *IDB*, IV p. 46.
[132] Kirsopp Lake, *The Historical Evidence for the Resurrection of Jesus Christ* (1907), ch. VI.

theological interpretation, of the relation between the physical and the non-physical, and between resurrection and exaltation. The impression given in some accounts is of a figure who has been resuscitated to a fully physical, visible and tangible state, and in other accounts of one who is not immediately recognizable as what he had been except through specific acts and words. The manner of the Risen One's 'coming' and 'going', his being present and being absent, are presented in different ways and without explanation. While the risen Christ of Luke moves towards ascension, the ascended Christ of Matthew stays with men until the end of the age, but not as the bodily risen one. The one element which the traditions, in all their variety, have in common is that the appearance of the risen Lord issued in an explicit command to evangelize the world, yet the early decades of the history of the church, in so far as they are known to us, make it difficult to suppose that the apostles were aware of any such command.

In one sense, therefore, the Easter tradition may be said to be strong. It is multiple and varied, and has a wide spread. It is not single, uniform or stereotyped. Whatever the Easter event was, it must be supposed to be of such a kind as to be responsible for the production of these traditions as its deposit at whatever remove. The events themselves, however, both the resurrection appearances and the empty tomb, lie so deeply concealed within the traditions that they can be glimpsed only very indirectly, so that the principal difficulty here is not to believe, but to know what it is which offers itself for belief. To say either that it was exactly like what any of the traditions describe it as being, or, on the contrary, that 'it had nothing to do with the rising of a dead body from the tomb',[133] would be in both cases far more dogmatic than we are allowed to be. There is a marked contrast between the centrality of the Easter faith in the New Testament, and the almost fortuitous character of the traditions which now support it; and between the events on the one hand, which remain so shadowy because the narratives (with one or two exceptions of an apologetic kind) are so casual about the risen Lord's state and condition, and their interpretation

[133] G. W. H. Lampe, in G. W. H. Lampe and D. M. Mackinnon, *The Resurrection* (1966), pp. 8ff.; N. Clark, *Interpreting the Resurrection*, p. 97f.: 'The event of the Resurrection has nothing to do with the resuscitation of a corpse.' While the resurrection of Jesus is not simply the reanimation of a corpse, it cannot be ruled out that reanimation might have had some sort of connection with it.

on the other hand, which is expressed so eloquently through the mouth of the risen Lord speaking in Matthaean, Lukan and Johannine tones respectively. The reader of the gospels or preacher of the gospel is likely to be able to appreciate and use this eloquence to the extent that he is not over-preoccupied with historical considerations.[134]

[134] Cf. H. Grass, *op. cit.*, pp. 542f.

III

THE RESURRECTION FAITH

THE central place of the resurrection faith in the New Testament is hardly what was to be expected either from contemporary Judaism or from the preaching and teaching of Jesus as it has been recorded. In the resurrection narratives of the gospels this centrality is already reflected, and the reason for it begins to appear in the fact that they already incorporate in themselves what came to be apprehended only later and gradually as central Christian truth – the exaltation of Jesus to universal status and authority, the effusion of the Spirit, the apostolic mission of the church to the world, and the understanding of the gospel in the light of scripture. While it is the incorporation of these themes in the narratives which renders them such difficult media for discerning what precisely the resurrection was, it also shows that the first Christians saw the resurrection to be connected with, and creative of, the fundamental elements of Christian belief and life. The resurrection was both corroborated by, and was itself known through, that to which it gave rise, and it is part of Christian knowledge of the resurrection to trace these effects, and to see how they are the effects of this particular cause.

A rudimentary form of resurrection belief is that which has been called the 're-active', and takes the form of 'man did that, God in reply did this'. The truth is stated by a double action, at the hands of men and of God, with the second cancelling the first. Resurrection is the divine reversal of the Cross as life is the opposite of death. This is on the whole the form taken in the preaching in Acts: 'You by the hands of lawless men did slay; him God raised up' – either because this is how in fact it was first apprehended, or because it is how the author of Acts understood it and how his probably non-Christian readers were most likely to receive it. It brings to a head over the person of Jesus what is a familiar theme of the Old Testament, where God is frequently he who contradicts and overrules the thoughts and actions of men. It prevents Christianity from becoming what in the Hellenistic milieu, with its 'gods many and lords many', there was inevitably great pressure for it to become, viz. a cult of Jesus, and ensures that the resurrection is primarily about God, who is known for the living God that he is in his act of raising Jesus (only in John 10.17 is Jesus said to raise himself). This re-active form is, however, rudimentary and in itself not particularly creative, since it says so little about the Cross except as something to be reversed; there is little positive doctrine of the Cross in Acts, or even of the risen life which the resurrection brings to light. Positive doctrine is in Acts rather attached to the Spirit.

This re-active aspect is brought out in a study by M. Barth and V. H. Fletcher, *Acquittal by Resurrection*, whose theme is the resurrection 'understood as the foundation of righteousness and justice'.[1] This is different from the view of U. Wilckens[2] that the resurrection was the divine eschatological ratification and endorsement appropriate to and demanded by the earthly ministry of Jesus, which, as Marxsen objects, makes the earthly ministry no more than a prelude to something else. Barth and Fletcher connect the resurrection with the juridical setting in Acts in which apostles lay emphasis on the resurrection in their defence before the courts (Acts 3–5), and they point to the strong forensic element in the Old Testament picture of God's righteousness. In their defence the apostles go over to prosecution, and represent their captors as themselves on trial. The resurrection is presented both as the confounding by God of the enemies of Christ in his reversal of their criminal act of crucifixion, and also, paradoxically, as the offer of forgiveness to those same enemies, whether they are Israel as a whole or Israel's leaders. It is doubtful, however, whether this is the source of the moral understanding of the resurrection, and of its association with the remission of sins, and whether there is a straight line from here to the Pauline statements which associate resurrection with the justification of men from sin (Rom. 4.25).

[1] M. Barth and V. H. Fletcher, *Acquittal by Resurrection* (1964), p. v.
[2] U. Wilckens, 'Das Offenbarungsverständnis in der Geschichte des Unchristentums', in W. Pannenberg (ed.), *Offenbarung als Geschichte* (1963²), pp. 42–90.

The character and status of these speeches in Acts are, of course, much debated. They may be relatively late stereotyped forms of kerygma in Luke's own day. The death of Jesus is presented in them not on its positive side but on its external side as a stumbling block which has to be got over by appeal to Old Testament texts about the resurrection of the Messiah; and since it has been brought about by the Jewish leaders, the forgiveness of sins, perhaps already associated with it in Christian thought, is directed to the exoneration of Israel and Israel's leaders from the crime of crucifixion (Acts 3.13, 17, 19–26; 5.30–32). That this rests on a stereotyped pattern is suggested by the fact that the same kind of speech is found even when the speakers are not on trial, and that there also the remission of sins is the upshot of the Christian message, even if somewhat loosely attached to it (Acts 2.22f., 36–83; 10.40–43; 13.27–33, 38f.). That the pattern can be given a slant in the direction of the exoneration of Israel would correspond with the apologetic intention of Acts, and with Luke's stress on the church as composed of believing Israel as well as Gentiles. The prominence of the resurrection in Acts may be due to the author seeing it as a decisive proof of the resurrection belief which he holds to be one of the chief hallmarks of true Judaism, which the Pharisees underlined and from which only the Sadducees maintained themselves aloof (Acts 4.1–2; 23.6–8; 24.14–16; 26.22–27). The compressed statement in Acts 4.2 should probably be taken to mean that the Sadducees were exasperated because the apostles proclaimed the doctrine of the general resurrection by reference to the case of Jesus.[3] But in that case the situation depicted is artificial and the arrest of the apostles must have had some other ground, since, as Haenchen observes, if the proclamation of resurrection as such was a ground for arrest the Sadducees would have had to arrest all the Pharisees. Similarly, what is said in Acts 26.2f. to be the burden of the law and the prophets, viz. that the Christ should suffer and as the first from the dead would announce light to the world, does not have the Pauline implication that as the firstfruits the risen Christ initiates and guarantees the resurrection of believers, but

---

[3] Not the Pauline sentiment that through the resurrection of Jesus the resurrection of the dead had begun to take place, as Hooke suggests, *op. cit.*, p. 49.

means rather that through his resurrection he is established as Messiah and Son of God and dispenses forgiveness of sins (Acts 26.18; cf. 13.33–38). Although a thoroughly Jewish tenet, resurrection is for Luke the one most capable of being translated for the Gentile world in the form that through his resurrection Jesus is established as the universal Lord through whom all men may receive forgiveness of sins, and as the divinely appointed judge of all men living and dead (Acts 10.36, 42f.; 17.18, 30f.; 26.17f., 23). But whether presented to Jews or Gentiles, resurrection has to do primarily with God, and this is the more forcibly emphasized by the re-active form.

Nevertheless there is more in the re-active view than simply the idea of reversal, since the resurrection has positive significance of its own, in that it is announced as that which establishes the messiahship and lordship of Jesus, or even as that by which he becomes Messiah and Lord, and the announcement being made in the context of polemical or semi-polemical speeches implies that the whole of Israel should accept what is announced, and is guilty if it does not. There are two difficulties here. The first is to discern the relation between the concepts of resurrection and exaltation. There are passages in the New Testament which virtually ignore resurrection and pass straight to an exaltation to God or to his right hand as the most adequate expression of what has to be said. This is so already in the reply to the high priest's question in Mark 14.62: 'I am; and ye shall see the Son of man sitting at the right hand of God, and coming with the clouds of heaven.' It is so also in the Epistle to the Hebrews, which contains only one somewhat oblique reference to resurrection in its concluding blessing, but which in its opening declaration about the Son of God passes from 'having made purification for sins' straight to 'sat down at the right hand of the Majesty on high' (1.3), and can state as the summary or chief point of its argument that 'we have such a high priest, who sat down on the right hand of the throne of the Majesty in the heavens' (8.1). It is so also in the possibly pre-Pauline hymn about Christ in Phil. 2, where the response to the self-negation of Jesus is that 'God highly exalted him, and gave unto him the name which is above every name (Kyrios)', so that the whole universe should acknowledge that Jesus Christ is Lord. It is also so, after its own fashion, in the Fourth Gospel, where the Son of man who descends from heaven ascends thither, does so by the Cross when he is lifted up, goes on a journey to prepare a place for the disciples and to bring them where he himself is, and who after resurrection speaks, as also in Matthew, as the Lord from the other side of exaltation.

The impression left by these and other passages is that exaltation is the primary and inclusive concept, and that resurrection is subordinate and contained within it. On the other hand, there are passages where Jesus' lordship is derived from his resurrection, as in the kerymatic statement, possibly pre-Pauline, in Rom. 10.9: 'If thou shalt confess with thy mouth Jesus as Lord, and shalt believe in thy heart that God raised him from the dead, thou shalt be saved', or in the description in I Thess. 1.10 of the Christian state as one of 'waiting for his Son from heaven, whom he raised from the dead, even Jesus, who delivers us from the wrath to come'. In the sermon in Acts 13 the theme is Jesus, the Son of God and saviour, as the perpetual ruler on the throne of David in fulfilment of Israel's divinely governed history, and the climax is reached in the statement that God has fulfilled his promise without remainder in raising Jesus, and in raising him from the dead incorruptible. Elsewhere the two conceptions of exaltation and resurrection jostle one another. This can be seen in a brief and simple form in I Peter 1.21: 'God who raised him from the dead, and gave him glory', or in Acts 3.13: 'the God of our Fathers hath glorified (exalted) his servant Jesus; whom ye delivered . . . ye killed the Prince of life; whom God raised from the dead', or Acts 5.30f.: 'The God of our fathers raised up Jesus, whom ye slew . . . Him did God exalt with his right hand to be a Prince and a Saviour, for to give repentance to Israel, and remission of sins.' It can be seen in a more extended and complex form, as in the remarkable passage in Eph. 1.19ff.: '. . . and what the exceeding greatness of his power to us-ward who believe, according to that working of the strength of his might which he wrought in Christ, when he raised him from the dead, and made him to sit at his right hand in the heavenly places, far above all rule and authority and power, and dominion, and every name that is named, not only in this world, but also in that which is to come', or even in I Cor. 15, where the argument from Christ's resurrection passes eventually into an argument from his lordship and reign through which all his enemies are subdued.

They jostle one another also in Peter's speech at Pentecost. The main thrust of the speech in its context is undoubtedly towards exaltation as the means to the gift of the Spirit ('being therefore by the right hand of God exalted, and having received of the Father the promise of the Holy Ghost, he hath poured forth this, which ye see and hear' . . . 'Let all the house of Israel therefore know assuredly, that God hath made him both Lord and Christ, this Jesus whom ye crucified', Acts 2.33–36), but on the way to this goal the resurrection is argued at some length on the basis of Psalm 16 (Acts 2.24–32). Only in the Lukan writings is a relation between resurrection and exaltation firmly established. There the resurrection has the character of an interim, limited in purpose to providing visible proofs that Jesus is alive and a programme for the future, and limited in time to forty days, when it is succeeded by exaltation in the form of a further visible and describable event, the ascension, which brings the temporary resurrection period to a close. It is thus possible that the concept of exaltation to the right hand of God and of the consequent share in God's authority and rule was prior to the idea of resurrection in establishing belief in Jesus' lordship and messiahship, for it leads directly to it, while resurrection from the dead, as such, does not.

G. Bertram[4] argues from a survey of New Testament texts that coincidental with the belief in the resurrection of Jesus from the grave and in his subsequent ascension, or emerging in a shorter or longer time from it, was a belief in his ascension to heaven direct from the Cross. The title of Bertram's essay is, as E. Lohmeyer observed,[5] misleading, since what these texts are concerned with is not deliverance from the Cross as such but from death in general, and not with 'ascension' (*Himmelfahrt*) in its ordinary sense but with exaltation.[6] The question is whether death-exaltation was always simply a synonym for, or an extension to its furthest point of death-resurrection, or was a parallel, independent and alternative conception in its own right. The question could also be raised whether it was not in certain respects the prior conception in being responsible, in a way the resurrection by itself is not likely to have been, for the belief

[4] G. Bertram, 'Die Himmelfahrt Jesu vom Kreuz aus und der Glaube an seine Auferstehung', in *Festgabe für Adolf Deissmann* (1927), pp. 187ff.
[5] E. Lohmeyer, *Kyrios Jesus* (1961²), p. 48, n.2.
[6] H. Grass, *op. cit.,* reviews the literature on this since Bertram.

in the imminent return of the exalted Lord to meet his own 'in the air' (I Thess. 4.17), and in serving to distinguish the living again of Jesus from other 'resurrections' (e.g. of Jairus's daughter), as eschatological and as involving the whole world – unless, on the contrary, it was as 'the Christ' that the 'Coming One' was expected, and as 'Lord' that he was rather experienced as already present with his church. Involved here are the vexed questions of the origin of the title 'the Lord' in the church, of why, when, where and by whom it was first applied to Jesus, of the significance of the Aramaic 'maran' ('Our Lord', I Cor. 16.22) in this development, and of the way Ps. 110.1 was used in this connection.[7]

Resurrection and exaltation have in common that they are God's action and have their source in him. E. Fascher[8] sees this as the essential point, and anything further, whether exaltation to God's right hand or bodily resurrection appearances, simply as different ways of attempting to express the inexpressible. The two are found apart: e.g. exaltation without reference to resurrection in Phil. 2.10f., and resurrection without reference to exaltation in Rom. 1.4. They are also found in combination (e.g. Acts 2.32f.; 5.30f.; Rom. 8.34; Eph. 1.20; Col. 3.1), although at times the combination is not without a certain awkwardness, e.g. in Col. 3.1 and Acts 2.30ff., where the citation from Ps. 16, as well as that from Ps. 110.1, bears more naturally on an immediate removal by God from the power and corruption of death than on resurrection from a grave, or Rom. 8.34, where the main thought is that the previously dead Jesus is now at the right hand of God to intercede for and not to condemn the elect, and the words 'rather is raised' are interjected. Despite Rom. 10.9, exaltation is more fitted for the proclamation of Jesus as Lord, as in Phil. 2.5–11, where the reversal of a self-abnegation which has led to death is by means of exaltation by the hand of God to a lordship acknowledged by the cosmic powers, and I Peter 3.21f., where 'Jesus Christ, who has gone into heaven and is at the right hand of God, with angels, authorities and powers subject to him' reads like a separate

[7] See O. Cullmann, *The Christology of the New Testament* (1959), pp. 203ff.; R. H. Fuller, *The Foundations of New Testament Christology* (1965), pp. 184ff.; F. Hahn, *Christologische Hoheitstitel* (1966³), ch. 2.

[8] E. Fascher, 'Die Auferstehung Jesu und ihr Verhältnis zur urchristlichen Verkündigung', *ZNTW* 26 (1927), pp. 25f.

confessional formula tacked on. In the Fourth Gospel, the expression 'lifted up' (exalted) is applied to the Cross itself to denote that the death of Jesus was itself his journey to the Father, which brings about his separation from his disciples but which is also his preparation of a place for them and his return to them through the Paraclete (John 7.33ff.; 8.21; 12.32; 14.3f.). For this exaltation a synonym is glorification, i.e. a removal into the divine sphere and life (John 7.39; 12.16; 13.31, etc.; cf. Isa. 52.13), and both exaltation and glorification are predicted of the Son of man (John 3.14; 8.28; 12.23–12.34; 13.31; cf. 6.62, 'ascending where he was before'). This, no doubt, is all Johannine theology rather than the preservation of any primitive conception, but it may be that these were always more appropriate expressions for the Son of man, and that the prophecies of the Son of man's resurrection in the synoptic tradition are accommodations to a settled belief in terms of death-resurrection (Mark 8.31; 9.31; 10.34 par.; contrast Mark 8.38; 13.26, 'his glory', and 14.62 = Luke 22.69, his heavenly exaltation). The same accent is evident in Hebrews, where the theology is, with the exception of the finale in 13.20f., entirely in terms of Jesus' exaltation (1.3f., 13; 2.5–10 – the Son of man, 5. 5), and also in Revelation (3.21); even in Luke the kerygma can be represented as the necessary suffering of the Christ and his entry into his glory (24.26; cf. I Peter 1.11). Bertram considers that in Matt. 27.52f., the words 'after his resurrection' are an adaptation to a later standpoint, and that the legend originally meant that the death of Jesus itself released the pious dead from Hades, and that this could only be so if his death and exaltation went together. In this connection may also belong other possible expressions of an immediate transition to a heavenly sphere such as Mark 14.25, 62, and Luke 23.43.

E. Schweizer has called attention to the part played in Judaism by the theme humiliation/exaltation, and sees it as to a great extent determining the church's early understanding of Christ. In Judaism the humiliation could take various forms, including suffering and death, and the exaltation could be represented as a transfiguration, an ascension or assumption into heaven, or as being taken by the angels at death, but not, apparently, as resurrection, though in the Wisdom of Solomon it is represented as the gift of immortality. In this connection

Schweizer comments, 'that the exaltation really dominated the thought of the early Church is also shown by the fact that the oldest tradition barely distinguishes between Easter and Ascension . . . in the Gospel according to St Matthew the risen Christ appears to his disciples as the One to whom all authority in heaven and on earth has already been given (Matt. 28.18). Also according to John (John 20.17), the ascension takes place on Easter morning before the appearances. It may well be asked if the reports of the first appearances (I Cor. 15.5f.) have been lost because they told of Jesus' exaltation to God and on account of that were not sufficiently realistic in the eyes of a later generation. At any rate, this would explain that Paul places his appearance on the road to Damascus entirely on the same level as the appareances to the twelve . . . The view that the event of Easter was the appointment to heavenly glory can still be traced behind the Synoptic tradition of the resurrection. This is the case especially with the Son of man tradition.'[9]

This is important, since all statements of exaltation (except Luke's account of a visible ascension), like all doxological statements, are necessarily figurative, as is Paul's statement that he had 'seen Jesus our Lord', if this seeing at all corresponded with the visionary experience of light and voice in the Acts accounts of the Damascus road. On the other hand, there is no attempt in the gospel resurrection narratives to depict Jesus as the Lord in a body of glory – he does not appear as the Lord but only speaks as the Lord – and they are not of such a kind as to suggest lordship either as a corollary of resurrection or as its furthest theological extension. A. M. Ramsey[10] poses the question, 'Upon what event or series of events did the doctrine of his exaltation rest, and what was its relation to those events?' After examining the texts and the language involved his conclusion, based chiefly on John's gospel but also more tentatively on those of Mark and Matthew, is that the account of the Ascension in Acts 1 does not stand alone as 'evidence that the disciples saw an appearance which brought home to them not only the Resurrection but also the glorious heavenly status of their Master'. He sees the relevant passages in the epistles and Acts

[9] E. Schweizer, *Lordship and Discipleship* (1960), pp. 38ff.
[10] A. M. Ramsey, 'What was the Ascension?', in M. C. Perry (ed.), *Historicity and Chronology in the New Testament*, Theological Collections 6 (1965), p. 135.

as giving no 'clear testimony to a belief that there had been an event of ascension distinct in time from the event of resurrection', but as giving testimony to 'the belief of the Church in a concept or θεολογούμενον expressed in the imagery of exaltation'.[11] The two images of resurrection and exaltation represent, he thinks, two distinct truths, and reference is made to H. Sasse's essay in *Mysterium Christi*, where it is said to be 'of profound significance that the New Testament distinguishes the resurrection and exaltation of Christ. . . His "Lordship" would be inconceivable apart from the resurrection, but it would not be accounted for by it alone.'[12] Nevertheless, the awkwardness of the combination of these two themes remains, and the attempt to derive from the gospels a resurrection appearance which brought home the truth not only of the resurrection but of the heavenly status of Jesus, other than the legendary narrative of Acts 1, is not very convincing. It may be too easily assumed that exaltation to share the authority of God in the last things was a corollary, or extension of resurrection, whereas what may have been prior as a theologumenon or concept was 'seeing Jesus our Lord' (*maran*) as the exalted and coming One, and resurrection a corollary or extension of that.

[11] *Op. cit.*, pp. 139f. It is difficult to follow B. M. Metzger, *Historical and Literary Studies*, p. 84, that 'the ascension of Jesus follows necessarily as part of the logic of his bodily resurrection. For, if Jesus rose from the dead not with a natural, but with a spiritual (or glorified) body – and this is undoubtedly the teaching of the New Testament – then it would appear to be inappropriate for him to remain permanently on earth.' The New Testament does not give the impression that during the period of resurrection appearances Jesus was 'on earth', or in some intermediate state between earth and heaven. The logic of 'he appeared' would seem to be that he made himself visible from the invisible heavenly sphere. And if he rose with a 'glorified' body, would he have to be further 'glorified' for the ascended state? Metzger quotes the judgment of W. A. Whitehouse that 'the final item in the life-story, the Ascension, does not add to the difficulty (of the bodily resurrection) . . . The intellectual difficulty about the physical facts entailed by His bodily resurrection and His appearances is not increased by this last withdrawal.' But there is surely a difference between the resurrection and the ascension. In the case of the former no description is given of the resurrection itself, which remains a hidden and mysterious act of God, and even the appearances are of such a kind that for the ancient as well as the modern mind there was not a complete identity between them and what they pointed to. In the case of the ascension, however, the actual heavenly glorification is itself depicted in physical terms ('as he went . . .' Acts 1.10), and there is an identity between physical fact and spiritual truth.

[12] H. Sasse, 'Jesus Christ the Lord', in G. K. A. Bell and A. Deissmann, (eds.), *Mysterium Christi* (1930), pp. 93ff.

If this is the case, then exaltation will have lent its weight to resurrection. For exaltation in respect of Christ is genuinely eschatological; being exaltation to the throne of Godhead it is final, in the sense that it is impossible to think beyond it. It is not temporary but permanent, and is to a rule without end. Resurrection, however, falls short of finality in so far as it is to a temporary state *en route* to the end. Yet New Testament writers clearly intend to portray the resurrection as itself eschatological; not as a further event, however extraordinary, but as the entry of the eschatologically new into the old, and as a sign of the end of the old. It is precisely this which involves them in difficulties, for how can such an event be described in historical and human terms? There is, for this reason, one respect in which the concept of resurrection proves superior to, and more creative than, the concept of exaltation. While the latter intends to proclaim the elevation to the position of ultimate authority not of some unknown X, but of the man Jesus – as when in Phil. 2 it is in virtue of his self-negation and obedience to death that God exalts him to lordship ('wherefore God highly exalted him'), so that his self-emptying and obedience are not simply qualifications for, but the substance of, his lordship – exaltation in itself could mean an extrication from this world into the other world, and it inevitably directs attention upwards and forwards, either to Christ's permanent state, as in the Epistle to the Hebrews, or to his parousia after a brief interval, as in Revelation.

Resurrection, on the other hand, as the more concrete and cruder term, directs attention not only forwards but backwards also. As reversal and resuscitation it is the recovery intact from death of this particular man, and of what made him the particular man he was. Like Janus, it looks both ways, and in opening into what is new brings with it that which is old and otherwise past. The historical past is not discarded as a snake sloughs off its skin, but is recovered. The showing by the Lord of his hands and side (feet) has been taken as a symbolic expression of this truth, and led to the comment of Scott Holland that at the resurrection it was not only Jesus who rose, but his whole life with him. It is perhaps involved in any concept of bodily resurrection, whatever particular meaning may be given to the word 'body'. It was this sense of the recovery of the past as the raw material of the eschatological future which led to the repetition and transmission in tradition of the words and deeds of Jesus, and eventually to the writing of the gospels, in their present form of accounts of his earthly ministry, as accessories to belief in the risen Lord. For gnostics, who must reject a genuinely earthly redeemer and his resurrection, a gospel could begin only the other side of his exaltation or extrication from the material world, and did indeed often take the form of the impartation of private esoteric truths by a purely other-worldly figure, who is raised for this purpose.

It is here, however, that a second difficulty appears. Did the resurrection create the lordship and messiahship of Jesus, or simply establish from God what was already there?

This question, of course, lies at the heart of New Testament studies, and is probably in the end unanswerable. For once it is granted that the gospels have been written, and their material previously moulded, in the light of the post-Easter faith, it becomes very difficult to dissect with any certainty what is pre-Easter from what is post-Easter, especially with relation to the central point of the person of Jesus. That Jesus did not refer to himself as the Lord of his disciples or of a future Christian community is probable, and the use of 'the Lord' for him in the gospels, which is largely confined to Luke, seems to be anachronistic. It is a title which came to belong particularly to the resurrection tradition (Luke 24.34; Acts 4.33, and its sudden appearance in John 20–21). The title Son of man, which seems to belong to the pre-Easter tradition in the synoptic gospels (the usage in John is different) and hardly at all outside (Acts 7.56), could on one interpretation come near to what 'Lord' means if the 'coming' of the Son of man means his coming before God for vindication (cf. its combination with sitting at the right hand of God in Mark 14.62), but the origin of this title, its locus in the tradition and its meaning are notoriously obscure problems, and its connection with resurrection is confined to the stereotyped statements in Mark 8.31; 9.31; 10.34 and Mark 9.11, which at least in their present form are probably later Christian formulations. If 'the Christ' (the Messiah) is to be strictly defined as a political figure, a son of David and king of Israel in the coming age who will conquer Israel's enemies and rule with an earthly rule, then resurrection cannot be held to have either confirmed or established the messiahship of Jesus, since he is not proclaimed as Messiah in this sense after or as a result of his resurrection. The problem therefore arises of the origins of the different conception or conceptions of messiahship involved in the application of this title to Jesus so as eventually to become his proper name. For if messiahship in its original sense was either claimed by or attributed to Jesus, and the resurrection was to be understood as divine vindication of what Jesus had been, then no new or 'Christianized' conception of messiahship could arise. That Jesus was himself responsible for a Christianizing of the concept which was to be vindicated by his resurrection has only a slender basis in the gospels. There is no statement which amounts to this, and there are few references to Messiah which do not reflect an already Christianized conception (e.g. Mark 9.41; Luke 24.26; 4.41). The confession elicited from Peter at Caesarea Philippi is, as it stands, a confession of messiahship upon which there is no comment. For the evangelist it is probably a statement of what he held to be true in the light of an already Christianized understanding of messiahship, though it was to be kept secret for the time being. Only by a critical dissection of the whole section Mark 8.27–9.1, which is undoubtedly a construction of the evangelist, can it be maintained that originally 'Get thee behind me Satan' was Jesus' reply to the affirmation 'Thou art the Christ' and so a repudiation of it.[13] The juxtaposition of this confession with the statement of the divinely ordained suffering of the Son of man and his resurrection may not have constituted for Mark the substitution of one conception for another, nor the modification of the one by the other, but the combination of two conceptions, both of which are true for him. Similarly, the reply to the question of the high priest whether he is the Christ, further defined as 'the Son of the Blessed One' (possibly in the sense of the king of Israel, since the king had been so designated), is according to Mark in the affirmative, and there is added that as a result of his being Messiah they will see the Son of man with kingly power and rule at the right hand of God and coming on the clouds of heaven. Here also is a juxtaposition which may amount to an assertion of two conceptions at the same time,

[13] So E. Dinkler, 'Petrusbekenntnis und Satanswort. Das Problem des Messianität Jesu', in E. Dinkler (ed.), *Zeit und Geschichte* (Bultmann Festschrift), pp. 127ff.

though of such a kind that messiahship supplies the basis of, and is defined as, a future rule and coming (especially if 'I am' is to be taken as a future in connection with 'You shall see'). Whether this juxtaposition goes back to Jesus himself is bound up with the difficult question of the authenticity of the trial scene, of which no disciple could have been an observer. It may already represent an interpretation in the church of what messiahship now meant, viz. the exaltation of Jesus as Lord and his coming as Lord. 'The interrogation before the Sanhedrin – it can hardly be called a trial in the strict sense of the word – appears to be one of the rare instances in which Mark felt compelled to fill in a gap in his knowledge by an implausible, theologically motivated invention.'[14]

On the other hand, the resurrection of a man would not as such constitute him the future King–Messiah or the coming Son of man, unless that man was somehow to be seen as an eschatological figure and his resurrection therefore as the beginning of the end events, nor could the resurrection of one who had claimed to be the future King–Messiah and the coming one of itself establish his claim, since at best resurrection would be only a preparation for the exercise of such an office. Resurrection is, after all, concerned with death and with whatever is signified by death. Hence F. Hahn[15] and others see the origin of the Christianizing of the concept of Messiah in the historical fact that Jesus was put to death on the charge of being 'the king of the Jews', i.e. as a messianic pretender. This was the original connotation of his death before it was further interpreted as being 'for our sins', and the resurrection both reversed the action of men in putting him to death and was divine confirmation of the truth of his kingship. The Messiah thus becomes a Christian Messiah, i.e. a suffering Messiah vindicated by resurrection.

It is this point that Paul takes up, and it is for him and for others the starting point (I Cor. 15.3ff.). It is not easy to decide how often in the more than two hundred instances in which Paul uses the word 'Christ' without the article it is or is not any more than a surname for Jesus, but in view of the pregnant phrases 'in Christ', 'with Christ', etc., it is probable that in most cases there is a theological significance. According to G.

[14] R. P. Casey, 'The Earliest Christologies', *JTS NS* ix (1958), p. 256.
[15] F. Hahn, *Christologische Hoheitstitel*, pp. 195ff.

Bornkamm,[16] it is at times a proper name, but for the most part is used in a titular sense, almost always in kerygmatic expressions, where it concerns the death and resurrection of Christ in the plan of salvation. The messiahship which Paul had once rejected and which he embraced at his conversion, had, so far as we can see from his letters (and this probably means also for his converts), nothing to do with a messianic earthly humanity of Jesus but only with a messiahship grounded in his death and resurrection, and although Paul both inherited, and added to, interpretations of the death of Jesus in relation to sin, suffering, etc., there is still probably to be seen beneath his argument in Gal. 3.13f. and his application to the Cross of Deut. 21.23, 'Cursed be he that hangs on a tree', the sense that historically the Cross was the excommunication by Israel of one accused of leading Israel astray. Only at a later stage is the earthly life of Jesus seen and presented as the earthly life of the (Christianized) Christ, which is interrupted by death and certified by resurrection. In this sense the gospels are accounts 'not of an historical Jesus but of an historical Christ'.[17]

J. A. T. Robinson has suggested[18] that there is to be found embedded in the speech of Peter in Acts 3 the most primitive christology of all – that of Jesus as the prophet and servant who through death and resurrection became the future Messiah-to-be – 'that he may send the Christ appointed for you, Jesus' (Acts 3.20). This cannot, of course, be what was intended by the author of Acts himself, for whom Jesus had been the Christ already in his earthly life (Luke 2.11, 26; 4.41; 9.20; 24.26, 46), and Robinson has to suppose a somewhat wooden procedure on Luke's part by which he adds the words of 3.18, 'But what God foretold by the mouth of all the prophets, that his Christ should suffer, he thus fulfilled', to an already existing speech in order to bring it into line with his own christology. But it is unlikely that the removal of these words leaves us with an already existing speech untouched by Luke, for the words of 3.21, 'whom heaven must receive until the time for establishing

16 G. Bornkamm, 'Baptism and New Life in Paul', *Early Christian Experience* (1969), p. 76.
17 E. Heitsch, 'Jesus aus Nazareth als Christus', in H. Ristow and K. Matthiae (eds.), *Der historische Jesus and der kerygmatische Christus* (1961), p. 78.
18 J. A. T. Robinson, 'The Most Primitive Christology of All?', *Twelve New Testament Studies* (1962), pp. 139ff.

all that God spoke by the mouth of his holy prophets from of old', are also probably due to Luke and refer back to his previous narrative of the ascension with its promise of a return (the phrase 'establishment of all things', like 'times of refreshing' in 3.20, is a literary phrase which is probably to be assigned to Luke's hand). Moreover, the crucial expression 'the Christ appointed for you' may well itself be due to Luke, since the word 'appointed' occurs only twice again in the New Testament (Acts 22.14; 26.16), and the concepts of divine appointment, foreordination and prevenience are especially characteristic of Luke's theology (cf. Acts 2.22; 17.31), the language which goes with them being common in his writing. Rather, the speech may be explained as falling into two parts. The first part, 3.12–16, follows the usual pattern of the glorification (cf. Luke 24.26) of Jesus the servant, the holy and righteous one, by resurrection, in virtue of which his name is powerful for healing. The second part, 3.17–26, is a special appeal to Israel in the light of this, in accordance with a pronounced tendency in Acts towards this kind of appeal. To them Jesus had been sent first in blessing (v. 26) and their negation of him is excused as due to ignorance, but of this they are to repent, so as to make way for God's blessing and to be ready to receive him the second time; they will thus be of the true Israel still, and will be found among those who listen to the prophet like Moses whom God promises (vv. 22ff.), and among the sons of the prophets who spoke of these days and of the covenant of God with Abraham. This doctrine of a double manifestation of Jesus as the Christ to Israel would appear to be among the least primitive of the christologies and one which was evolved from the exigencies of the continued appeal which is made to Israel in Acts.

Was the resurrection creative, or was it simply probative? The impression left by the gospels as they now stand is that it was the latter; it proved what was already there. In them Jesus claims messiahship, instructs on the divine necessity of his death, and acts and speaks as one who is in full knowledge of his certain vindication either by resurrection or exaltation. The resurrection sets the seal on all this. The gospels, however, are christological works written out of faith in the risen Lord, and they are able to maintain their picture only by a measure of artificiality, either by stressing the complete failure of the disciples to understand what they had heard so constantly and clearly repeated, or by injunctions given to them to be silent about what they had seen and heard. A critical examination of the gospels and of their sources would suggest that the christological element has been considerably increased in them, and that when later interpretation has been allowed for, we are uncertain how Jesus thought of himself in relation to messiahship and lordship, and how he conceived of his own future. Moreover, in certain expressions of Christian faith the resurrection is given a more creative role. This is the natural interpretation of Peter's Pentecost speech, with its argumentation by way of resurrection and subsequent exaltation to its climax: 'Lord and Messiah has God made him, this Jesus whom ye crucified', as also of his speech in Acts 3.13ff., with its climax in the expectation that God 'may send the Christ who hath been appointed for you, even Jesus: whom the heaven must receive until the times of the restoration of all things'. It may also be reflected in the kerygmatic statement, possibly pre-Pauline, with which the Epistle to the Romans opens: 'concerning his Son, who was born of the seed of David according to the flesh, who was declared to be the Son of God with power, according to the spirit of holiness, by the resurrection of the dead'. If this is so, then attention is focused even more fiercely on the resurrection, for whatever it may have been as an event it is now seen to be the *fons et origo* of Christian faith in the lordship of Jesus. However little we may be able, from the nature of our sources, to reconstruct what happened at the resurrection, it must be presupposed to be of such a kind as to impart to the earthly ministry and death of Jesus the eschatological import which was deemed proper to them. It made both him and his work new. How far, and in what way, he may himself have contemplated this it is hardly possible to say, since our sources seldom, if ever, ascribe faith to him, but only certain knowledge in advance.

But lordship and messiahship are in Christian thought unintelligible apart from those to whom Jesus is Lord and Messiah. The word κύριος (lord) is inseparable from its correlative δοῦλος (slave), and appears to have begun its life in the Christian church not as 'the Lord', but as 'our Lord' ('*maran*', I Cor. 16.22). Messiah also, though it begins as God's Messiah or anointed one, is inseparable from its correlative Israel – this is the force of the statement, 'let the whole house of Israel, therefore, know assuredly that God made him both Lord and Christ' (Acts 2.36). If, then, resurrection is the principal source of faith in the lordship and messiahship of Jesus, it follows that resurrection is also the source of the existence of the church, and its knowledge of itself as the community of the risen Lord and Messiah, the community of the last days. Again, this refers both backwards and forwards. It refers backwards particularly in being resurrection rather than exaltation, for while exaltation speaks of the elevation of Jesus out of this world to heavenly and universal status, resurrection, as the resurrection of the man Jesus, speaks of the climax and fulfilment of the intention of his earthly mission. If in the life, work and death of Jesus is to be seen the most complete form of God's coming to men, of his presence with them, and of his embracing his own created world, then in the resurrection of Jesus at God's hands, as resurrection in this world and not out of it or beyond it, is to be seen the continuation and climax of the movement of God towards men and of his union with them. Of this truth the empty tomb is a powerful symbol, as is the fact that the appearances recorded are confined to those who had previously been disciples – 'not to all the people, but unto witnesses that were chosen before of God, even to us, who did eat and drink with him after he rose from the dead' is how Luke can express it (Acts 10.41) – and whose discipleship was re-established and freshly minted after temporary unbelief. That Jesus appears only to disciples has often, and not unnaturally been accounted a suspicious factor in the tradition, but is it necessarily so? On the contrary, the most untrustworthy and legendary elements in the tradition are precisely those, for example in Matthew, which would make the resurrection a terrifying visible portent compelling the acknowledgement of all, irrespective of whether they have had any previous relation to Jesus or faith in the living God. For all that it is thought of as a reversal of the action of men the resurrection is not, apparently, in the New Testament to be regarded as designed to confute publicly the enemies of Jesus, or to restore a visible kingdom to Israel. It is domestic to the church, and subsequent to the crucifixion nothing happens so far as the world is concerned and in the face of the world until Pentecost, with the emergence of a spirit-filled church, of which the world is forced to take cognizance that they are filled with new wine. God's dealings with and movement towards the world is indirect and by way of his direct dealings with and movement towards Jesus and his disciples. From this point of view the resurrection body of Jesus is simply the church.

This aspect of the church as the immediate and primary reality of the resurrection has been particularly explored by John Knox in his writings,[19] and full value must be given to it alongside the lordship of Christ. Indeed, the two belong inseparably together if the origin of the conception of Jesus as the Lord is to be seen in a prior conviction of the Christian community that he is its or 'our' Lord.[20] It is probably to be seen as lying somewhere behind the Pauline designation of the church as the body of Christ, and as the continuing presence of Christ in the world until the parousia.[21] This aspect may also lie behind what appears to be the one common element of the gospel resurrection narratives, the missionary command and commission of the risen Lord to his disciples. The resurrection of Jesus is his effective presence now with believers and the continuance in some form in this world of what he had been. He is risen in the world and not out of it. It is true that the gospels, including in the end the Fourth Gospel, differ from gnostic gospels, in which the post-resurrection period exhibits a spiritual Christ liberated from the natural world and delivering to his hearers for the first time the hitherto secret doctrines of the spiritual world as the essence of the gospel. It is true also that the resurrection is responsible for that characteristic of Christianity which has been called 'the scandal of particularity', since it predicates of a particular historical event a kind of continuity and permanence which otherwise history does not know. In the gospels, however, this continuity of Christ in the church, and the reference

[19] Especially John Knox, *The Church and the Reality of Christ* (1963); cf. G. Koch, *op. cit.*, pp. 241, 335.

[20] See John Knox, *op. cit.*, p. 92, and the literature there cited.

[21] Though the central contention of J. A. T. Robinson's book *The Body* (1952), that the body of Christ in Paul actually means the resurrection body of Christ, which is always to be thought of as a corporate entity, and that there is no distinction between the two, seems hardly tenable. It involves strained exegesis of passages in I Cor. 15; II Cor. 5 and Phil. 3 in order to get a corporate rather than an individual sense out of them, while the words 'Saul, Saul, why persecutest thou me?', to which Augustine appealed as suggesting the identity of Christ and Christians, come from Acts, and cannot be taken as primary evidence of Paul's thinking, if evidence at all. See the critique of D. E. H. Whiteley, *The Theology of St Paul* (1964), pp. 193ff.

back to him of its experience, which was eventually to be responsible for the writing of the gospels themselves, has taken concrete forms. The 'reading back' of a church's experience into the resurrection narratives, and the differences in those narratives themselves, to some extent reflect different evaluations of what elements in Christian experience were central and were to be seen as evidence of Christ's continuing and effective presence. Thus in Matthew it is baptism and the recapitulation of all Christ's commandments as the substance of Christian catechetical instruction; in Luke it is the dynamic operation of the Spirit in the missionary church and the interpretation of the gospel by reference to the Old Testament; in John it is the Spirit as the interpreter of Christ's mind, the forgiveness of sins and the inauguration of the new creation. The Lukan construction is the most definite, for there the most concrete sign of the effective presence of the risen Lord is the apostolate, which in a sense is essential to and creative of the church. The chief accent of the sermons in Acts, with the exception of Stephen's which is not apostolic, is on the resurrection; and the witness the apostles give (Luke 24.48; Acts 1.8) is particularly concentrated in a witness to the resurrection (Acts 2.32; 3.15; 5.32; 10.40f.), so that at this point even Paul, in contrast to his own words in I Cor. 15.11, is made dependent on their witness (Acts 13.31). Membership of the twelve, which for Luke is identified with apostleship (Luke 6.13f.; Acts 1.2, 13) is especially for witness to the resurrection, and is limited to those who have acquaintance with the history of Jesus from John's baptism onwards (Acts 1.21–26). Their function in Acts is as much to witness to Jesus' past by witnessing to the resurrection which ratifies it as it is to be missionaries of the gospel. This very precise theory of apostleship, which makes out of the twelve as co-judges with Christ of Israel (Matt. 19.28 = Luke 22.30) the guarantors of the history of Jesus, was to be of immense importance, particularly when it led to the idea of an apostolic tradition and to the creation of a canonical New Testament which was (falsely) believed to be apostolic through and through. Its connection with the resurrection, whereby the resurrection is the renewal and extension by the risen Lord of an office and function which he had already established in the course of his earthly ministry, becomes evident only in Luke's two volumes, and may be a Lukan creation. But the questions of the nature of the apostolate and of the group of 'the twelve', of the connection between them, and of their origins, whether in the actions and life of Jesus or in the post-Easter church, are wide open questions, and on the evidence available they are very difficult to answer.[22] In begetting the church, the resurrection also points forwards, since the church is the body of Christ in the world and towards the world. That the church's mission is to the whole world was a conviction arrived at only later and by degrees, and that it was read back into the resurrection narratives is highly probable.

Nevertheless, it has to be explained why the church did not develop into a sect within or outside Judaism like the Qumran sect, in this case a Jewish sect with resurrection leanings. From the somewhat meagre evidence available we may perhaps conclude that with the apprehension through the resurrection of Jesus as Israel's Messiah, the church was conscious of itself as being not a pious or reformist group, but the Messiah's people, and therefore the true Israel, with an urgent mission to the rest of Israel, and ultimately, since this was Israel's vocation, with a mission to the world. This, at least, may be the significance of the story of the election of Matthias to be witness of the resurrection and to make up the number of the twelve, if the twelve are to be seen as a standing symbol of the direction of the mission of Jesus to Israel. The whole question, however, is a signal illustration of how fugitive the gospel material can be at decisive points, since whether Jesus contemplated a church at all is, on the evidence available, a much disputed question. There is one text which could be of decisive importance, but which proves to be more than ordinarily elusive. According to Mark, who is followed with some variations by Matthew, the first charge brought against Jesus at his trial was that he had been heard to declare 'I will destroy this temple that is made with hands, and in three days I will build another made without hands' (Mark 14.58), and the words are thrown as a taunt at Jesus on the cross by passers-by (Mark 15.29). Luke omits the charge, only to substitute something like it – 'we have heard him say, that this Jesus of Nazareth shall destroy this place' (Acts 6.14) – as the charge against Stephen, whose martyrdom is for Luke the historical occasion of the beginning of the break between the church and Israel. John, in the special place he assigns to the cleansing of the Temple at the beginning of his gospel, has a variant version, 'Destroy this temple, and in three days I will raise it up' (John 2.19), which he proceeds to interpret of the temple of Christ's body, which in this gospel, speaking as it does on more levels than one, could be the resurrection body of Christ, or the church, or both.

If Jesus did say something of this kind, then in view of the unique place in Jewish religion of the Temple as the special abode of the divine presence, it is difficult to imagine a more revolutionary statement, and it could provide an important clue to what Jesus envisaged as the outcome of his mission to Israel. Was it to be the reconstitution of God's people at the central point of its attachment to God and of God to it (the Temple), of which he was to be the agent ('I will build'), which was to be eschatological (or whatever is implied in 'made without hands'), and which in the phrase 'three days' was connected with the resurrection?[23] Did some such saying work underground until it came to the surface with Stephen, and did it lie behind the various expressions in the New Testament of the church as the temple of God, the abode of the Holy Spirit, and of Christians as the several stones in a building held together by the corner-stone which had been rejected by Israel (Mark 12.10f.; Acts 4.11f.; I Peter 2.4ff.; I Cor. 3.9, 16; Eph. 2.19ff.)? We cannot know the answer, because we do not know what the original saying may have been, in view both of the variant versions we now have of it, and of the

[23] See esp. R. J. McKelvey, *The New Temple* (1969), chs. I–III; cf. also W. G. Kümmel, *Promise and Fulfilment* (1957), p. 101: 'That this saying can be understood only in a strictly eschatological sense as a prediction of the messianic temple is incontestable in view of the Old Testament and Jewish hope of the building of a new temple in the messianic age'. It is frequently difficult to decide whether the passages in the Apocrypha and Pseudepigrapha which express this hope refer to a temple in heaven, or one which is to descend from heaven to earth. McKelvey draws attention (pp. 46ff.) to the Qumran Scrolls as evidence for a Jewish interpretation of the temple to mean the community. Kümmel thinks that it can hardly be decided whether the new building in the saying of Jesus 'is thought only to be the coming upon the scene of the messianic community, or to be the rise of a heavenly temple as well'.

fact that Mark, in recording his version, reports it as the statement of witnesses who were false, and whose assertions in any
case did not tally.

However it may have come about, the emergence of the church
from the resurrection was responsible for a certain fragmentation
in Christian thought, and for a fresh orientation which was to
prove very fruitful. In Jewish thinking, resurrection, the judgment and the final consummation came to belong inseparably
together as a single divine action towards men. In Christian
thinking, while still belonging closely together, they could also
be thought of as distinct, and each could to some extent go its own
way and produce its own effects. All are eschatological, for resurrection, especially in combination with such concepts as
Messiah and kingdom, is the beginning of the new final creation
of the world, and exaltation is to universal lordship and to the
position of judge at the last judgment, while the Spirit, as forming
and informing the church, is the gift of the last days and the
pledge of what is to come. Hence the church as the body of Christ
is not simply his prolongation or continuity in history, nor is its
relation to him solely that of effects to cause on the historical
plane, as for example in the relation of Platonism to Plato or of the
subsequent history of France to Napoleon. As the body of Christ
in and to the world, it is the reminder to itself and to the world
that all history stands under the judgment and lordship of the man
Jesus, and in looking forward its message does not consist just
in the repetition of his words, but arises from the new situation
created by his resurrection. The various elements can also be
found in various combinations. Thus to be risen with Christ is
also to sit with him in the heavenly places (Col. 3.1; Eph. 2.6); the
church is his body, but he is Lord over it (Eph. 1.22; Col. 1.18);
the saints stand under his judgment but will assist him in the
judgment (II Cor. 5.10; I Cor. 6.3); the Spirit which informs the
church is the Spirit of him who raised Jesus from the dead
(Rom. 8.2–11); the Cross is already the exaltation of Christ and
his judgment of the world (John 12.23–32); with the advent of
the Spirit the parousia of Christ has in some sense taken place
(John 14.16–20), and so on. Since, however, they are not all
necessarily contemporaneous they can be thought of as distinct,
if not in isolation, and each has its own special truth to convey.
Resurrection, along with the doctrine of the Spirit, moves more

and more into the centre of Christian faith, and imparts to it a special quality. This can be observed in the Pauline epistles.[24]

Paul's contribution to the New Testament doctrine of resurrection would appear to lie along two distinct lines.

(a) The first is formal and dogmatic, involving a fixed eschatological schema, though this is modified according to circumstances. Paul sharpens the eschatological element. This would seem to be in part due to the way he views himself as an eschatological figure and his mission to the Gentiles as a now unique and integral part of an eschatological programme. To judge from such passages as Gal. 1–2 and Rom. 11.15ff., Paul envisaged the Christian mission, divided into a mission to Israel under Peter and his companions and a mission to all that was not Israel under himself and his own companions, as the immediate gathering of the elect which is the prelude to the parousia. His own part in this had been thrown into relief by his being imparted the divine secret of the reversal of what would have been the normal procedure. Whereas the conversion of Israel should have preceded and led to the conversion of the Gentiles, the gospel of the cross and resurrection was paradoxically to secure first the fulness or representative sum of the Gentiles, which was preceding, and would lead to, the conversion of Israel. This eschatological perspective would be further heightened if II Thessalonians were Pauline, and if the exegesis of II Thess. 2.6f., found in some of the fathers and revived by O. Cullmann, were correct, whereby 'he who holds back' and 'that which holds back' the final manifestation of evil and the appearance of the Antichrist figure, the man of lawlessness whom Christ will slay at his parousia, refers to the apostle himself and the gospel he preaches. In more than one passage, Paul states his ultimate object as being the presentation of his churches to Christ (presumably at the judgment), and it is this primary intention rather than simply pastoral care in the ordinary sense which involves him in writing letters at all, and

---

[24] An outstanding study of the complex question of Paul's resurrection belief and its development is D. M. Stanley, *Christ's Resurrection in Pauline Soteriology* (1961), from which the expression 'along the axis of the parousia' is taken. His earlier dating of Philippians, which makes a development more easily traceable, is disputable.

which gives his letters their particular tone.[25] In this context resurrection doctrine will be largely that of the second type referred to in ch. I. It will lack depth because it will be concerned with resurrection as one element in an eschatological schema, viz. the means of being present at the final *rendezvous*.

This is the position in I Thessalonians, where the problem (4.13ff.) is how Christians who have died can take part in the reunion of the Lord with his elect, and the resurrection of Jesus is simply appealed to as a guarantee that the same God as raised Jesus will bring along with Jesus those who have died 'through Jesus' (perhaps an expression for 'the Christian dead'). These will thus not be left out as hopeless, but will be raised first in order to be able to join those still alive at the parousia in a reunion with the Lord and a permanent existence with him beyond the judgment and the divine wrath, from both of which they had already been delivered (1.10). The expression 'for a meeting with the Lord in the air' is a remarkable one for the parousia. Both in the word 'meeting', which could be a technical Hellenistic term for the public ceremony of welcoming royal personages, and in the expression 'in the air' used of a region of elements and spirits between earth and heaven, it may reflect Greek rather than Hebrew ideas. Whether the elect when reunited proceed from 'the air' to heaven or to earth is not apparent, but it is probably intended that together they exercise the judgment (cf. I Cor. 6.2f.). The perspective is not essentially different in I Cor. 15. The situation in the Corinthian church which led to the resurrection being one of the subjects to be treated in I Corinthians is obscure and much debated.[26] Some, at least, of the Corinthian Christians were maintaining that 'there is no resurrection of the dead' (15.12). This can hardly have been the Sadducaean position, as they could not have become Christians at all without accepting at least the resurrection of Christ, of which Paul begins by reminding them (15.1–4). It may be that they denied any future resurrection on the ground that they believed themselves to be in a resurrection

[25] J. Munck, *Paul and the Salvation of Mankind* (1959), p. 190, thinks that Paul considered the possibility of excommunicating the whole Corinthian church by separating it from Christ and consigning it to Satan.

[26] See the references to variant views in J. C. Hurd, *The Origin of I Corinthians* (1965), pp. 91, 195ff.

existence already (cf. II Tim. 2.18), and if so, this belief could have had one of two possible origins, in each case traceable to Paul himself. It could either have stemmed from the conviction, for which there is evidence elsewhere in I Corinthians, that the believer was already living 'proleptically in the kingdom',[27] with all the spiritual freedom which that implied,[28] or it could have been a survival of a previously held conviction that the parousia was so imminent as not to require any resurrection to enter the kingdom. Profound as the exposition of the resurrection body in I Cor. 15 proved to be for subsequent Christian generations in suggesting some form of 'somatic' and personal identity between the present and the future, it is in the chapter itself limited in its scope. The perspective is, as in I Thessalonians, the apocalyptic one of the last trumpet (15.52), and the possibility of some Christians having died before the parousia – indeed, it may be even more primitive if the correct reading in 15.51 is πάντες οὐ κοιμηθησόμεθα and is to be rendered 'all shall not sleep', sc. 'none of us shall die'. What is added as a secret revealed to Paul (15.51ff.), and against any idea of a reunion of the Lord in his glorious state with an elect in their present earthly condition (flesh and blood), is that all without exception are to be prepared for the parousia, the dead by resurrection to incorruption and the mortal living by transformation into immortality, and the certainty that this will take place immediately at the parousia (15.52). The manner of this change is suggested by appeal to various kinds of variation and mutation, including reference to a second Adam or heavenly man who is lifegiving spirit, and who is identified with Christ.

The perspective is substantially the same in Philippians, at any rate in the present form of that letter, and probably also even if 3.20f. and 4.5 belong to different letters. 'The Lord is near', i.e. for the parousia, and he is expected from heaven, but whereas the passive verbs in I Cor. 15 suggest that the author of the necessary transformation is God (cf. also 'God gives it a body', 15.38), here Christ himself as the future saviour is to carry out the transformation, into the likeness of his own body of glory, and by the exercise of his power to subdue all things to himself, by which in I Cor. 15.24f. also he subdues all the enemies of God,

[27] J. C. Hurd, *op. cit.*, p. 285.
[28] See W. Schmithals, *Die Gnosis in Korinth* (1965), esp. pp. 206ff.

including death. II Cor. 5.1–10 is more complex, and is difficult to interpret both in itself and in relation to the question whether Paul's outlook had altered to any great extent from that in I Cor. 15. The context is the special one of Paul's estimation of his present temporary sufferings in the light of future permanent glory. The concern is still primarily with the possibility of resurrection and of how it may come about – hence the conditional clauses in vv. 1, 3, and the expression of aspiration in v. 4. The parousia is not immediately in view, though it may be hinted at in a rather different manner in the concepts of 'being absent from the body', and of 'being present with the Lord'. Further, a qualification is introduced that the elect, who in I Thess. 1.10 have already been delivered from the wrath to come and in I Cor. 6.2f. are said to be destined to judge angels and the world, must themselves stand before the judgment seat of Christ. Here also there is no mention of an ultimate transformation of present existence at resurrection, but, as in I Cor. 15, of a 'putting on' or 'putting over'. What is put on or over, however, is surprisingly not clothing but 'a building from God', a 'heavenly house eternal in the heavens', and a 'dwelling place from heaven'. The interpretation of these remarkable mixed metaphors, not of the individual's clothing with a resurrection existence, but in a corporate sense as denoting the whole body of Christ, the church, in its glorified state[29] is not convincing. The word οἰκοδομή (building) might possibly be given such a sense on the ground that elsewhere in Paul it refers to the church and its 'edification' – though of the only two real parallels, I Cor. 3.9 means rather 'You (the Corinthian community) are of God's constructing', and Eph. 2.21 is dubiously Pauline. This corporate sense can hardly attach to οἰκία (house) and οἰκητήριον (dwelling place), for these are not said to be places where Christians dwell together, but something to be put on (a corporate sense could be present in the reference to 'being away from the body' and 'present with the Lord'). The words 'if our earthly tent house is demolished' (v. 1) can hardly refer to anything else than the death of the individual. That Paul was

[29] As by J. A. T. Robinson, *The Body*, pp. 76ff.; E. E. Ellis, *Paul and his Recent Interpreters* (1961), pp. 38ff. Similarly, 1 Cor. 15.35, 'with (not 'in') what body do they come?', must surely refer to the form in which the elect as individuals accompany the Lord as his attendants when he appears and is glorified in his saints (II Thess. 1.10).

thinking here in individual terms would also seem to be indicated by his somewhat surprising conclusion to the passage,
that each one is to appear before the judgment seat of Christ
to receive according to what he has done through the body.
The idea of heavenly clothing (though not of heavenly house),
prepared in advance for the elect, is found in apocalyptic writing
(1 Enoch 62.15; 108.12; 11 Enoch 22.8; Asc. Isa. 9.2; Rev. 3.4,
etc.). The nearest parallel to the heavenly body as a house
appears to be Iranian.[30] It is partly the fact that on its eschatological side, Paul, and the New Testament in general, stopped
short at a certain stage in Christian modification of the Jewish
eschatological drama, that made it possible, and almost
inevitable, for the vacuum to be filled later by the importation of
further apocalyptic elements, and for Christian eschatology first
to become elaborately schematized down the centuries, and
then, with the abandonment of much of the scheme and its
details, to arrive at its present chaotic condition.

(*b*) The second line of Paul's thought on resurrection is the
opposite of formal, and is thoroughly empirical and experiential.
This is not so much in relation to himself and to his own private
experience. As Marxsen observes,[31] when speaking of his own
conversion Paul does not refer specially to having seen Jesus as
the Risen One, and conversely, when speaking of the resurrection he does not refer to his own conversion experience.
The connection is rather with the Christian life as such as being
life in the spirit. For Paul, the hallmark of Christian experience
is that it is existence in the spirit of those who have received the
Spirit, i.e. the effective power and presence of God. How strong
this is in Paul can be seen from the fact that he bases his whole
appeal to the Galatians upon it. The starting-point of this appeal
is that they have received, and know that they have received,
the Spirit, and can be asked whether they received it as a result
of the performance of law or from the hearing of the gospel
with faith (Gal. 3.2); and they can be exhorted to return to life
in the spirit as those who have been begotten according to the
spirit (Gal. 4.29–5.25). Even in I Cor. 15.1–20, the primary

[30] So R. Reitzenstein, *Die hellenistichen Mysterienreligionen* (1910), p. 355; P.
Vielhauer, *Oikodome* (1939), pp. 107ff.
[31] W. Marxsen, 'The Resurrection of Jesus as a Historical and Theological
Problem' in C. F. D. Moule (ed.), *The Significance of the Message of the Resurrection for Faith in Jesus Christ*, p. 23.

appeal is not to the fact of Jesus' resurrection, but to the experience of the Corinthians; for them to rule out the possibility of resurrection is to deny the resurrection of Christ, and with it the effective working of the gospel as evidenced in their present faith and the forgiveness of their sins. Similarly, in II Cor. 3, the whole apostolic ministry of the new covenant is characterized as a permanent ministry of spirit, in contrast to the transitory ministry of law, and a progressive transformation into the likeness of the Lord's image is possible, because the Lord who brings it about is himself spirit, or effective divine power, and the communicator of it.

This life of spirit has three particular characteristics: (i) it is characterized by 'newness' (cf. Rom. 7.6, 'to serve in the newness of spirit') as opposed to the oldness of the letter (law), and something of what this newness consists in is indicated in the several statements about the Christian life in Rom. 8; (ii) the spirit imparts life and makes alive in contrast to both the letter (law) which kills and the flesh (natural life) which has the mind of death. The moral content of this life is righteousness, in contrast with the death worked by the law in only bringing unrighteousness to light and with the flesh's total absence of righteousness (Rom. 7.6ff.; II Cor. 3.6ff.; Rom. 8.6–11; Gal. 3.21); (iii) the spirit is called a 'first instalment' (ἀρραβών II Cor. 1.22; 5.5) and 'first-fruit' (ἀπαρχή Rom. 8.23), and by these technical terms from finance and the cultus is not meant that the present possession of spirit is a guarantee of further instalments of spirit, but that the present possession of spirit, which is all there is, is a foretaste and promise of something further, which is the full life of 'glory', an eschatological term which comes nearest to denoting the divine life itself (Rom. 8.21ff.; II Cor. 3.17f.; 5.5ff.). Since resurrection also spells for Paul newness, life and the promise of glory, it can for that reason be brought into close connection with this life of, and in, the spirit of which it is a proximate cause. This is so first of Christ himself, who is said, in a highly compressed statement (Rom. 1.4), to have been appointed or designated Son of God with effective power both as a result of resurrection and by a spirit of holiness, and through resurrection and exaltation he is able to perform the work of spirit in interceding (Rom. 8.34). But as the risen and exalted Lord, he does or will impart the resurrection life to believers, and in doing so imparts newness and righteousness, life and glory. Thus in certain passages the characteristics of life in the spirit are drawn together under the heading of resurrection. In Rom. 6.4ff., union with Christ's death in baptism carries with it that 'as Christ was raised through the glory of the Father so also we shall walk in newness of life', and shall be in the likeness of his resurrection and live with his resurrection existence to God. Dying to the law means belonging to the one who was raised from the dead and bearing fruit to God through the newness of spirit (Rom. 7.4ff.), and in Rom. 8.9–11 the Spirit of God, which is also the Spirit of Christ, dwells in the believer to produce life and righteousness. It is itself the Spirit of him who raised Jesus from the dead, and in virtue of this present indwelling of his Spirit God will quicken the mortal body in resurrection. In II Cor. 4.10ff., the apostolic ministry of the spirit and of progressive transformation into the divine glory described in ch. 3 is said to be a treasure contained in earthen vessels; it therefore issues in a constant experience of the death and life of Jesus, and the apostle's confidence in the midst of sufferings derives from the spirit of faith that 'he who raised Jesus from the dead will raise us up with Jesus', and those who 'live' live to him who for them died and was raised.

Paul nowhere brings these two lines of thought, the formal eschatological and the empirical experiential, into a systematic relationship. When he is arguing for the possibility of resurrection, as in I Thess. 4 or I Cor. 15, he makes little direct appeal to the Christian life of the spirit, and when he is talking of life in the spirit he does not expressly place it on an eschatological basis. Nevertheless the two at times overlap, and in some instances it is not certain which line he is pursuing. Thus the statement 'if any man is in Christ there is a new creation' could be taken, and is generally taken, to be a technical eschatological statement to the effect that for any to be 'in Christ' means that the new and final age of the world has begun. H. Schwantes[32] adduces, however, rabbinic parallels in which the expression 'new creation' is used in a non-technical and purely metaphorical sense with a number of possible nuances. Thus an unexpected deliverance from danger, or a fresh start in forgiveness, is called a new creation. He maintains that both in

[32] H. Schwantes, *Schöpfung und Endzeit* (1963), pp. 26ff.

Gal. 6.15 and II Cor. 5.17 (old things have passed away, new
things have come into being) the emphasis is not on κτίσις
(creation) but on καινή (new), and that Paul is arguing from the
experienced newness of the life in Christ. There is some overlap
in I Cor. 15, in that the possibility of a future resurrection body
lies in the certainty that as the believers have borne the image of
the earthly they will also bear the image of the eschatological
heavenly Adam, who is himself 'lifegiving spirit', and the
future 'body' is a spiritual one. The overlap is greatest in II
Cor. 5.1–10, and contributes somewhat to the difficulties of
that passage. Whereas Paul generally speaks of the resurrection
of the believer as future (unless Col. 3.1 is Pauline), there are
statements, especially about the pressure of distress, opposition
and suffering, where the boundary line between the future and
the present is crossed, and the resultant picture is blurred. Thus
it is not clear what is the relation between the present participa-
tion in Christ's resurrection and the future hoped–for resurrection when these are brought into conjunction in a single
sentence in Phil. 3.10f., or between the new man who is being
daily renewed at the expense of the old man's destruction and
the house-garment through which what is mortal is completely
swallowed up by life in a single passage, II Cor. 4.16–5.4.[33]

Paul's epistles are *ad hoc* letters, and what he says in them arises
from the several situations to which they are addressed. One of
the earliest situations appears to be that reflected in I Thessalonians, where the crisis for faith is the death of some Christians
before the parousia, and what is said about resurrection is determined by this problem. Paul reminds them that their conversion
had meant a turning from (dead) idols to be the slaves of a God who
is living and true, and to await his Son from heaven, whom he
raised from the dead, Jesus, their deliverer from the wrath of the
judgment (1.9f). Here the orientation is towards the future consummation. To be a Christian is to be waiting for the Lord's
coming from heaven as the deliverer in, as well as the judge at, the
coming judgment, his resurrection being a medium to that end.
The problem of the Christians who have died is solved along these

[33] I. Hermann, *Kyrios und Pneuma* (1961), pp. 61ff., stresses with reference
to the 'spiritual body' of I Cor. 15.44 that 'spirit' is an eschatological term,
and could itself describe the resurrection state, which is also eschatological.

lines. The problem is not that they are dead, but that being dead they may miss the reunion between the Lord and the living. It is answered by what Paul calls a 'word of the Lord'; there will be no essential difference between living and dead, for as Jesus died and rose, those who have died 'through' Jesus, as Christians, God will bring along with Jesus through resurrection to join the living (4.15ff.). Further, they are exhorted to the practice of virtue in the interim because God has not destined them for wrath, but for the final salvation 'through our Lord Jesus Christ, who died for us, that, whether we are alive or dead we may live along with him' (5.9f.). So long as resurrection was thought of, as here, almost entirely 'along the axis of the parousia' and as a phenomenon of the end, it could play only a limited part in Christian thinking, but even here there was promise of something further. In the statement 'that whether dead or alive we may live along with him' there is already a hint of resurrection as standing more in its own right; as not merely a means to a further end, but as a new and permanent form of existence characterized by the relationship expressed in the words 'with Christ'. The preposition 'with', especially as a prefix to the verb, marks for Paul the parallelism between the career of Christ and that of the Christian, who co-suffers, co-dies, is con-crucified and co-buried with Christ, is raised with him, lives with him, is conformed to him and made to sit with him, is co-heir, co-ruler and is con-glorified with him (Rom. 8.17; 6.1–9; Gal. 2.20; Col. 2.12; 3.1; Eph. 2.6; Phil. 3.10, 21 cf. from its own point of view of resurrection as escape from the temporal, Epistle to Rheginos, 45.19–28, 36–38). It is instructive to note that this parallelism breaks down precisely at the point of resurrection, so that at one time it can be said that the Christian has already risen with Christ (Col. 3.1) and at another that he will rise with him (Rom. 6.8). This is because in the case of Christ resurrection was followed immediately by exaltation, to be soon followed by parousia, while in the case of the Christian it is followed by continued life in this world. While the expectation of the parousia remained with Paul all his life, and so determined his thought on resurrection, the realization of what was involved in being here and now 'in Christ' or 'with Christ' served to unhook some of the links which tied resurrection to apocalyptic expectation, and to allow it to play a more creative role of its own.

This is evident in Philippians. The expectation of the end is still there. 'The Lord is at hand', he tells them (Phil. 4.5), and in warning them against the wordliness of their opponents he refers them to their citizenship in heaven whence they expect 'a Saviour, the Lord Jesus Christ, who shall fashion anew the body of our humiliation, that it may be conformed to the body of his glory, according to the working whereby he is able even to subject all things unto himself' (3.20f.). Here Christ is Lord and Saviour, not as in I Thessalonians because he delivers from the future wrath of judgment, but because he will in the future resurrection impart to them the same divine glory with which he has himself been clothed, and by which he subdues the universe. But this future resurrection is also a matter of present experience, so that in the same epistle, speaking of himself, he can say that his aim is 'to know Christ and the power of his resurrection and the fellowship of his sufferings, being conformed unto his death; if by any means I may attain unto the resurrection of the dead' (3.10f.). Here resurrection is being used in two ways in a single sentence; it is both what the apostle already experiences in close conjunction with Christ's suffering and death, and also that which he hopes to attain, and the first is now giving substance to the second. This transition is also evident in Galatians, though in more incidental statements. When he begins with 'Paul, an apostle (not from men, neither through man, but through Jesus Christ, and God the Father, who raised him from the dead) . . . grace and peace from God the Father, and our Lord Jesus Christ, who gave himself for our sins, that he might deliver us out of this present evil world' (Gal. 1.1ff.), he bases the divine origin of his apostleship on his understanding of Christ as one raised from the dead by God, and Christ is here presented as deliverer, not as in I Thessalonians from the coming wrath, nor as in Philippians from earthly to heavenly existence, but from the present evil of the world. When he goes on to speak of himself as con-crucified with Christ, and as having died to the law in order to live to God with a life which is not his own but the life of Christ in him (2.19f.), it is not resurrection in relation to parousia which is dominant, but resurrection in relation to death, resurrection as a means not to a further end but to a life which continues because it is life in and with Christ.[34]

[34] The relation of resurrection and parousia is inescapable in the New Testament, and especially in the Pauline epistles. It does not follow that this

The way thus becomes open for a consideration of resurrection itself as a mark of Christian life, and for its application to the basic issues of Christian truth. The notion of power is inseparable from the term, but as the power of Christ's resurrection in conjunction with his suffering and death, and as God's power through these things, it is related internally, and not simply formally, to the moral purposes of God in the gospel, and this in a variety of ways. Thus in II Corinthians, Paul finds in dying and rising with Christ the clue to the understanding of what has been happening to him, and the means of drawing from it the positive conclusion of complete confidence in God. He has been spiritually, and perhaps physically, as hard pressed as he believed it possible to be. 'The burden of it was too heavy for us to bear, so heavy that we even despaired of life. Indeed, we felt in our hearts that we had received a death-sentence. This was meant to teach us not to place reliance on ourselves, but on God who raises the dead' (II Cor. 1.8f.). In a passage which has been called the deepest and most directly practical in the epistles he analyses in a series of paradoxes the apostolic, and by implication the Christian, life as being 'hard-pressed on every side, we are never hemmed in, bewildered, we are never at our wits' end; hunted, we are never abandoned to our fate; struck down, we are not left to die. Wherever we go we carry death with us in our body, the death that Jesus died, that in this body also life may reveal itself, the life that Jesus lives. For continually, while still alive, we are being surrendered into the hands of death, for Jesus' sake, so that the life of Jesus also may be revealed in this mortal body of ours' (4.8ff.). Behind this analysis lies Christ himself, to whom Paul refers at the close of the epistle as the justification and source for the apostolic authority he wields – 'He died on the cross in weakness, but he lives by the

---

is a permanent aspect of the matter. The parousia expectation presupposed that the world and history were of a certain kind, and were to receive a certain kind of consummation. This was already eroded to some extent in the New Testament itself, and other conceptions of the consummation substituted e.g. in Ephesians. It has now irretrievably collapsed, along with the view of the world and history which goes with it, and it has again to be replaced by something else. Thus N. Clark (*op. cit.,* pp. 113ff.) is convincing when, in exploring the implications of the New Testament resurrection belief for modern preaching, he considers it in relation to the death of the individual (where the New Testament gives little help), or to the consummation of the natural order (where it offers some signposts), but not when he asserts that 'the unveiling of the resurrection awaits the parousia'.

power of God; and we who share in his weakness shall by the power of God live with him in your service' (13.4). Life through death and life in death is the secret both of Christ and of the apostle, and in this way God is apprehended as God. Further, since for Paul death was associated with sin in a way it cannot be for us, death and resurrection expose to view the ultimate issues of human life under God.[35]

Paul does not say that the death of Christ was brought about by sin, but that it was on account of sin and for the purpose of dealing with it (Rom. 8.3; 1 Cor. 15.3; II Cor. 5.21; Gal. 1.4). This it does because it is not a passive suffering but an active onslaught, which condemns sin in the flesh and puts it to death by dying to it. The resurrection which God confers is, then, not simply God's answer to it or reversal of it, but that which brings to light the inner moral quality of obedience and righteousness which was in it. This is expounded in Rom. 6, not directly with reference to Christ but to the Christian. Baptized into Christ the Christian is baptized into the Christ who died and was buried, and so dies and is buried with him. For Paul, the miracle of resurrection, which is far greater than any miracle such as the raising of Lazarus could be, is that it is the resurrection of him who dies to sin once and finally and is the destruction of sin. The death of the Christian with Christ is death to sin, a con-crucifixion of the old man and the destruction of the body of sin. But the resurrection life which Christ lives is life to God. At this point Paul hovers between the present and the future. He can refer in the course of the same paragraph both to the Christian's resurrection as future ('that like as Christ was raised from the dead through the glory of the Father, so we also may walk in newness of life. For if we have become united with him by the likeness of his death, we shall be also by the likeness of his resurrection . . . if we died with Christ, we believe that we shall also live with him'; Rom. 6.4–8), and to the Christian's resurrection as present ('Even so reckon ye also yourselves to be dead to sin, but alive unto God in Christ Jesus'; 6.11). It would be foolish to attempt to discriminate between death and resurrection in this complex of thought and to assign more importance to one

[35] For resurrection in relation to sin and its conquest, see N. Clarke, *op. cit.*, pp. 52ff. It remains a stubborn fact that this close inter-connection of sin and death is not an idea which modern man can share, and that the New Testament is bound to lose something of its force here.

than to the other, but in view of the long-standing tendency to stress the death of Christ in Paul's thought almost to the exclusion of everything else, it may be observed that in one respect resurrection is here more important.

The ultimate goal must always be life, and death is the way to it. The death which Christ died to sin once issues in a life which is lived permanently to God. In reference to the Christian this can become: 'For if, while we were enemies, we were reconciled to God through the death of his Son, much more being reconciled, shall we be saved by his life' (Rom. 5.10) or: 'Ye also were made dead to the law through the body of Christ; that ye should be joined to another, even to him who was raised from the dead, that we might bring forth fruit unto God' (Rom. 7.4). Here we have a glimpse of the interior quality which resurrection has now taken on. To be 'in Christ' is to be of the new creation, and this means to belong through death and resurrection to him who through death and resurrection lays claim to all men, dead or alive (II Cor. 5.14ff.; Rom. 14.7ff.). But Christ's resurrection is more than the vindication of him *ab extra* by God: it brings to light the quality of his death as a death to sin and as an act of supreme obedience and righteousness, in revealing his life as a life to God. To live with his life is to live to God. Paul can therefore see resurrection as underlying that justification by faith which is the only proper relationship between man and God. In Rom. 4 this is expounded over the figure of Abraham, who is the prototype of such a relationship, and who, in contrast to Adam, the parent of that life of all men in which they die, is the parent of all believing men. The faith in question here is not faith in general, but a specific trust in the God who is able and powerful to fulfil his purpose and his promises, in this case his purpose of blessing the whole world by way of Abraham and his promise that Abraham shall have the necessary child. What stands in the way, humanly speaking, is death, in the form of the deadness of Abraham's body and of Sarah's womb for the purposes of begetting a child. In this situation faith in God must take the form of faith in him as the one who raises the dead in imitation of his original act of creation and of calling the non-existent into existence (Rom. 4.16–21). Such faith, which is foreshadowed in Abraham at the very beginning of the Jewish religion, Paul sees as having sprung to life and as having been established at the heart of things in Christian faith. This is faith in 'him that raised Jesus our Lord from the dead, who was delivered up for our trespasses, and was raised for our justification' (4.23ff.). In so far as the two statements in the last clause are to be taken separately, justification is connected causally not with death but with resurrection, so that Paul can go on to call it 'justification of life' (5.18). In Rom. 8.1–18, deliverance from the law, sin and death, justification, righteousness, life, the possession of the Spirit and the sonship of God which goes with it, are all drawn together, and the pivot of the thought is the resurrection life already conveyed to mortals by the Spirit. ('Shall quicken' in v. 11 should probably be taken not as an eschatological future, but as a future possibility in this life; cf. 'you shall live' in v. 13.) We have too little evidence to be able to speak with any confidence of a gradual evolution of Paul's thought, but it is possible to see resurrection, from being primarily an adjunct of the end, become the centre of Christian life, indeed its starting-point, which is to govern what lies between beginning and end. So far from it being an adjunct of the end, the end is now read off from it, whether (as in I Cor. 15) as the final putting on of the spiritual body of the glorified heavenly man, who is both the eschatological Adam and a life-conferring spirit, or (as in II Cor. 5) as the clothing with a heavenly habitation and as the climax of a process of the wearing away of the old or outer man of this creation by the constant renewal of the new man in Christ. The word 'body' here means essentially 'person', and need not bind Christian hope to the particular anthropology which Paul and his contemporaries may have held. It secures the permanence after an eternal mode of whatever the person is, and is revealed to be, by life in Christ, and the way is left open for each generation to attempt a definition of what it is which constitutes the person.

It is thus of the essence of the Christian faith that within the temporal order a real beginning is possible which is new, and which is from God. Paul expressed this in terms of death and resurrection with Christ. There are two other forceful expressions of it in a somewhat different mode. The author of I Peter introduces all that he has to say about the Christian life by the praise of God for having given the believer a new birth to a living hope and to an imperishable inheritance by the resurrection of Jesus Christ from the dead (I Peter 1.3ff.). Rebirth is almost certainly a pagan conception, which is here drawn into the Christian vocabulary and baptized into Christian thought – baptized, indeed, in a special sense, if those are right who see a very close relationship between this epistle and initiation into the Christian life through baptism. The author of the Fourth Gospel opens his account of the public ministry of Jesus with the interview with Nicodemus. Its theme is the kingdom of God, which is mentioned only here in this gospel, and over against the statement of the law of the temporal order that a man cannot enter a second time into his mother's womb and be reborn it is insisted that to see or enter the kingdom of God there must be a birth which is both birth a second time and from above, a birth by spirit and into life, of which the Son of man, who alone spans heaven and earth, is cognizant, and of which he will be the instrument through his exaltation. At the outset of his gospel, the author insists that this veritable new beginning is the index of Christianity; in making the raising of Lazarus the climax of the public ministry he also indicates that Christianity reaches its most satisfactory definition as life from the dead. These insights, which close the New Testament, are heard again in St Augustine's word: 'In the natural order things rise into being and then die; in Christianity they die and rise into being', and in those of the modern poet: 'What we call the beginning is often the end, And to make an end is to make a beginning. The end is where we start.'

Appendix

THE RESURRECTION:
THEOLOGY AND HISTORY

PREOCCUPATION with the problem of historicity in the resurrection tradition is apparent in much of the best modern writing on the subject. This is hardly surprising, since the specifically modern debate over the relation between the historical and the non-historical, between fact and faith in Christianity (or, as it should probably be phrased, over the amount, place and character of the historical in it) comes to a head here. This is so both as regards the resurrection itself as a very special case of the relation between historical and non-historical, and also as regards the decisive role which belief in the risen Lord has played in shaping the Christian message as a whole and in preserving and shaping the gospel material as a whole. Here, as W. Marxsen observes, 'the discussion is specifically concerned with the relation of the historical to the theological and of the theological to the historical'.[1] Thus, in what is probably the best known study in English, A. M. Ramsey's *The Resurrection of Christ*, it is the theological chapters which stand out as the most convincing, those, namely, on resurrection as a scriptural theme, on the various theologies of the separate gospels, and on the resurrection and the church. The theological and spiritual significance of aspects of the resurrection is also the strength of the writings of Bishop Westcott which Ramsey commends, as also of H. A. Williams' penetrating little book *Jesus and the Resurrection* (1961[2]).

Similarly, the strength of Dr Künneth's *The Theology of the Resurrection*, which the author describes as 'an attempt to expound in a strictly systematic way the word of the resurrection of the Kyrios without curtailing what was proclaimed in the primitive

[1] 'The Resurrection of Jesus as a Historical and Theological Problem', *The Significance of the Message of the Resurrection*, p. 15.

church as the resurrection message', lies in its second and third parts, where the resurrection is expounded doctrinally in relation to christology and to the Christian understanding of the world and time, rather than in the first part, where the ground is being cleared for such an exposition. Here, indeed, he makes a number of important preliminary points, such as that in Christianity resurrection is the starting-point for thought and means 'the genuine life to which all other life bears a secondary relation',[2] and where he notes the ways in which the concept of resurrection both approximates to, and is distinct from, certain other concepts – the idea of life, immortality, myth, etc. – which have often accompanied it and been confused with it. On the other hand, the tradition in its details contributes little to this theological exposition, and Künneth is somewhat uncomfortable with it. Thus it is hardly a solution of the problems involved simply to insist that 'the thing is, to understand the ultimate concern of the resurrection witness, expressed as it was precisely also in plastic, concrete form, and to expound it theologically in the light of the concept of the primal miracle of the resurrection',[3] when that witness is inseparable from 'the abundance of concrete detailed statements in the tradition', which he admits are not all to be accepted uncritically. If 'what makes the witness of the resurrection different from other statements lies beyond the historic plane', it does not follow that 'there can be no more talk of the science of history threatening the truth of the resurrection event, if the latter is a revelational reality of an absolute character',[4] since the resurrection as known through its witness is not of an absolute character. This he admits when he differentiates between the reality of the resurrection as such and its 'appearance', as also between the immediate full revelation which the disciples still await and a fragmentary revealing in unveiled form which they received in the appearances. But in that case, it is not clear why it follows that 'the question of "how" the appearances took place is unanswerable, just as a detailed portrayal of the event remains out of the question'.[5] Indeed, the opposite would seem to be required by the further assertion that 'we must not diminish the difference between the primary testimony to the

---

[2] 'What real life is, is known for the first time on the ground of the resurrection of Jesus, in which is established the underivable primal reality of life', *op. cit.*, p. 75.

[3] *Op. cit.*, p. 85.   [4] *Op. cit.*, pp. 3of.   [5] *Op. cit.*, p. 87.

resurrection in the *"verbum visibile"* of the appearances, as the foundation of the original believing knowledge, and the subsequent secondary proclamation of the resurrection which presupposes that fundamental testimony . . . the chosen believers' special nearness to the revelation as eye-witnesses is the precondition of all later resurrection faith',[6] since the contribution of eye-witnesses would lie presumably in the possibility of a portrayal of events, and the question for 'believing knowledge' is not so much whether to believe but what it is which is to be believed. Again, it is not evident why the fact that the resurrection narratives are to be understood as confessional statements liberates us 'from the interminable theological dispute on the significance of the differences in the resurrection narratives',[7] since the question remains open how far these statements are a precipitate of faith. Is it not a romantic reconstruction that 'the interest of the primitive Church surely centred solely on handing on the witness of the apostles as unspoiled as possible, and most especially the witness to the resurrection of Jesus which was of such decisive importance. Here the very details of the account were of priceless worth, and invention by the Church contrary to the apostolic witness had no place among the Church's interests, nor could it have failed to be sharply contradicted by the apostles or their pupils'?[8] Here terms like 'the primitive Church', 'the witness of the apostles', 'the apostles or their pupils', need to be carefully scrutinized, and the statement as a whole would seem to have little relevance to the matter over which it is made, the tradition of the empty tomb, since here freedom of adaptation for theological purposes is on any showing at its greatest.

In a careful and sensitive study,[9] S. H. Hooke is also happiest in a theological treatment of the resurrection as a transaction between the Father and the Son, historically unverifiable and incapable of description, which is responsible for immense and unique consequences in the apprehension of the man Jesus of Nazareth in a new form of existence as the Lord; and it is the Johannine tradition with its symbolic character and the Pauline conception of the Lord as the life-giving spirit in a body of glory which belong with this apprehension rather than the Lukan picture, where the intention of identifying the Lord with Jesus has

[6] *Op. cit.*, p. 102. [7] *Op. cit.*, p. 105. [8] *Op. cit.*, p. 93.
[9] S. H. Hooke, *The Resurrection of Christ* (1967).

led to crudity. Of the Johannine account of the tomb he writes, 'We cannot tell whether the author thought he was writing history, or intended to present to faith a symbol of the victory of the Resurrection and the Life over the power of death.'[10] He observes that the weakness of theories of the resurrection appearances as 'visions' lies in the fact that what stands out in a vision and is remembered in detail is precisely what is seen, whereas for the most part no attempt is made to describe the form of the risen Lord, as is done, for example, in the visions in Revelation. 'The emphasis all lies not on *what* they saw, but on *whom* they saw. It was not an object of sense-perception that they 'saw', but a Person, a Presence that removed their fear, and flooded their consciousness with joy.'[11] Nevertheless, with due caution, he appeals to the visionary experience of the Transfiguration as providing something of a key to what he calls 'the misty borderland between what must seem a slender body of historical material capable of verification, and a realm whose reality lies beyond the criteria of historical criticism',[12] noting both the close connection made by Mark between the Transfiguration and the resurrection from the dead (Mark 9.9f.), and by Luke between the night of Jesus' glory there and the description of the resurrection as entry into glory (Luke 9.32; 24.26). By this he does not mean that the Transfiguration is to be taken, as by some, as a misplaced resurrection appearance, but that 'knowing that the right time had come to prepare the future witnesses of the resurrection, Jesus took the three disciples up the mountain. There, after praying, he exercised that control over his physical conditions which he possessed, always in complete surrender to the Father's will, and allowed himself to be seen by the disciples in a condition which could only be described as "glory".'[13] In this way, they were themselves subject to a metamorphosis of perception which prepared them to be witnesses of what was to be called resurrection. This could, of course, be to expound one mystery by another even more mysterious and more heavily laden with symbolism, and strictly speaking it would seem to involve the preparation of only these three disciples, who must then presumably be regarded as the original witnesses of the resurrection faith. He does not develop in detail the corollary of his observation on the weakness of the vision theory, namely that the resur-

[10] *Op. cit.*, p. 133.   [11] *Op. cit.*, p. 142.   [12] *Op. cit.*, p. 148.
[13] *Op. cit.*, p. 127.

rection comes into sharp focus not in what was seen but in what was said and heard, but one gets the impression from his treatment as a whole that this element belongs to the subsequent interpretation of the resurrection in the church.

Significant in this respect is Karl Barth's change of view.[14] It was integral to Barth's thought in his *Epistle to the Romans* that the resurrection was not an historical event, but a symbol of the transcendent ground of the historical life and death of Jesus as revelation. 'In the Resurrection the new world of the Holy Spirit touches the old world of the flesh, but touches it as a tangent touches a circle, that is, without touching it. And, precisely because it does not touch it, it touches it as its frontier – as the new world. The Resurrection is therefore an occurrence in history, which took place outside the gates of Jerusalem in the year AD 30, inasmuch as it there "came to pass", was discovered and recognized. But inasmuch as the occurrence was conditioned by the Resurrection, in so far, that is, as it was not the "coming to pass", or the discovery, or the recognition, which conditioned its necessity and appearance and revelation, the Resurrection is not an event in history at all.'[15] 'As history, it lies on the frontier of that which is not history; as non-history, it lies on the frontier of history.'[16]

In the *Church Dogmatics*,[17] where the subject is treated under the heading of 'Jesus, Lord of Time', and with respect to the question of the possibility of a continuity in Christ of past, present and future, it is again said that the Easter time is 'simply the time of the revelation of the mystery of the preceding time of the life and death of the man Jesus';[18] but for the history of the man Jesus to be recounted as salvation history, which is the key for our whole understanding of the man Jesus in his time, Barth now asserts that 'Jesus has a further history beginning on the third day after His death, and therefore after the time of His first history had clearly come to an end. In temporal sequence it is a second history – or rather the fragments of a second history – of Jesus.'[19] Here the resurrection is no longer a tangent but a prism 'through which the apostles and their communities saw the man Jesus in every aspect

[14] Cf. the comments of Van A. Harvey, *The Historian and the Believer* (1967), pp. 153ff., and the critique by C. Hartlich and W. Sachs, in H. W. Bartsch (ed.), *Kerygma und Mythos* II (1952), pp. 113ff.
[15] Karl Barth, *The Epistle to the Romans* (1933), p. 30. [16] *Op. cit.*, p. 222.
[17] Karl Barth, *Church Dogmatics* III 2 (1960), pp. 437ff.
[18] *Op. cit.*, p. 455. [19] *Op. cit.*, p. 441.

of his relation to them – as the One who "was, and is, and is to come"', but 'we are here in the sphere of history and time no less than in the case of the words and acts or even the death of Jesus'.[20] What is meant by 'history' here? In clearing the ground, Barth makes a number of criticisms of Bultmann which have a certain validity. He asks why it should be true 'that an event alleged to have happened in time can be accepted as historical only if it can be proved to be a " 'historical' fact" in Bultmann's sense – i.e. when it is open to verification by the methods, and above all the tacit assumptions of modern historical scholarship'; or why it should be thought that the modern world-view is so binding and so incompatible with the mythical world-view of the past that we are incapable of receiving the resurrection witness. But the purpose of this criticism is to make room for a 'higher history', which 'good taste prevents us from calling "historical fact"', and he adduces as examples of this higher history the narratives of Gen. 1–2. 'So too is the Easter story, except for a tiny "historical" margin.' 'This is the act of God – the act in which He appeared objectively in the glory of His incarnate Word . . . the *man* Jesus was manifested among them in the mode of God.'[21]

Further, of the resurrection traditions themselves Barth states that they are fragmentary and contradictory, and that 'it is impossible to extract from the various accounts a nucleus of genuine history'; and of the forty days, which he elsewhere calls the *evangelium quadraginta dierum*, he says that they are to be taken not literally but typically. There are two difficulties here. The first is the propriety of the use of the phrase 'higher history' to establish an event as both having the character of the historical in the usual sense of that word and at the same time as being immune from historical investigation. The creation narrative of Gen. 1–2 has, since New Testament times, been appealed to as a theological analogue to the resurrection; but in what sense of the word 'history' can it be called an historical analogue? Secondly, and more important, the difficulty is not, as Barth seems to think, whether to believe in the resurrection, but what it is that is to be believed. Can one appeal to the traditions to establish the factuality of the resurrection and as telling us what is to be believed even in the sphere of 'higher history' if they are fragmentary, contradictory, and 'couched in the imaginative, poetic style of his-

[20] *Op. cit.*, p. 442.　　[21] *Op. cit.*, pp. 445, 446, 448.

torical saga?' Harvey sees Barth's view as basically contradictory: 'On the one hand, in order to justify the heavy assent of the believer he appeals to the hearing and seeing of the risen Jesus by the apostles, an appeal that achieves its force just by virtue of its employment of certain familiar common-sense categories like touching, hearing and seeing. On the other hand, the stories are immediately immunized against assessment by the concession that they are not literal or historical. He offers with his right hand something that he takes away with the left. The result is that the machinery of the argument grinds to a halt as soon as it is taken seriously as an argument. It is no longer clear what would count as data and warrants and backings for, or a legitimate qualification of, the argument. Consequently, it is impossible to give any kind of weighted assent, because it is simply not clear what would be an appropriate one.'[22]

R. R. Niebuhr sees the resurrection as raising precisely these questions of the nature of the category of 'the historical', of historical causality and of the principles of historical interpretation. It is his thesis that 'all conceptions of history and of historical reason that do not begin with the resurrection can neither gain from nor contribute to the resurrection faith any significant light'.[23] From a review of the approaches made to the historical by Protestant theology in this and the previous centuries, he concludes that its understanding has been stultified because its model has been sought in the natural sciences, and theology 'has made the canons of natural science do duty as the principles of historiography also, and treated the data of history as though they were the phenomena of nature and nothing more'.[24] The way out of this is not to have recourse to a *Heilsgeschichte* (sacred history) as running alongside and intersecting ordinary or profane history, since such a sacred history lacks one of the necessary constitutents of anything which is to be called historical, namely contingency and irregularity. It runs too much according to plan. The category of the historical is *sui generis*. It has to do with what is individual, spontaneous and unrepeatable, conveyed by memory; it must be approached for its own sake and as standing in its own right. Thus 'the resurrection shares in the arbitrariness, irrationality and independence which

[22] Van A. Harvey, *The Historian and the Believer*, p. 159.
[23] R. R. Niebuhr, *Resurrection and Historical Reason*, p. 3.
[24] *Op. cit.*, p. 78.

characterize all events to some degree; and like them, it is problematic'.[25] But while these considerations may pave the way for a more receptive attitude to the resurrection tradition, they do not in themselves supply warrants for accepting it. Thus Niebuhr pronounces the resurrection an anomaly without parallel, though as an event in history it 'must contain elements that historical reason can recognize'.[26] Here the difficulty is both that we have no criteria for judging an event which is strictly without parallel, even if the quality of the historical is that it is individual and unrepeatable, while the ability to call anything an anomaly without parallel depends upon the ability to appeal to commonly recognized human experiences as generally making up the historical. 'The elements which historical reason can recognize' he sees in the corporeal details of the resurrection appearances, which are to be interpreted as 'historical signs' concerned with recognition and identification, which bring to life in the present what was till then only past in the disciples' memory, and which open up the future for them. When, however, he makes an exception of the incident of Jesus himself eating fish, and (probably) of the empty tomb as a later tradition, in not fulfilling this function, it is again open to question whether the stories with their corporeal details are not historicizations of the truth that it is Jesus of Nazareth who is the object of faith as the risen Lord.

The boldest attempt to solve the problem is to be found in the positions which Wolfhart Pannenberg and his school have elaborated in a number of works, precisely because they see the resurrection as the fulcrum and model of a total view which identifies theology and history.[27] In this view the distinctions between history as objective fact and its evaluation by faith, or between secular history and sacred history (*Heilsgeschichte*), or between ordinary history and 'primal history', or between history as chronicle of past event and history as present existential living, are all false. They either make faith a necessary supplement to history before it can be used as history, or else they divorce faith from history and ground faith in itself. These contend on the contrary that history

---

[25] *Op. cit.*, p. 171.   [26] *Op. cit.*, p. 162.
[27] See esp. Pannenberg's *Jesus God and Man* (1968), and James M. Robinson and John B. Cobb, Jr. (eds.), *Theology as History* (New Frontiers in Theology Vol. III, 1967), which contains a focal essay by Pannenberg on the resurrection, critical evaluations of this, and references to, and discussions of, the writings of Pannenberg and those associated with him.

is 'reality in its totality', and that the whole of reality is history. There are no 'mere' historical facts, since history brings its own meaning with it and speaks a 'language of facts'. The historical is constituted by events and their meaning together and by the same process. This is so because events are available to us only through the transmission of traditions in which the events are already inseparable from the context in which they have been interpreted, and apart from which they cannot be grasped. This context itself provides for further events to be expected and to happen, and this brings about the continuity of history. Its unity and sweep as universal history are secured only by the eschatological goal and completion to which it is directed, and through which its universal character in relation to God will be revealed by God himself. The significance of the present derives from that present's future. God is the future of every present and was the future of every event now past. His kingdom means the power which he exerts upon the present as the future coming One, and the proof of his existence now lies in the ultimacy of his coming kingdom. Thus for Pannenberg the appeal to God from history conceived of as the whole of reality eschatologically directed performs something of the same function as the arguments in natural theology, when they have inferred God from the unity, order and purpose of the world. The postulate that history is to be seen eschatologically and grasped proleptically is held to be demanded by human experience, since men are unable to find satisfaction in this life alone; and it is already present in the traditions of Israel. But it is clearest in Jesus, because within the apocalyptic tradition of Israel which alone makes this type of thinking possible he is seen to be, and declares himself to be, the one in whom the kingdom of God enters our time. In his history the end of things takes place proleptically as a personal event.

Of this total view the resurrection is for Pannenberg the paradigm. If the historical is to be thought of eschatologically, and so as revelatory of God, the resurrection, as the confirmation of Jesus' proclamation of the coming kingdom of God, is supremely the point where the unity and universality of history can be grasped, and God's presence discerned. For this reason the resurrection must itself be historical, and is to be established by the kind of investigation proper to the historical. Therefore the concept of the historical must be expanded to make room for an event which is without analogy, viz. the coming to life again of a man by the action of God in such a way that he lives for ever. Such an historical event can be apprehended as revelatory in this sense because it is known through the transmission of tradition, in this case a tradition governed by the Jewish apocalyptic expectation of the general resurrection of the dead as the climax of history. The resurrection of Jesus is unintelligible apart from this expectation; in the context of this expectation it cannot appear as a random event affecting a private individual, but only as the beginning of the end. Thus in contrast to W. Marxsen's hypothesis[28] that we must distinguish the essence of the Easter faith as the permanent presence of Jesus as the living one from 'resurrection' as a mode of conceptualizing this conditioned by a first-century apocalyptic we cannot share, Pannenberg insists that the Easter event is not to be separated from apocalyptic categories of thought (the last judgment, the general resurrection, the parousia etc.), which remain valid and may not be exchanged for others. Similarly, while 'resurrection' is a metaphor (he identifies it with waking from sleep), it is an 'absolute metaphor' which is not replaceable.

These theses are argued with an impressive sweep and force, and by way of a thoroughly detailed examination of evidence. They constitute a bold attempt to close the gap between fact and interpretation which the critical-historical method has opened up, and they demand something of a conversion for those brought up in that method. Thus Pannenberg's position rests upon a predominantly receptive attitude towards traditions and their continuity, whereas the critical-historical method has frequently felt itself able to advance only by a suspicious attitude towards tradition and by uncovering discontinuities. Further, the inference of God as cause from the supposed universality of history has the added weakness to similar arguments in natural theology that the history from which the inference is made is not yet a totality, but is incomplete and short of its consummation.[29] Surprisingly, how-

---

[28] *Op. cit.* (see n. 1).

[29] It is not clear whether Pannenberg thinks that a corollary of his position is that the Christian theologian ought to be prepared to offer an interpretation of all the history there has been, a prospect from which even O. Cullmann, with his conception of 'salvation history', shrinks (O. Cullmann, *Salvation in History*, 1967, pp. 293ff.). For a critical analysis of Pannenberg's criteria for establishing events, and in particular the resurrection, as historical, and of the view that only the historical has theological and spiritual influence upon

ever, Pannenberg's thinking in general is not matched in its boldness by his treatment of what is crucial to it, the resurrection as an historical event. The chapter on the resurrection stands significantly at the beginning of his great work on christology, *Jesus God and Man*, since his whole christology arises from there, but in this chapter, as elsewhere on the same subject, he is forced to speak with considerable hesitation and reserve. The structure which he builds includes a number of shaky and considerably qualified propositions, and leans heavily at times on indirect evidence and suppositions. Thus it has been justly observed that he speaks a great deal more, and a great deal more confidently, about resurrection in general than about the resurrection of Jesus in particular. The following is typical: 'Thus the resurrection of Jesus would be designated as a historical event in this sense: If the emergence of primitive Christianity, which, apart from other traditions, is also traced back by Paul to appearances of the resurrected Jesus, can be understood in spite of all critical examination of the tradition only if one examines it in the light of the eschatological hope for a resurrection from the dead, then that which is so designated is a historical event, even if we do not know anything more about it in particular.'[30] But is this soundly based? If our previous assessment of the evidence in ch. I is at all accurate, then it would seem doubtful whether the general resurrection from the dead was a sufficiently fixed theologoumenon in Jewish tradition (or was sufficiently 'cultivated', in Pannenberg's language) to provide the necessary context from which the resurrection of Jesus would be immediately read off. Such an apocalyptic fundamentalism may have lain behind the original Easter faith, but the New Testament documents do not on the whole bear witness to this, and the doctrine of the general resurrection does not figure prominently in them.[31] Indeed, to the extent that the resurrection of Jesus was thought of as the beginning and ground of the general resurrection, there

---

us, see G. G. O'Collins, 'Revelation as History', *Heythrop Journal* VII (1966), pp. 394ff.; 'Is the Resurrection an "Historical" Event?', *ibid.* VIII (1967), pp. 381ff.

[30] *Jesus God and Man*, p. 98.
[31] It is perhaps significant that N. Clark, *op. cit.*, p. 51, in support of a similar argument, quotes only the late texts, John 11.25; Acts 4.2; 17.18, apart from Rom. 1.4, and it is not certain that this last carries the required meaning.

would be no need of a tradition either of an empty tomb or of corporeal appearances, for as the beginning of the resurrection of the dead Jesus would be in heaven, or wherever the final judgment and the bestowal of eternal life were to take place.

Pannenberg admits that for what he calls the second generation witnesses, who comprise most of the New Testament writers – Mark, Matthew, Luke, John, the authors of the deutero-Pauline letters and of Hebrews – it has become clear that 'the resurrection of Jesus was not yet the beginning of the immediately continuous sequence of the eschatological events, but was a special event which happened to Jesus alone.'[32] Hence he leans heavily on Paul as the one for whom the resurrection of Jesus did not need to be interpreted, since in the necessary context of the expectation of universal resurrection it already carried its meaning in itself, and Paul was able to read off from it the whole of the gospel he was subsequently to preach. But is this even clear in Paul? In reply to those Corinthian Christians who asserted that there was no resurrection (whatever they may have meant by that) he certainly argues both ways, that if Christ is not raised there is no resurrection and that if there is no resurrection Christ is not raised, but the fact that he begins with a rehearsal of the resurrection appearances might be held to indicate that his emphasis lies on the first statement and that the second is a complement to it. In I Thess. 4.15–17, as also possibly in I Cor. 15 (18, 23, 51), what is in the foreground is an appeal not to the universal resurrection but to the certain union of Christ with his own, whether they are the dead in Christ or believers still alive, and this appears to be grounded on the view that Jesus as Lord and Messiah is an inclusive person whose destiny is valid for others. This could also be the emphasis in the expression 'first-born from the dead' (Col. 1.18; Rev. 1.5), especially if interpreted in the light of Rom. 8.29, 'to be conformed to the image of his Son, that he might be the first-born among many brethren', as also of the expression 'firstfruits of those who sleep' (I Cor. 15.20, i.e. the Christian dead). And why does Paul find it necessary to make the distinction, first Christ, then those who are Christ's, then the handing over the kingdom to the Father (I Cor. 15.23f.)?

With respect to Jesus himself Pannenberg may be right in his assessment of the eschatology of the gospels when he affirms that

[32] *Op. cit.*, p. 66.

'the question of the ultimate confirmation of Jesus' claim to authority stands over his entire path', and that 'the whole of Jesus' work aimed at the future verification of his claim to authority'.[33] Nevertheless, the statement that 'Jesus in any case reckoned with the imminent end of the world and the resurrection of the dead and judgment of the Son of Man which were associated with that',[34] is curious, for while an imminent denouement and the coming judgment are clearly the basis of much that is said in the gospels, the universal resurrection is not so, and this despite the fact that the gospels are written from a belief in the resurrection of Jesus. And would the universal resurrection account for the alternative conception of the exaltation and lordship of Jesus?

In his assessment of the gospel evidence for the resurrection of Jesus Pannenberg again relies heavily on supposition. Thus, when he appeals to the empty tomb tradition it is very little to the gospel accounts, which he thinks may be late and legendary,[35] but to the *a priori* considerations that the first Christians were bound to have satisfied themselves at an early stage about the emptiness of the tomb, and that the situation must have been of such and such a kind in the first Jerusalem community for the resurrection kerygma to have been preached there, viz. they must have known that the tomb was empty. For the basis of the resurrection as historical, he appeals less to the appearances, which he is content to categorize as 'visions' provided that the word is not understood in a purely subjective sense, than to the need to supply an adequate cause for the change in the disciples. The greatest weight is put on I Cor. 15.1–8, since we can deduce from Paul's own words that the experiences of the others he names was the same as his own, that these others were still there to be interrogated, and that we know enough about Paul's own experience to say that it was an historical event. This last point involves reliance on the Acts account of the Damascus road experience. Finally Pannenberg deals with the words of the risen Lord by the assertion that in the resurrection of Jesus word and event belong together, and express the same content, so that

---

[33] *Op. cit.*, p. 65.   [34] *Op. cit.*, pp. 65f.

[35] *Op. cit.*, p. 102: 'The deviations in Matthew and Luke are all understandable from dogmatical or redactional motives, and, therefore, can be left out of consideration for an historical enquiry.' In the Markan version, 16.7 is to be disregarded as a Markan addition to the tradition, and the message of the angel reduced to 16.6 – though Pannenberg does not say how this angelic message is to be adjudged historically.

'the words of the risen Jesus add nothing new to the significance inherent in the event itself, but, rather, state this significance'.[36] He does not, however, attempt to substantiate this in detail, except with reference to the Gentile mission, but this only in the form in which it appears in prophetic eschatology of the nations flocking to Zion, and this nowhere appears in the words of the risen Lord.

[36] *Op. cit.*, p. 72.

INDEX OF NAMES

INDEX OF BIBLICAL REFERENCES

Old Testament

Genesis
2.7 — 12, 125
18.2 — 102, 105
18.15 — 73
45.3 — 73, 78

Exodus
3.12 — 91

Deuteronomy
1.1 — 109
21.23 — 146
30.13 — 25

Joshua
1.5ff. — 91
5.14 — 102

II Samuel
7.14 — 13

II Kings
4.31 — 20

Psalms
2.7 — 13
2.8 — 14
16.10 — 12f., 49
110.1 — 13, 138
118.22 — 13

Isaiah
26.19 — 11, 20, 21, 29
29.6 — 86
52.13–
53.12 — 45, 48, 139
55.3 — 13

Daniel
7.9 — 86
7.14 — 88

Daniel
10.6 — 86
12.2 — 11, 16, 20, 23

Hosea
6.2 — 13, 48f.
13.14 — 12

Ecclesiasticus
48.5 — 20, 24

Wisdom
5.11 — 111
15.11 — 125
19.13 — 111

II Maccabees
3 — 26
7.14–38 — 15, 18, 21
12.43 — 21
14.46 — 15

New Testament

Matthew
1.20 — 86
1.23 — 91
1.24 — 86
2.13 — 86
2.19 — 86
4.8 — 83, 89
4.12ff. — 84
5.1 — 88

Matthew
5.20ff. — 83
5.46–48 — 33
7.21f. — 91
8.11f. — 90
9.25 — 24
10.6 — 84, 88, 90
10.24 — 91
11.27 — 89f.

Matthew
12.11 — 25
12.18ff. — 90
12.39f. — 33, 48f.
13.38 — 90
13.52 — 91
14.23 — 83, 88
14.28ff. — 53
15.24 — 84, 88, 90